P9-CRH-493

ARNULFO L. OLIVEIRA MEMORIAL LIBRARY
1825 MAY STREET
BROWNSVILLE, TEXAS 78520

SPECIAL SCIENCE MEMORIAL LIBRARY
13TH BUILDING
SERIES IN BUSINESS

College
Financial
Management

College Financial Management

Basics for Administrators

E. Eugene Carter
University of Illinois
at Chicago Circle

LexingtonBooks
D.C. Heath and Company
Lexington, Massachusetts
Toronto

ARNULFO L. OLIVEIRA MEMORIAL LIBRARY
1025 MAY STREET
BROWNSVILLE, TEXAS 78520

Library of Congress Cataloging in Publication Data

Carter, E Eugene.
  College financial management.

  Bibliography: p.
  Includes index.
   1.   Universities and colleges—United States—Finance. I. Title.
LB2342.C322   378'.02'0973   80–7465
ISBN 0–669–03700–1

Copyright © 1980 by D.C. Heath and Company

All rights reserved. No part of this publication may be reproduced or trans-
mitted in any form or by any means, electronic or mechanical, including pho-
tocopy, recording, or any information storage or retrieval system, without
permission in writing from the publisher.

Published simultaneously in Canada.

Printed in the United States of America.

International Standard Book Number: 0–669–03700–1

Library of Congress Catalog Card Number: 80–7465

*This book is dedicated to
Lotte and Paul Boschan,
with the respect and affection of their
granddaughter's father*

Contents

List of Figures

List of Tables

Preface and
Acknowledgments

As a trained economist and teacher in a management school, I have often wondered about the basic concepts from economics and finance that might benefit an educational administrator not trained in these fields. As I indicate in chapter 1, that curiosity led to this book. I do not want to imply that an educational institution should be managed as a business, with prime if not exclusive attention to the profit-and-loss statement. Nor do I wish to suggest that the institution be run as a production line, with emphasis on engineering efficiency. Rather, I simply wish to suggest that administrators consider various means of measuring costs of scarce resources and that they consider alternative uses of those resources. In this book, then, I present some basic economic concepts, an analysis of some institutional factors relating to the security markets and portfolio theory, and a discussion in the context of several case examples of how some colleges have coped with issues such as dormitory projects, endowment management, and long-run planning with an emphasis on tenure considerations.

Many of these materials were developed while I taught in the Institute for Educational Management at the Harvard School of Education. The dean, Paul Ylvisaker, and several of my colleagues, including Richard Chait, now at Pennsylvania State University, George Weathersby, and Frederick Jacobs, contributed to my understanding of many of the educational issues and helped me refine my own thoughts with their friendly probing of my assertions. Two Harvard professors who preceded me in teaching finance in this program, Dwight B. Crane and Samuel L. Hayes, also contributed to my education through the development of several cases, some of which I have revised for this book. I thank them for their insights into the issues and for their permission to include their cases.

Drs. John B. Breazeale and George Houston of Wichita State University and Georgetown University, respectively, contributed much of their own time and smoothed the process of my developing the two cases included here that deal with their institutions. With no reward other than the hope that perhaps other academic administrators might profit from their own experiences, these two men deserve a special thanks for their patience.

Many of my academic colleagues at the University of Illinois at Chicago Circle read all of the manuscript and commented in great detail on it. They have helped me to sharpen the focus and to present my ideas in a more lucid manner. I offer my particular thanks to Richard A. Cohn, associate professor of finance; Rita M. Rodriguez, visiting professor of finance; Ralph

Westfall, dean of the College of Business Administration; and Vernon A. Miller, director of the Office of Academic planning.

My special thanks go to Norman Cantor, who conducted a seminar on university governance in the 1980s during his tenure at the University of Illinois at Chicago Circle as vice chancellor for academic affairs. He now serves as dean of the Graduate School of Arts and Sciences at New York University. Dr. Cantor's seminar enabled many of us on this campus to meet our counterparts in other departments and, more importantly, to discuss our ideas developed from the books he offered. As Herbert Simon once remarked, the real value of a teacher is not found in any student survey; rather, the question is answered in terms of the quality of the reading list given to students. In that sense, Norman was a first-rate instructor for us.

Mr. Floyd Beatty, vice-president of A.G. Edwards and Sons, Inc., provided various tabulations of security yields included in the text, and I thank him for his patience and thoroughness.

Cynthia McMillan served as an extraordinarily talented research assistant, checking sources, compiling exhibits, and editing the final manuscript with great patience and attention to detail. I gratefully acknowledge her efforts. Holly Heim reviewed an earlier draft of the manuscript and offered many good suggestions, and I thank her for these comments.

I also express my gratitude to Elizabeth Mott Bollier of Lexington Books. As production editor for the book, she carefully arranged mailings to four different addresses. Marci Nugent carefully edited the manuscript for final production, and her efforts are appreciated by me and even more by the readers.

Finally, I accept responsibility for the merits or demerits of these ideas. It is my hope that other academic administrators will find a thought here or there that proves of value. More importantly, I hope this book provokes further attention to the issues of economic and financial analysis as they bear on academic administration. One only has to view the financial situation of many private schools and the testiness of many public funding bodies to recognize that this field is a fruitful one for analysis.

College
Financial
Management

1 Introduction

Faced with serious inflation, declining student enrollments, shifting demands for undergraduate fields, reduced graduate demand for Ph.D. programs, and a loss of federally sponsored research programs, many of America's colleges and universities today confront financial problems more serious than anyone had ever imagined. Virtually every college president has experienced some of the preceding litany of ills. In part, the inability of many college administrators to face these problems stems from lethargy; some of them feel that the boom years of the sixties will somehow return if they ignore the problem, maybe it will evaporate with time. The sixties was a period of unprecedented growth for American higher education: Enrollments doubled; campuses expanded, often due to generous state legislators' responding to public demand for higher education; and public funding for research soared, in part in reaction to the Soviet space challenge. The enrollment increase derived from both an enlarging pool of high school graduates (a cohort that forms the common pool from which students go on to higher education) and the fact that the percentage of high school graduates enrolled in programs of higher education increased, rising from 31 percent of the high school class in the late 1950s to 43 percent in 1969. That the further expansion was not likely to continue and that the eighteen year-old high school cohort would actually drop 19 percent from 4.2 million in 1980 to 3.4 million in 1990 should have been reasonably apparent, but most faculty and administrators (unchecked by trustees or legislators) chose to ignore these patterns.[1]

Why was the problem so difficult to face in the 1970s? In part, the difficulty came from moving to a no-growth (or, at least, to a selective-growth) from a rapid-growth environment; the mental state for the latter ill-fit the former. Of greater significance was the issue posed by economics: The heavy (and heady) expansion of the 1960s created fixed costs and inflexibility that made response to the changed environment tardy and incomplete. The situation was exacerbated by other issues:

1. The end of the draft deferment for a man enrolled in higher education coupled with the diminution of the conflict in Southeast Asia meant that the influx of many males to higher education was reduced. No longer was there the incentive to continue higher education in order to postpone military service.

2. The record inflation of the 1970s, unprecedented by historical standards in the United States, created pressure on American universities because of their operating-cost structure. To some degree, a productivity increase in the creation of any service or product can offset some amount of cost increase. However, service industries such as education are notoriously resistant to attempts to increase productivity. As a result, the cost of education rose even more than the increase in the general price level. There are differences of opinion on how much of this cost increase was passed on to students. If it took the form of higher fees and charges, potential students were even less likely to enroll. If it was absorbed by the educational institution, serious funding problems for the institution itself resulted.

3. Related to the preceding issue, the periods of declining stock market and a severe recession during the 1970s created problems for student and institution alike. Private (independent) institutions witnessed the loss of their endowments with the declining securities market. Because many of these institutions depended on investment income to provide the difference between their operating income and expenses, this erosion of value was serious. Institutions heavily invested in bonds often saw their endowment wither as well when rising interest rates reduced bond prices. Although not as critical, many public institutions also depended on small endowments to provide seed money for faculty recruiting and research, experimental programs, special library facilities, and building expansion. The loss of these endowments reduced the already limited flexibility of many public university administrators. The recession meant that taxpayers and potential students alike were reluctant to contribute more money to higher education because their own budgets were severely pressed. Finally, the recession meant reduced job opportunities for many graduates, and this loss was translated into a rejection of college by many first-generation college-bound students: Why go if the meal ticket was not there?[2]

University Problems and Management Practices

Many of the problems that colleges and universities face are susceptible to the analysis of an applied economist, for the issues parallel problems faced by small businesses, giant corporations, insurance company pension-fund managers, mutual-fund managers, and municipal government officials. Corporations continuously face a problem of trading off income and cash today for future opportunities. Pension-fund managers have to estimate the likely ranges of benefits that will be paid in the future and consider how those benefits can be funded. Portfolio managers have to consider how to invest their funds: fixed income, short term or long term, common stocks with growth potential, general common stocks, and so forth. Even government officials have tried to consider some of these same problems, both from the standpoint of financing public employees' pension benefits as well as from a cost-benefit analysis of various project proposals under consideration by the budget authority.

There is a common theme among these various situations related to university management: The dollar is a *numeraire*. In other words, the problems and issues are often related to each other by a dollar standard, or counting chip. Contrary to the polemic often hurled at an economist or manager, this dollar numeraire does not mean that the cheapest way is always the "right" way or the "best" way. Rather, a fair conclusion would be that the dollar-cost figure, within the range of an accurate estimate, provides information about the cost of one option over another. If the more costly option is more desirable (better quality, better morale, or some other "better" that is not often counted in dollar terms), then the relevant question becomes: If option *A* is more desirable than option *B*, but option *A* also costs $5,000 more than option *B*, *are the intangibles that create that greater desirability worth at least $5,000?*

Placed in that context, much of the financial analysis may become far less controversial. A bookkeeper's mentality is not desired; indeed, a noted economist, Arthur Okun, once observed that economists are the only people who have to be reminded that not everything has a price. On the other hand, some idea of relative costs, of the amounts of money being involved or committed by a decision relative to the total amount that is available, ought to be useful to a decision maker.

Chapter-by-Chapter Overview

It is with the perspective of an applied economist in the area of finance that I have written this book. Most people thrust into administrative roles in colleges and universities have their backgrounds in education, often as distinguished teachers and scholars. These people are often unfamiliar with the concepts, terms, and possibilities of economic analysis, and they cannot reasonably be expected to know these areas. Faced with the pressure of many management issues, these administrators often absorb such knowledge by accident: a casual remark from a local banker at lunch; the observations of the local accountant when preparing some material for the trustees or for a committee; the remarks of a legislative aide when item vetoing a particular budget request.

This chapter will outline some of the concepts from economics that seem most applicable to universities. These definitions let us approach a range of issues faced by university administrators at various times. Chapter 2 will review the characteristics of various financial instruments available to universities that have money to invest for the short term (between tuition receipts in the fall and the disbursement for payrolls over several following months, for example) or the long term (the establishment of an endowment fund for a chaired professorship). Some instruments also are relevant to university administrators who wish to borrow for scholarship-funding pools, building construction, or short-term bridge financing between summer payrolls and tuition payments by students in the fall, for example. Within this area of financial instruments, the discussion of various financial securities provides information for the endowment manager who has to select among various financial instruments.

Chapters 1 and 2 present basic ideas about economics and basic facts about securities that will already be known by many college administrators who read this book. Such readers may skim these chapters, moving directly to chapter 3, which discusses the issues of short-term cash management. As an example, universities have a seasonal need for funds as well as a seasonal receipt of funds. *Seasonal* means that the funds that are required to meet obligations that come to the school from various sources such as tuition do not occur evenly throughout the year; one twelfth of the annual amount does not flow in or out each month. The issues of risk and return for various securities described in chapter 2 will be discussed further in chapter 3. Finally, we will discuss *pooled funds*, which are available for balances of relatively small amounts (for example, under $100,000).

Chapters 4 and 5 approach two common areas that are particularly good examples of the analysis of specific projects: dormitory (or building) financing and student-aid financing. We treat both of these topics with an extended analysis of two simple cases. These cases outline the issues faced by university administrators confronting these problems. We discuss the institutional facts: what procedures and choices are open for solving these problems. Then we confront the institutional problems: One university might decide to solve a problem by one means whereas another school with a different funding source, student body, or risk attitude on the part of its administrators might decide on a different solution. Finally, we outline general approaches to these problems in the context of cash management, risk considerations, and alternative goals. Such general approaches provide the administrator with a framework for analysis that is all too often lost when simple "case stories" are presented. The particular elements of a given situation may not generalize to other institutions in other times.

Chapters 6 and 7 present a topic of major concern to many private institutions today: the problem of endowment management and spending rules. Endowment management once consisted of simply selecting a broad portfolio of securities, all of which individually met the risk profile of the owner: bonds for widows and orphans versus growth stocks for young executives, for example. Universities could follow the same pattern, usually biased toward the fixed-income securities favored by conservative pension-fund managers. In recent years research from financial theory has suggested a number of different ways of evaluating risk, and empirical data from actual returns to security holders of different types of portfolios have been analyzed. This chapter summarizes this research for the academic adminis-trator, and provides another case example of the sophisticated endowment-management evaluation procedures followed by one college, Georgetown University. Chapter 7 discusses risk and return over time for financial administrators adopting various types of spending rules. For example, drawing a certain percentage of the endowment each year compared with drawing a percentage of a five-year average of endowment value each year provides different probabilities for the value of the portfolio in thirty years. We discuss this risk evaluation in relation to the risk of a single investor's facing the same problem of withdrawing money from his or her portfolio.

Finally, chapter 8 discusses long-run financial strategy for a university. An extended case, Wichita State University, illustrates the type of data that may be useful to the administrator planning for various contingencies. In addition, we present some comparisons of tenure in light of our financial concepts, indicating today's present value of some long-run tenure deci-sions, and how such decisions may be evaluated in light of the financial mobility of the institution.

Throughout this text, the emphasis is on providing information that the university administration should find useful in financial management. The issues often will involve matters of general education policy. The purposes of the book then are to present a framework for analyzing information about strictly financial problems and, more importantly, to show the finan-cial implications of many educational-policy decisions.

Some Basic Concepts

Eight specific terms transfer from the field of economics to the analysis of financial problems confronting educational administrators. Although we cannot discuss these concepts in the detail provided in many accounting, economics, and corporate-finance textbooks, their importance requires at least some formal presentation. These concepts are:

Marginal versus average cost and revenue

Fixed and variable cost and revenue

Long-run and short-run analysis

Opportunity cost

Cash versus accrual accounting

Time value of money

Liquidity

Risk and risk premiums

Marginal Versus Average Cost Revenue

A school that spends $10 million for wages to educate 10,000 students has an *average cost* of $1,000 per student ($10 million divided by 10,000). This may be considered as the average unit cost of a production line—a consideration not likely to endear the concept to humanists! Average cost differs from an important thought from economics, *marginal cost*. Marginal cost may be thought of as "incremental" or "extra" cost: In the position of the institution now, what is the extra cost of one more student? The marginal cost may be more or less than the average cost: Adding one more student to a half-empty classroom involves zero additional wages for the instructor. Adding a student who requires individual tutorial instruction because of the student's class choice or a government-mandated special educational program may cost several times the average cost of all students. Furthermore, adding a student may be distinguished from subtracting one student. For example, once a program is established, subtracting one student may save no money. Thus for the administrator, it is useful to focus on *which* type of marginal change will be made—an increase or a decrease—and to note that the impact of the marginal change may differ depending on the type of cost subcategory involved. Costs are not homogeneous.

Related to cost is the issue of revenue. The *average revenue* per student depends on factors such as what percentage of the existing student body is financed by external sources and what group is financed by the school's financial-aid program. That is, average revenue is total revenue divided by the number of students. On the other hand, the marginal revenue of an additional student may be higher, lower, or the same as the average revenue per student. Marginal revenue depends on the financing sources for that additional student. Is the student completely supported by a scholarship from internal funds, or is the student financed by parents or outside funding authorities?

In most decisions we compare the marginal cost and the marginal revenue associated with a given decision. Thus the *average* student may provide $1,100 of income and cost $1,000. But average figures may not be at all relevant to our decision on whether to add five additional students in history, for example. The relevant consideration then is how much do these students bring to the school in dollar terms relative to how much they cost? That is, what are the marginal revenue and the marginal cost of adding these students?

Fixed Versus Variable Costs and Revenues

The time period also affects whether costs are fixed or variable. In the short run, many costs are *fixed*. That is, the costs do not change with small alterations in the number of people served or units produced. The situation cited previously involving the additional classroom student is a good example. If a classroom holds 30 students and faculty are permitted to teach this number of students, then once a single student is in the classroom, instructional salaries, heating, and the like are probably fixed. However, the cost of housing those students can have a sizable variable component. For example, if dormitories are full and additional students must be housed, a local apartment building may be willing to take students at the university room rate only if the school pays the difference between that rate and the commercial rate. In this case each additional student is associated with a specific variable housing cost beyond the normal room bill.

Long-run and Short-run Analysis

As a famous economist once observed, in the long run we are all dead. However, we still should think about the distinction between the long run and the short run. Traditionally, *long run* refers to a time period for which fixed costs can become variable: Teachers retire or buildings are shifted to other uses. Usually the time period is associated with the years required for existing fixed costs to become variable: What is fixed in the short run always becomes variable at some point. Notice that the break between long run and short run may differ among the costs. Further, the long run for *revenue* items may reflect many other events beyond the influence of the college administrator. A strategy that provides short-run revenue increases may ultimately do much less in the long run. For example, raising tuition by 30 percent may generate more short-term income from students who will have educational, social, and economic objections to transferring their credits to another institution. In the long run (two years?), there may be a net loss if this increase stimulates a substantial number of students to move to another institution. (We examine just this sort of issue in more detail in chapter 5 where we review student-aid financing and the tuition strategy of an institution.)

Opportunity Cost

One tenet of any economic philosophy is scarcity. No society can do every-thing; some people will receive more than others, some goods will be produced and others not produced. So too for the school, there will always be an opportunity cost, funds invested one way could be spent another way. Public schools often know that X dollars will be allocated to the university system this year, and the division of these X dollars between salary increases versus new program funding provides a vivid example of opportunity cost. Something must be lost for something else to be gained. Sometimes the opportunity cost is management or faculty time in that there are only so many hours, and innovative teaching will be at the cost of research commit-ments. More time spent raising funds means less time spent counseling faculty. Opportunity cost coupled with the concepts of marginal cost and revenue often provide a useful insight into the main variables affecting a decision: Should Ms. A's time be spent in this way, at the margin? What will time spent in that manner provide, what will it cost in dollars, and what other ways might she spend her time with what benefits—the opportunity costs.

Cash Versus Accrual Accounting

The economist will define income as the cash receipts in a period plus or minus any change in the wealth of a person or institution. The accountant, facing the same problem, will follow a prescribed set of rules that seeks to define income in a consistent way, a way that will not necessarily reflect the economist's views. For example, the accountant will value a school building at cost of construction, and will depreciate the building over its estimated useful life, perhaps thirty years. Depreciation merely represents a way to allocate an *expenditure* (the money spent on the building) as an *expense* (the cost of something for a particular period of time). What is the "some-thing"? One might term it the service provided by the use of the building in that period. Perhaps the building will be used for a much longer or shorter time period. Perhaps because of inflation, it could be sold to a nearby factory for several times its construction cost. To the accountant these issues are interesting but not part of the problem, which is that the accrued expense of the building for a particular period is the assigned depreciation charged for that period, regardless of the current value of the building.

The accountant then typically studies the institution as a going concern and looks at the accrued amounts for a particular period. These may differ sharply from the actual cash in and cash out for a period and may differ again from the change in wealth of the institution reflected in appreciation or depreciation of buildings, security portfolios, or the like. *Cash accounting* looks at the cash inflow and outflows for each period; *accrual accounting* reflects the income and expenses attributable to that period according to specific accounting rules, whether or not they were reflected by cash changes.

This distinction is especially important in businesses, but the distinction is somewhat blurred because of the fund-accounting system used in many schools. In colleges, the balance sheet reflects fund balances, and transfers into and out of those funds may reflect arbitrary accounting practices aside from the accrual concepts noted above. This issue is beyond the scope of this book, but several excellent references discuss fund accounting.[3] What is important is that the cost calculated by the accountant for the school may not reflect the cost in an economic sense. This difference between "book" figures and "economic" figures needs to be kept in mind as we think about various financial decisions.

However, the foolishness of a slavish devotion to formulas in college budgeting is well captured by Chambers.

> Every year brings needs for innovations not embraced in the formula; therefore even a newly devised formula should never be used as a substitute for thought (though it often is!). This year's formula will be out of date next year. Any formula needs constant revision, especially in a field undergoing rapid change, as is true of higher education now.

> No magic formula can excuse an abdication of reason by responsible public officers. The formula fad is a menace to progress.[4]

Time Value of Money

Probably no concept has had a larger impact on the field of finance than the idea of the time value of money, also reflected in such terms as the "present value" or "present worth" of some item. Originally part of insurance actuarial analysis in the 1600s, the concept moved to mining, engineering, and economics in the last century, and became popularized in finance in the 1930s and 1940s. The advent of the high-speed computer in the 1950s and the small calculator in the 1960s meant that many individuals from very diverse backgrounds were able to use these concepts to aid their financial decision making.[5]

Why is the time value of money important? Our concern here is not with inflation, although changes in the value of the dollar can easily be placed in the analysis as we shall show in chapter 7. Rather, the problem is considering the opportunity costs and benefits of several choices that may have different lifetimes and different cash flows associated with each year, choices that must be compared in order to reach a decision. Usually the analysis is based on yearly cash flows, although monthly or weekly data can be used. In addition, some opportunity cost of money must be selected, which also may be called a *discount rate* or *rate of return*. As an example, if a university wants to build a dormitory, perhaps money will cost 9 percent. If a university has idle cash, perhaps it can be invested at 8 percent. In the long run, the common stocks may return 10 percent. Thus there may be different rates for different purposes, although we shall usually use a common rate for many different decisions under review at any time.

The sort of problem that present-value analysis enables us to consider is the following. Suppose a donor offers to give us $1,000 now or $1,200 at the end of three years. Which is preferable? We might immediately think that the $1,000 could be invested at, for example, 8 percent, providing $80 in interest the first year, another $86 in interest the second year, and $94 in interest the third year, for a total value of principal and interest in three years of $1,260. Under this analysis, we prefer the $1,000 now, for the total amount we would have in three years is more than the $1,200 offered under that alternative. Thus our *opportunity cost* of taking the $1,200 in three years is $60.

Algebraically, this analysis could be done as follows:

$$(\$1,000) \times (1.08) = \$1,080 \text{ at the end of one year}$$

$$(\$1,080) \times (1.08) = \$1,166 \text{ at the end of two years}$$

$$(\$1,166) \times (1.08) = \$1,260 \text{ at the end of three years}$$

But suppose we recognize that the analysis is clumsy: different opportunities might have different lives. Perhaps the alternative is not $1,200 in three years but $500 for each of years 3, 4, and 5. Then we may see that a more useful value to calculate is the worth *today* of various choices. We ask: What sum, invested today at a given rate, would have the same value as this future cash flow? In our case, what is $1,200 at the *end* of three years worth *today*? That amount is:

$$X \times (1.08)^3 = \$1,200$$

The term $(1.08)^3$ equals 1.08 times 1.08 times 1.08, which reflects the compounding of interest and must be reversed for the present-value analysis. Rearranging terms, we have

$$X = \frac{\$1,200}{(1.08)^3}$$

and X is equal to $953.

Fortunately, tables exist for calculating the present values of cash flows. These tables are shown in the appendix to this chapter. For example, if we want to know the value today of $1 received in three years when the opportunity cost of money is 10 percent, the 10-percent column in table 1A–5 shows .75131 on the third row, for the third-year receipt. In other words, the dollar received at the end of three years is worth about 75 cents today. Alternatively, $0.75131 invested at 10 percent for three years is worth $1 (0.75131 $\times$ 1.10^3 = 1.00). Table 1A–6 shows us the value today of $1 received every year for so many years. Thus $1 per year for three years when the opportunity cost is 10 percent is worth $2.4868, which is also the sum of the three terms in table 1A–5 for $1 received at the end of one year, plus a second year, plus a third year (0.90909 + 0.82645 + 0.75131).

Sometimes people compare an outflow now with several inflows and compute the opportunity rate to make the present value of all those future cash flows equal to the current outflow. This rate is often called the *internal rate of return,* or *rate of return.* The algebra describing these concepts and exercises involving present value are part of the appendix to this chapter. What is important is that one can reduce cash flows received several years in the future to a single number that permits comparisons of various opportunities open to the school.

Liquidity

Whatever the present-value or opportunity-cost aspects of decisions, there is always the issue of liquidity, that is, of being able to raise cash when needed. Corporations have often faced bankruptcy and so, increasingly, are schools. A balance sheet of a business is composed of assets on one side and liabilities (or obligations to others) and the shareholder's equity on the other side. Bankruptcy can occur either when the debts exceed the assets (meaning the owners have a negative worth in the business) or when the firm is unable to meet obligations as they come due. Both New York City and most corporations reflect the latter type of financial stringency and/or bankruptcy: The assets are not sufficiently liquid to meet the obligations. Sometimes assets can be liquidated only at a much lower figure than their cost value or their true "market value," which means the price agreed upon between a willing buyer and a willing seller not acting under duress. Hence liquidity is an issue that we must bear in mind in making financial decisions for a college.

Risk and Risk Premiums

Risk can take many forms. Sometimes it is a liquidity risk such as when a school administrator cannot have the money when it is needed. Sometimes it is a bad outcome such as when common-stock returns are notoriously more risky in the sense of having very high or very low returns than, for example, bonds. The fact that someone earns more for a particular job may mean that it is simply riskier; for example, one may argue that formalized tenure procedures for professors or public employees may mean that their salaries should be lower than they would be otherwise since they are in a less risky position.[6] Often we say that the higher risk investment in real estate or common stocks should return more as a reward for taking risk. This issue is elaborated on in chapter 6. Of course, we will probably earn more or less than we estimate. The point is that the *estimate* of a likely return should be sufficiently high to compensate for bearing that risk. This issue too has become a major part of formalized corporate and investment finance in the last two decades, and it has applications to the college administrator facing a variety of choices with alternative risk patterns. Its application will be part of the continuing exposition in this book.

As we move to specific topics covering issues of concern to university administrators, the preceding eight economic concepts will be useful. Sometimes we will discuss them in detail, sometimes merely mention them, and other times assume them without citation. However, when they become an automatic way of viewing problems, a way to measure choices without requiring a particular decision, then the first step will have been taken toward using the tools of economics in considering educational problems. Many of these ideas represent common sense, or a method that seems subconscious; it is only when one has sat through corporate board or faculty committee meetings that one realizes how uncommon "common" sense is. Usually, people of good will and great competence will look at the world in different ways. There often is ignorance and venality and sometimes just plain stupidity. However, there also frequently will be fundamentally different value systems at work. Perhaps placing some of these issues explicitly before a group will permit a more rational analysis of some aspects of the issues, and that may lead to better decisions. It is my hope that such an outcome will occur.

Notes

1. See Joseph Ben-David, *American Higher Education: Directions Old and New* (New York: McGraw-Hill, 1972), and the *Chronicle of Higher Education,* 5 September 1978, p. 1. The problem with the expansion of doctoral programs in the 1960s and the continued flow of new Ph.D.s who may think they have academic jobs waiting is captured in one short article. Thus the hiring of junior faculty averaged 27,000 between 1962 and 1972, yet it will average no more than 10,000 from 1982 to 1992, in large part because

of the enrollment drop cited above. However, the forecast is for 46,000 new Ph.D.s to be produced *per year* in the 1980s. This forecast implies that less than one-fifth of the new Ph.D.s will have jobs in academics in this period versus about one-half in the 1960s. Again there will be sharply divergent patterns in various disciplines; some will have virtually no jobs for the new Ph.D.s (for example, history, classics?) and others will continue to have shortages (for example, accounting?). See Allan M. Cartter and Lewis C. Solmon, "Implications for Faculty," *Change,* September 1976, pp. 37–38. The agony of the unavailability of tenured positions and the creation of an army of "gypsy scholars" is captured in a front-page *Wall Street Journal* column, 13 March 1979. Also see "Can't Somebody Turn the Damned Thing Off?" *Forbes,* 7 August 1978, pp. 47–53.

2. There is some evidence that in a recession *viewed as short-term,* initially students will attend college for want of anything more lucrative to do with their time. Since a recession often coincides with declining state-tax revenues, a public-school enrollment surge in a recession can be extremely difficult to fund. This issue is discussed as part of the Wichita State University analysis in chapter 8.

3. Problems of accounting-data assimilation and the use of accounting data are well summarized in Anthony J. Gambino, *Planning and Control in Higher Education,* National Association of Accountants, New York, 1979. The study is summarized in *Management Accounting,* January 1979, pp. 53–54.

Budgets are not new in general, not even in the education field. Sidney G. Tickton recounted a budgeting plan for a small college. As he discussed it, the standard pattern familiar in the private business sector was followed. First, compute current levels of enrollments, faculty salaries, and so on. Next, project for the society as a whole. Third, project for the individual college, and then analyze the final results. The major benefit is often in the analysis itself, seeing the interrelationships between class sizes, market attractiveness to student and faculty. There is usually a rerunning of the ten-year budgets in various periods as one updates the inputs; these data are not immutable. Various options can be calculated such as alternative student-faculty ratios, growth in student bodies, and class size. The key to the analysis I am presenting is an emphasis on the importance of returning *flexibility* for the future years to college funding. Then a university official may be very concerned about what commitments of funding have been made, both for next year's budget and for the following years. See Sidney G. Ticketon, "The Ashford College Case Study," chapter 7 in *Financing Higher Education 1960–1970,* ed. Dexter M. Keezer (New York: McGraw–Hill, 1959).

The American Financial Accounting Standards Board has considered some of the accounting-statement issues for nonprofit organizations. For a summary of their discussion memorandum on the key issues about what statements should be provided, for whom, and for what purpose, see "Objectives of Financial Reporting by Non-business Organizations," *Management Accounting,* February 1979, pp. 53–56. Also see Robert N. Anthony, *Financial Accounting in Non-business Organizations,* research report of the Financial Accounting Standards Board, Stamford, Conn., 1978; and Robert N. Anthony and Regina Herzlinger, *Management Control in Nonprofit Organizations* (Homewood, Ill.: R.D. Irwin, 1975).

One account of management control using budget information for long-run resource planning is found in David S.P. Hopkins and William F. Massy, "A Model for Planning the Transition to Equilibrium of a University Budget," *Management Science,* July 1977, pp. 1161–1168. Also see Richard C. Grinold, David S.P. Hopkins, and William F. Massy, "A Model for Long-range University Budget Planning under Uncertainty," *Bell Journal of Economics,* Autumn 1978, pp. 396–420; and Joseph A. Maciariello and Willard F. Enteman, "A System for Management Control in Private Colleges," *Journal of Higher Education,* November 1974, pp. 594–606.

4. M.M. Chambers, *Higher Education: Who Pays? Who Gains?* (Danville, Ill.: Interstate Printers and Publishers, 1968), p. 269.

5. For a more detailed account of the evolution of present value, see pp. 37–38 of E. Eugene Carter, *Portfolio Aspects of Corporate Capital Budgeting* (Lexington, Mass.: D.C. Heath and Company, 1974).

6. There is some good analysis that indicates that municipal employees in the U.S. civil service earn far more than their skills would justify in the private sector, presumably because of bargaining power and/or weak legislators.

Appendix 1A: Discounting: Net Present Value and Internal Rate of Return

Once the cash flows are determined, we need to appraise the cash flows in consideration of the time value of money. Net Present Value (NPV) and Rate of Return (ROR) are two means by which to discount cash flows.

Suppose one has X dollars (for example, $10) and the ROR (discount rate) is r (for example, 10 percent). At the end of one year, the value Y_1 of the holding is

$$Y_1 = X(1 + r) \qquad Y_1 = \$10(1 + 0.10) = \$11.00$$

At the end of two years,

$$Y_2 = Y_1(1 + r) = X(1 + r)^2 \qquad Y_2 = \$10(1 + 0.10)^2 = \$12.10$$

The term Y_2 represents the *terminal value* of investment X at the end of the second year compounded annually at the rate r. One can reverse the procedure. Given Y_2 dollars at the end of two years and the rate of discount r, then X, the amount of money equivalent to Y_2 dollars two years hence, can be found:

$$X = \frac{Y_2}{(1 + r)^2} \qquad X = \frac{\$12.10}{(1 + 0.10)^2} = \$10.00$$

and X is the present value of Y_2.

In capital budgeting, we estimate the Y values (yearly net cash flows) for the investment. We select a discount rate that is the opportunity cost of funds to the school (the cost of capital) r. Then X can be computed, where X is the net present value of the stream of cash flows. This stream includes the initial investment Y_0, which is negative, and the other Y_i s that may be negative or positive.

$$X = Y_0 + \frac{Y_1}{(1 + r)} + \frac{Y_2}{(1 + r)^2} + \cdots + \frac{Y_n}{(1 + r)^n}$$

This appendix is drawn from E. Eugene Carter, *Portfolio Aspects of Corporate Capital Budgeting* (Lexington, MA.: D.C. Heath and Company, 1974). See also chapters 10 and 11 of Rita M. Rodriguez and E. Eugene Carter, *International Financial Management,* 2d. ed. (Englewood Cliffs, N.J.: Prentice Hall, 1979).

If the present value is positive ($X > 0$), the investment is considered desirable, as it covers the cost of funds of the school.

The ROR is also called the "discounted rate of return," "internal rate of return," or "return on investment"; the ROR is the rate at which the future cash flows can be discounted to equal the investment. It is obtained using the same equation but slightly different analysis. Instead of assigning a discount rate r, the equation is solved for that rate for which the present value of the stream of cash outflows and inflows of an investment equals zero. That is, we find r such that

$$0 = Y_0 + \frac{U_1}{(1 + r)} + \frac{Y_2}{(1 + r)^2} + \cdots + \frac{Y_n}{(1 + r)^n}$$

Again, Y_0 is negative, representing the cash investment in the project.

Present-value Examples

1. A student offers to pay $500 per year for five years in exchange for a $2,000 loan today. What interest rate is she paying?

2. The payments on a mortgage loan are computed so that the return to the lender and the cost to the borrower are both equal to the interest rate. For example, assume that you borrowed $1,000 at 5 percent and planned to repay the amount in four equal annual payments. The annual payment shown in a banker's mortgage table for this would be about $282.00. Convince yourself that the $282 would repay the loan in four years and cost 5 percent by filling in table 1A–1. Next, take the point of view of the lender and compute the present value of four annual payments of $282.00 using a discount rate of 5 percent, as started in the table 1A–2. If the present value is $1,000, the lender is earning 5 percent on the funds loaned to you.

3. A newly tenured faculty member is expected to earn $20,000 per year for the foreseeable future. Assuming the faculty member has associated support costs of $5,000 per year for secretarial services and the college has a 5-percent cost of funds, what is the present value of a thirty-year commitment to the professor? (Question: Which fringe benefits should also be included in the cost? How might we measure them?)

4. For $800, a university can buy a new typewriter that has a useful life of ten years and no salvage value. Alternatively, the manufacturer offers a lease of $120 per year that is noncancelable for ten years. Under either case, the school is responsible for maintenance. What is the imputed, the implied, interest rate in this lease? How should the college make the decision on whether to lease or buy the machine?

Table 1A–1
Loan Payment Schedule

End of Year	Total Payment	Interest Paid on Outstanding Balance of 5%	Principal Repaid	Outstanding Balance
0	–	–	–	$1,000.00
1	$282.00	$50.00	$232.00	768.00
2	282.00			
3	282.00			
4	282.00			

Table 1A–2
Loan Receipt Schedule

End of Year	Total Payment	Present-value Factor at 5%	Present Value
1	$282.00	0.952	$268.46
2	282.00	0.907	
3	282.00		
4	282.00		————
Total present value			════

5. A university vice-president wonders about the worth of a cash flow for a fire-insurance policy of $400, $600, and $700 if his institution can earn 10 percent on its money. What is the equivalent annual flow of these three premium payments?

Solutions to Present-value Examples

1. The present value of a five-year, $500 cash flow is to equal $2,000. Thus a factor Y in table 1A–6 should be found such that $500 times Y equals $2,000. Solving, Y equals $2,000 divided by $500, or 4.00. Looking across the line for five years, we find the factor nearest to 4.00 is 8 percent, with a factor of 3.9927.
2. See tables 1A–3 and 1A–4.
3. Although the tables include figures for only twenty-five years, we can solve this problem by noting that the cash paid to the professor and the secretary from years 26 through 30 are really the same as a year 1 to 5 series viewed from the twenty-fifth year. Thus the present value of

ARNULFO L. OLIVEIRA MEMORIAL LIBRARY
1825 MAY STREET
BROWNSVILLE, TEXAS 78520

Table 1A-3
Loan Payment Schedule

End of Year	Total Payment	Interest Paid on Outstanding Balance of 5%	Principal Paid	Outstanding Balance
0	–	–	–	$1,000.00
1	$282.00	$50.00	$232.00	768.00
2	282.00	38.40	243.60	524.40
3	282.00	26.22	255.78	268.62
4	282.00	13.43	268.57	.05
				(Approx. 0)

Table 1A-4
Loan Receipt Schedule

End of Year	Total Payment	Present-value Factor at 5%	Present Value
1	$282.00	0.952	$268.46
2	282.00	0.907	255.77
3	282.00	0.864	243.65
4	282.00	0.823	232.09
	$1128.00	3.546	$999.97
			(Approx. $1,000)

$25,000 per year for five years at 5 percent from table 1A-6 is $25,000 times 4.3295, or $108,238. The present value of $25,000 per year for twenty-five years at 5 percent from the same table is $25,000 times 14.0939, or $352,348. We can think of the first figure as deriving the present value of the last five years as of the twenty-fifth year, so we must discount this twenty-fifth-year present value to today's value. Using table 1A-5, the present value of $1 received at the end of twenty-five years, discounted at 5 percent, is 0.29530. Hence the value of this flow is 0.29530 times $108,238, or $31,963. Adding these two figures, the total commitment today in present value of future payments to this newly tenured professor is $31,963 plus $352,348, which equals $384,311. More realistic examples of these calculations under various assumptions are part of the discussion in chapter 8, which considers fringe-benefit costs.

Table 1A–5
Present Value of $1 Due at the End of N Years

N	1%	2%	3%	4%	5%	6%	7%	8%	9%	10%	12%	14%	N
1	0.99010	0.98039	0.97007	0.96154	0.95238	0.94340	0.93458	0.92593	0.91743	0.90909	0.89286	0.87719	1
2	.98030	.96117	.94260	.92456	.90703	.89000	.87344	.85734	.84168	.82645	.79719	.76947	2
3	.97059	.94232	.91514	.88900	.86384	.83962	.81630	.79383	.77218	.75131	.71178	.67497	3
4	.96098	.92385	.88849	.85480	.82270	.79209	.76290	.73503	.70843	.68301	.63552	.59208	4
5	.95147	.90573	.86261	.82193	.78353	.74726	.71299	.68058	.64993	.62092	.56743	.51937	5
6	.94204	.88797	.83748	.79031	.74622	.70496	.66634	.63017	.59627	.56447	.50663	.45559	6
7	.93272	.87056	.81309	.75992	.71068	.66506	.62275	.58349	.54703	.51316	.45235	.39964	7
8	.92348	.85349	.78941	.73069	.67684	.62741	.58201	.54027	.50187	.46651	.40388	.35056	8
9	.91434	.83675	.76642	.70259	.64461	.59190	.54393	.50025	.46043	.42410	.36061	.30751	9
10	.90529	.82035	.74409	.67556	.61391	.55839	.50835	.46319	.42241	.38554	.32197	.26974	10
11	.89632	.80425	.72242	.64958	.58468	.52679	.47509	.42888	.38753	.35049	.28748	.23662	11
12	.88745	.78849	.70138	.62460	.55684	.49697	.44401	.39711	.35553	.31863	.25667	.20756	12
13	.87866	.77303	.68095	.60057	.53032	.46384	.41496	.36770	.32618	.28966	.22917	.18207	13
14	.86996	.75787	.66112	.57747	.50507	.44230	.38782	.34046	.29925	.26333	.20462	.15971	14
15	.86135	.74301	.64186	.55526	.48102	.41726	.36245	.31524	.27454	.23939	.18270	.14010	15
16	.85282	.72845	.62317	.53391	.45811	.39365	.33873	.29189	.25187	.21763	.16312	.12289	16
17	.84438	.71416	.60502	.51337	.43630	.37136	.31657	.27027	.23107	.19784	.14564	.10780	17
18	.83602	.70016	.58739	.49363	.41552	.35034	.29586	.25025	.21199	.17986	.13004	.09456	18
19	.82774	.68643	.57029	.47464	.39573	.33051	.27651	.23171	.19449	.16351	.11611	.08295	19
20	.81954	.67297	.55367	.45639	.37689	.31180	.25842	.21455	.17843	.14864	.10367	.07276	20
21	.81143	.65978	.53755	.43883	.35894	.29415	.24151	.19866	.16370	.13513	.09256	.06383	21
22	.80340	.64684	.52189	.42195	.34185	.27750	.22571	.18394	.15018	.12285	.08264	.05599	22
23	.79544	.63416	.50669	.40573	.32557	.26180	.21095	.17031	.13778	.11168	.07379	.04911	23
24	.78757	.62172	.49193	.39012	.31007	.24698	.19715	.15770	.12640	.10153	.06588	.04308	24
25	.77977	.60953	.47760	.37512	.29530	.23300	.18425	.14602	.11597	.09230	.05882	.03779	25

Table 1A–5 continued

N	15%	16%	18%	20%	22%	24%	25%	26%	28%	30%	N
1	0.86957	0.86207	0.84746	0.83333	0.81967	0.80645	0.80000	0.79365	0.78125	0.76923	1
2	.75614	.74316	.71818	.69444	.67186	.65036	.64000	.62988	.61035	.59172	2
3	.65752	.64066	.60863	.57870	.55071	.52449	.51200	.49991	.47684	.45517	3
4	.57175	.55229	.51579	.48225	.45140	.42297	.40960	.39675	.37253	.35013	4
5	.49718	.47611	.43711	.40188	.37000	.34111	.32768	.31488	.29104	.26933	5
6	.43233	.41044	.37043	.33490	.30328	.27509	.26214	.24991	.22737	.20718	6
7	.37594	.35383	.31392	.27980	.24859	.22184	.20972	.19834	.17764	.15937	7
8	.32690	.30503	.26604	.23257	.20376	.17891	.16777	.15741	.13878	.12259	8
9	.28426	.26295	.22546	.19381	.16702	.14428	.13422	.12493	.10842	.09430	9
10	.24718	.22668	.19106	.16151	.13690	.11635	.10737	.09915	.08470	.07254	10
11	.21494	.19542	.16192	.13459	.11221	.09383	.08590	.07869	.06617	.05580	11
12	.18691	.16846	.13722	.11216	.09198	.07567	.06872	.06245	.05170	.04292	12
13	.16253	.14523	.11629	.09346	.07539	.06103	.05498	.04957	.04039	.03302	13
14	.14133	.12520	.09855	.07789	.06180	.04921	.04398	.03934	.03155	.02540	14
15	.12289	.10793	.08352	.06491	.05065	.03969	.03518	.03122	.02465	.01954	15
16	.10686	.09304	.07078	.05409	.04152	.03201	.02815	.02478	.01926	.01503	16
17	.09293	.08021	.05998	.04507	.03403	.02581	.02252	.01967	.01505	.01156	17
18	.08080	.06914	.05083	.03756	.02789	.02082	.01801	.01561	.01175	.00889	18
19	.07026	.05961	.04308	.03130	.02286	.01679	.01441	.01239	.00918	.00684	19
20	.06110	.05139	.03651	.02608	.01874	.01354	.01153	.00983	.00717	.00526	20
21	.05313	.04430	.03094	.02174	.01536	.01092	.00922	.00780	.00561	.00405	21
22	.04620	.03819	.02622	.01811	.01259	.00880	.00738	.00619	.00438	.00311	22
23	.04017	.03292	.02222	.01509	.01032	.00710	.00590	.00491	.00342	.00239	23
24	.03493	.02838	.01883	.01258	.00846	.00573	.00472	.00390	.00267	.00184	24
25	.03038	.02447	.01596	.01048	.00693	.00462	.00378	.00310	.00209	.00142	25

Table 1A–6
Present Value of $1 Received Annually for N Years

N	1%	2%	3%	4%	5%	6%	7%	8%	9%	10%	12%	14%	N
1	0.9901	0.9804	0.9709	0.9615	0.9524	0.9434	0.9346	0.9259	0.9174	0.9091	0.8929	0.8772	1
2	1.9704	1.9416	1.9135	1.8861	1.8594	1.8334	1.8080	1.7833	1.7591	1.7355	1.6901	1.6467	2
3	2.9410	2.8839	2.8286	2.7751	2.7232	2.6730	2.6243	2.5771	2.5313	2.4868	2.4018	2.3216	3
4	3.9020	3.8077	3.7171	3.6299	3.5459	3.4651	3.3872	3.3121	3.2397	3.1699	3.0373	2.9137	4
5	4.8535	4.7134	4.5797	4.4518	4.3295	4.2123	4.1002	3.9927	3.8896	3.7908	3.6048	3.4331	5
6	5.7955	5.6014	5.4172	5.2421	5.0757	4.9173	4.7665	4.6229	4.4859	4.3553	4.1114	3.8887	6
7	6.7282	6.4720	6.2302	6.0020	5.7863	5.5824	5.3893	5.2064	5.0329	4.8684	4.5638	4.2883	7
8	7.6517	7.3254	7.0196	6.7327	6.4632	6.2098	5.9713	5.7466	5.5348	5.3349	4.9676	4.6389	8
9	8.5661	8.1622	7.7861	7.4353	7.1078	6.8017	6.5152	6.2469	5.9952	5.7590	5.3282	4.9464	9
10	9.4714	8.9825	8.5302	8.1109	7.7217	7.3601	7.0236	6.7101	6.4176	6.1446	5.6502	5.2161	10
11	10.3677	9.7868	9.2526	8.7604	8.3064	7.8868	7.4987	7.1389	6.8052	6.4951	5.9377	5.4527	11
12	11.2552	10.5753	9.9539	9.3850	8.8632	8.3838	7.9427	7.5361	7.1607	6.8137	6.1944	5.6603	12
13	12.1338	11.3483	10.6349	9.9856	9.3935	8.8527	8.3576	7.9038	7.4869	7.1034	6.4235	5.8424	13
14	13.0038	12.1062	11.2960	10.5631	9.8986	9.2950	8.7454	8.2442	7.7861	7.3667	6.6282	6.0021	14
15	13.8651	12.8492	11.9379	11.1183	10.3796	9.7122	9.1079	8.5595	8.0607	7.6061	6.8109	6.1422	15
16	14.7180	13.5777	12.5610	11.6522	10.8377	10.1059	9.4466	8.8514	8.3125	7.8237	6.9740	6.2651	16
17	15.5624	14.2918	13.1660	12.1656	11.2740	10.4772	9.7632	9.1216	8.5436	8.0215	7.1196	6.3729	17
18	16.3984	14.9920	13.7534	12.6592	11.6895	10.8276	10.0591	9.3719	8.7556	8.2014	7.2497	6.4674	18
19	17.2261	15.6784	14.3237	13.1339	12.0853	11.1581	10.3356	9.6036	8.9501	8.3649	7.3658	6.5504	19
20	18.0457	16.3514	14.8774	13.5903	12.4622	11.4699	10.5940	9.8181	9.1285	8.5136	7.4694	6.6231	20
21	18.8571	17.0111	15.4149	14.0291	12.8211	11.7640	10.8355	10.0168	9.2922	8.6487	7.5620	6.6870	21
22	19.6605	17.6580	15.9368	14.4511	13.1630	12.0416	11.0612	10.2007	9.4424	8.7715	7.6446	6.7429	22
23	20.4559	18.2921	16.4435	14.8568	13.4885	12.3033	11.2722	10.3710	9.5802	8.8832	7.7184	6.7921	23
24	21.2435	18.9139	16.9355	15.2469	13.7986	12.5503	11.4693	10.5287	9.7066	8.9847	7.7843	6.8351	24
25	22.0233	19.5234	17.4131	15.6220	14.0939	12.7833	11.6536	10.6748	9.8226	9.0770	7.8431	6.8729	25

Table 1A–6 continued

N	15%	16%	18%	20%	22%	24%	25%	26%	28%	30%	N
1	0.8696	0.8621	0.8475	0.8333	0.8197	0.8065	0.8000	0.7937	0.7813	0.7692	1
2	1.6257	1.6052	1.5656	1.5278	1.4915	1.4568	1.4400	1.4235	1.3916	1.3609	2
3	2.2832	2.2459	2.1743	2.1065	2.0422	1.9813	1.9520	1.9234	1.8684	1.8161	3
4	2.8550	2.7982	2.6901	2.5887	2.4936	2.4043	2.3616	2.3202	2.2410	2.1662	4
5	3.3522	3.2743	3.1272	2.9906	2.8636	2.7454	2.6893	2.6351	2.5320	2.4356	5
6	3.7845	3.6847	3.4976	3.3255	3.1669	3.0205	2.9515	2.8850	2.7594	2.6427	6
7	4.1604	4.0386	3.8115	3.6046	3.4155	3.2423	3.1611	3.0833	2.9370	2.8021	7
8	4.4873	4.3436	4.0776	3.8372	3.6193	3.4212	3.3289	3.2407	3.0758	2.9247	8
9	4.7716	4.6065	4.3030	4.0310	3.7863	3.5655	3.4631	3.3657	3.1842	3.0190	9
10	5.0188	4.8332	4.4941	4.1925	3.9232	3.6819	3.5705	3.4648	3.2689	3.0915	10
11	5.2337	5.0286	4.6560	4.3271	4.0354	3.7757	3.6564	3.5435	3.3351	3.1473	11
12	5.4206	5.1971	4.7932	4.4392	4.1274	3.8514	3.7251	3.6060	3.3868	3.1903	12
13	5.5831	5.3423	4.9095	4.5327	4.2028	3.9124	3.7801	3.6555	3.4272	3.2233	13
14	5.7245	5.4675	5.0081	4.6106	4.2646	3.9616	3.8241	3.6949	3.4587	3.2487	14
15	5.8474	5.5755	5.0916	4.6755	4.3152	4.0013	3.8593	3.7261	3.4834	3.2682	15
16	5.9542	5.6685	5.1624	4.7296	4.3567	4.0333	3.8874	3.7509	3.5026	3.2832	16
17	6.0472	5.7487	5.2223	4.7746	4.3908	4.0591	3.9099	3.7705	3.5177	3.2948	17
18	6.1280	5.8178	5.2732	4.8122	4.4187	4.0799	3.9279	3.7861	3.5294	3.3037	18
19	6.1982	5.8775	5.3162	4.8435	4.4415	4.0967	3.9424	3.7985	3.5386	3.3105	19
20	6.2593	5.9288	5.3527	4.8696	4.4603	4.1103	3.9539	3.8083	3.5458	3.3158	20
21	6.3125	5.9731	5.3837	4.8913	4.4756	4.1212	3.9631	3.8161	3.5514	3.3198	21
22	6.3587	6.0113	5.4099	4.9094	4.4882	4.1300	3.9705	3.8223	3.5558	3.3230	22
23	6.3988	6.0442	5.4321	4.9245	4.4985	4.1371	3.9764	3.8273	3.5592	3.3254	23
24	6.4338	6.0726	5.4509	4.9371	4.5070	4.1428	3.9811	3.8312	3.5619	3.3272	24
25	6.4641	6.0971	5.4669	4.9476	4.5139	4.1474	3.9849	3.8342	3.5640	3.3286	25

Source: Excerpted from James C. Van Horne, *Financial Management and Policy*, 5th ed. (Englewood Cliffs, N.J.: Prentice-Hall, Inc., 1980), pp. 788–795. Reprinted by permission of the publisher.

4. First we find that $800 divided by $120 equals 6.67. Looking at table 1A-6, the closest factor to 6.67 for a ten-year cash flow is under the 8-percent heading. If the college believes its money is worth more than 8 percent, it should accept the lease: the difference in lease payments and the initial investment required to purchase the typewriter can be used profitably elsewhere. Alternatively, if it can borrow money to buy the typewriter at less than 8 percent, the administration probably will prefer to buy the machine. *Imputed* means the implied interest rate, which is about 8 percent.

5. The equivalent annual flow is a figure that many people like to use. Essentially, an uneven future cash flow is converted to its present worth. The present value is then divided by a factor from table 1A-6 that represents the number of years the cash flows will continue and the assumed interest rate. This calculation provides an annual cash flow that is equivalent to the present value of the original cash flows. In the example here, the present value of the three-year cash flow is

$$
\begin{array}{rcl}
\$400 \times 0.90909 & = \$ & 364 \\
600 \times 0.82645 & = & 496 \\
700 \times 0.75131 & = & \underline{526} \\
& & \$1,386
\end{array}
$$

from table 1A-5. The total is divided by 2.4868, the discount factor for $1 per year for three years at 10 percent from table 1A-6. The equivalent annual flow is then $1,386 divided by 2.4868, or $557 per year for three years. Many calculators include a present-value function or set of finance keys. The user inputs three or four of the five variables, and the calculator solves for the others. These keys are the number of years or periods, the interest rate, the payment per year, the present value, and the future accumulated value. When this function is absent, the most efficient way to find the present value of cash flows is not to multiply each year's cash flow by the appropriate factor from a table but rather to enter the figure for the present worth of $1 received in one year at the appropriate discount rate (for example, 0.92593 for 8 percent). This factor is stored as a constant where possible on the calculator, and is multiplied by the *farthest* year's cash flow. The cash flow for the next to last year is added to the resulting product and the sum again multiplied by the constant. This procedure is repeated until the present value of the total stream is calculated. Such a process eliminates redundant figures entries and reveals the present value relatively quickly.

2 Financial Instruments

The following two chapters outline the relationship between economic concepts introduced in chapter 1 and the short-run and long-run financial choices that colleges face. It would be useful, however, first to summarize the nature of some financial instruments that many school administrators will want to consider. These instruments vary as to the legal responsibilities of the borrower or investor, the basic risk of the returns, the form in which the return is received, and so forth. Many college financial officers will be investing some short-term money in these instruments such as funds received in February from spring tuition bills that will be disbursed over the second semester as various payrolls are met. At other times the school will require financing.

Longer run financing obligations involve the creation of a fund for erection of a building, the investment of funds segregated for a library acquisition program or an endowed chair for a professor, or the allocation of current funds for retirement income for salaried employees. Public and private colleges alike face these problems. The private school has an even more complex task in deciding among the instruments in which it will invest its portfolio. The endowment decision affects not only income today and in the future but also the total funds that will be available in the future. We approach this topic in chapter 6.

There are only two major types of investment securities. One type represents debt such as bonds and the other represents ownership, as is the case with common stock. This basic difference between stocks and bonds has a dramatic effect on the nature of the revenues provided by these two types of securities.

Stocks represent shares of ownership or *equity* in a business. A stockholder owns a share of the plant, equipment, and other assets of the company, and the profits the company makes. Therefore stock prices rise or fall based in large part on expectations of how much profit the company will make in future years. Most companies pay a portion of their profits to their stockholders as dividends, and firms with rising profits usually have dividends that increase with this growth. These dividends provide a stream of revenue each year to stockholders, thereby providing a dividend yield. In addition to this revenue, stockholders also benefit through increases in the market price of the stock, or they lose through declines in stock price. Thus the *total return* from holding a stock over a period of time consists of the dividend yield plus the capital gain or loss that resulted from changes in the market price of the stock.

Just as a company can sell stock to obtain funds, it also can issue bonds or other types of debt securities. Purchasers of bonds are essentially lending money to the company for a period of time. To obtain this money, companies promise to pay interest, usually every six months, and to repay the loan at some date in the future. Unlike dividends, which can rise or fall at the discretion of the company, interest payments are a legal obligation of the company to the bondholders and must be paid each year regardless of how much profit is made. The amount of the loan, called the *principal,* is sometimes repaid in installments over a specified period of time, but the total amount of principal must all be repaid by the maturity of the bond. In rare instances a company will default on the interest and principal of the bond because of severe financial problems. In such instances the bondholder stands ahead of the stockholder in the sense that all interest and principal due bondholders must be paid before stockholders can obtain any of the company's assets.[1] Bonds are like stocks in that their market value can rise or fall over time, but unlike stocks most of the returns to the bondholder come in the form of the interest payments rather than a capital gain or loss.

Primary Characteristics of Investments

In order to decide which type of security is appropriate for a particular purpose, one needs to have information about the primary characteristics of stocks and bonds. Not all bonds or stocks are alike, and the following four properties are useful in describing the differences: risk, maturity, return, and marketability.[2]

Risk to most people is epitomized by the purchase of Penn Central bonds three weeks before bankruptcy. However, risk is more than just the probability of bankruptcy. One important element of risk is the potential gain or loss of market value of the security. Stock prices rise and fall daily so that there is always some risk that the price of a stock may end up lower than anticipated. Bonds too have market-value risk since their prices can rise or fall between their issue date and their maturity. Bond prices depend primarily on the current interest rate. No one would pay full price for an old 5-percent interest rate bond when he or she could buy a new bond at 8 or 9 percent interest. Thus as interest rates on new bonds go up, prices on old bonds go down. If one continues to hold such bonds, their price will eventually return to their original value since the company must repay the full amount that it borrowed by maturity or face bankruptcy.

A second element of risk concerns the stability of annual income. Interest on long-term bonds, for example, provides a stable annual revenue since this payment is a legal obligation of the company. Dividends can rise or fall at the discretion of the company, but in most cases companies try to keep these payments stable over time.

Maturity is the date by which a bond issuer must repay its loan. Common stock has no maturity because the company never promises to repurchase the stock, but all debt instruments in the United States have a specific maturity. This maturity is usually thought of in terms of being short, intermediate, or long term. Short term is usually considered to be a maturity date within one year. Intermediate-term bonds are those maturing from one to seven or eight years in the future, and long-term bonds include all longer maturities.

Return consists of the annual yield from each security and its capital gain or loss over the investment period. The annual yield on bonds results from the interest paid, and the yield from common stock results from dividends. Dividends on common stock have averaged close to 3 percent to 4 percent of the selling price of stock over the past several years. Interest yields on bonds fluctuate with economic conditions, but bonds issued in the 1970s have had interest rates in the range of 7 percent to 11 percent. With these interest rates no one would buy common stock unless they expected the market price of stocks to rise over time. This has been the pattern historically as the market value of stocks over a long period of time has tended to increase about 5 percent to 6 percent each year. This increase means a total return on stocks of roughly 9 percent to 10 percent, but of course this return is in no way guaranteed each year. Since bonds also fluctuate in market value between the time they are issued and their maturity date, they provide an opportunity for interim gains and losses, but the total return on bonds held to maturity will be the annual interest rate received.[3]

Marketability is the fourth major characteristic of securities. It reflects the ease with which securities can be sold at the given market price. Most of the securities that would be held by an educational institution are readily marketable. Stocks of most companies are actively traded on one of the stock exchanges such as the New York Stock Exchange or in the over-the-counter market. Stocks can be readily purchased and sold through brokers. The market for bonds is somewhat different than that for stocks. Frequently bonds purchased for endowment funds are bought when they are newly issued by a corporation. Such purchases are considered to be a part of the primary market for bonds. When a bond purchaser then wants to sell such bonds, they must be sold in the secondary market. Although the secondary market for bonds is not as active as it is for common stocks, bonds of most large companies can be readily bought or sold in this market through brokers. There are, however, securities that are not easily marketable and therefore pose some potential problems to colleges and universities. These securities would include those that represent debt or ownership of small or little-known companies.

Short-term Debt Securities

Short-term securities are used increasingly as means of investing surplus operating funds that are temporarily available. Most schools, for example, have a large inflow of cash as tuition is received. These funds can be invested until they are needed for operating purposes. In addition, most endowment and other funds frequently have some share of the portfolio invested in short-term securities while waiting for a more permanent investment of funds or to have some liquid reserve in case of an emergency.

U.S. Treasury bills are a popular investment security for short-term investment purposes. As a debt obligation of the U.S. government, they are considered to be free of default risk. If necessary, the government can raise taxes or even print money to pay interest and principal on its debt. Because these Treasury bills are risk free, they pay a slightly lower interest rate than other short-term securities, but they are very easy to buy, and they are readily marketable in case they need to be sold to raise cash. One way to purchase Treasury bills is to buy them directly through one of the twelve Federal Reserve Banks in the weekly auction of new Treasury bills. This is the primary market. They are typically sold with maturities of 91, 182, or 365 days. Most institutions though would buy Treasury bills from a bank or a broker (that is, on the secondary market) since that is a more convenient way to purchase relatively small amounts. Figure 2-1, taken from the *Chicago Tribune,* shows the quotes on outstanding U.S. Treasury bills and other debt instruments of the government.

As an example, consider the bill maturing on July 10, 1980. This security could have been purchased on January 9 at a price that would give the purchaser an effective annual interest rate of about 12.65 percent. The bid and asked columns are computed on the basis of a 360-day year and represent the discounts based on the number of days the security has until payment. As a buyer, one would pay the asked price. Using the figure shown, the discount on a $10,000 face amount security would be (182 divided by

Treasury Securities

Wednesday, January 9, 1980

Rate	Mat.	date	Bid	Asked	BidChg	Yld
7.50	Jan	1980 n	99.22	99.26	.....	10.62
4.00	Feb	1980	98.3	99.6	— .27	12.43
6.50	Feb	1980 n	99.11	99.15+	.1	11.84
7.63	Feb	1980 n	99.8	99.12	.....	12.01
7.50	Mar	1980 n	98.26	98.30	.....	12.23
7.75	Apr	1980 n	98.16	98.20	.....	12.28
6.88	May	1980 n	98.4	98.8	.....	12.05
8.00	May	1980 n	98.10	98.14+	.2	12.13
7.63	Jun	1980 n	97.26	98.2 +	.2	11.95
8.25	Jun	1980 n	98.3	98.7 +	.1	12.23
8.50	Jul	1980 n	97.27	97.31+	.1	12.39
6.75	Aug	1980 n	96.22	96.30+	.1	12.22
9.00	Aug	1980 n	98.16	98.24	.....	11.22
8.38	Aug	1980 n	97.15	97.19+	.1	12.42
6.88	Sep	1980 n	96.9	96.17+	.3	12.03
8.63	Sep	1980 n	97.12	97.16+	.2	12.35
8.88	Oct	1980 n	97.14	97.22+	.2	11.98
3.50	Nov	1980	93.20	93.28	.....	11.29
7.13	Nov	1980 n	96.2	96.10+	.1	11.83
9.25	Nov	1980 n	97.23	97.31+	.1	11.73
5.88	Dec	1980 n	94.20	94.28+	.3	11.61
9.88	Dec	1980 n	98.8	98.16	.....	11.55
9.75	Jan	1981 n	97.31	98.7 +	.1	11.59
7.00	Feb	1981 n	95.8	95.16	.....	11.48
7.38	Feb	1981 n	95.18	95.26	.....	11.55
9.75	Feb	1981 n	97.30	98.6 +	.1	11.50
6.88	Mar	1981 n	94.24	95	.....	11.37
9.63	Mar	1981 n	97.27	98.3	.....	11.34
9.75	Apr	1981 n	97.28	98.4	.....	11.34
7.38	May	1981 n	94.28	95.4	.....	11.38
7.50	May	1981 n	95.4	95.12+	.4	11.30
9.75	May	1981 n	97.30	98.6 —	.1	11.20
6.75	Jun	1981 n	93.27	94.3 +	.3	11.21
9.13	Jun	1981 n	96.31	97.7 +	.3	11.23
9.38	Jul	1981 n	97.4	97.12	.....	11.26
7.00	Aug	1981	93.16	94.16	.....	10.84
7.63	Aug	1981 n	94.20	94.28+	.2	11.22
8.38	Aug	1981 n	95.20	95.28+	.2	11.21
9.63	Aug	1981 n	97.14	97.22+	.2	11.21
6.75	Sep	1981 n	92.26	93.2 +	.2	11.30
10.13	Sep	1981 n	98.2	98.10	.....	11.23
12.63	Oct	1981 n	101.28	102 +	.4	11.37
7.00	Nov	1981 n	92.26	93.2 +	.4	11.27
7.75	Nov	1981 n	94.4	94.12+	.2	11.27
12.13	Nov	1981 n	101.6	101.10+	.2	11.33
7.25	Dec	1981 n	93	93.8 +	.2	11.16
11.38	Dec	1981 n	100.7	100.9 +	.1	11.21
6.13	Feb	1982 n	91.2	91.10+	.2	10.87
6.38	Feb	1982	90.30	91.14—	.2	11.06
7.88	Mar	1982 n	93.3	94.6 —	.25	10.89

Rate	Mat.	date	Bid	Asked	BidChg	Yld
7.00	May	1982 n	92.4	92.12+	.4	10.76
8.00	May	1982 n	94.4	94.12+	.2	10.78
9.25	May	1982 n	96.28	97.4 +	.2	10.67
8.25	Jun	1982 n	94.16	94.24+	.1	10.73
8.13	Aug	1982 n	93.27	94.3 +	.1	10.80
9.00	Aug	1982 n	95.30	96.6	.....	10.72
8.38	Sep	1982 n	94.9	94.17+	.3	10.75
7.13	Nov	1982 n	91.6	91.14+	.1	10.69
7.88	Nov	1982 n	92.30	93.6 +	.3	10.72
9.38	Dec	1982 n	96.28	97.4 +	.2	10.54
8.00	Feb	1983 n	92.26	93.2	.....	10.69
9.25	Mar	1983 n	96.8	96.16+	.2	10.56
7.88	May	1983 n	92.10	92.18	.....	10.57
11.63	May	1983 n	102.25	103.1 —	.1	10.53
3.25	Jun	1978-83	81.8	82.8	.....	9.42
8.88	Jun	1983 n	95.3	95.11	.....	10.51
9.75	Sep	1983 n	97.20	97.28—	.2	10.45
7.00	Nov	1983 n	88.25	89.1 —	.1	10.54
10.50	Dec	1983 n	99.22	99.24—	.2	10.58
7.25	Feb	1984 n	89.8	89.16—	.3	10.47
8.25	May	1984 n	96.4	96.12	.....	10.31
6.38	Aug	1984	85.14	86.14+	.5	10.14
7.25	Aug	1984 n	89	89.8 —	.1	10.24
8.00	Feb	1985 n	90.10	90.18—	.2	10.44
3.25	May	1985	76.12	77.12—	.2	8.62
4.25	May	1975-85	77.18	78.18—	.2	9.45
10.38	May	1985 n	99.11	99.15—	.1	10.51
8.25	Aug	1985 n	90.13	90.21—	.3	10.50
7.88	Nov	1986 n	87.16	87.24—	.3	10.58
8.00	Aug	1986 n	88	88.8 —	.1	10.52
6.13	Nov	1986	82.14	83.14+	.2	9.46
9.00	Feb	1987 n	92.9	92.17—	.1	10.52
7.63	Nov	1987 n	85.20	85.28—	.3	10.28
8.25	May	1988 n	87.16	87.26—	.2	10.49
8.75	Nov	1988 n	89.28	90.4 +	.1	10.49
9.25	May	1989 n	92.18	92.26	.....	10.47
10.75	Nov	1989 n	101.1	101.5 —	.1	10.56
3.50	Feb	1990	76.19	77.19+	.2	6.57
8.25	May	1990	86.28	87.12—	.5	10.25
4.25	Aug	1987-92	77.8	78.8 +	.6	6.86
7.25	Aug	1992	77.30	78.14+	.3	10.36
4.00	Feb	1988-93	76.24	77.24+	.4	6.55
6.75	Feb	1993	74.30	75.30+	.3	10.10
7.88	Feb	1993	81.8	81.24—	.4	10.17
7.50	Aug	1988-93	78.2	79.2 —	.7	10.42
8.63	Aug	1993	86.4	86.20+	.2	10.49
8.63	Nov	1993	86.4	86.20	....	10.48
9.00	Feb	1994	88.26	89.10—	.3	10.47
4.13	May	1989-94	76.14	77.14—	.4	6.57
8.75	Aug	1994	86.26	87.26—	.5	10.39

Rate	Mat.	date	Bid	Asked	BidChg	Yld
10.13	Nov	1994	97.2	97.18—	.4	10.45
3.00	Feb	1995	76.14	77.14	.....	5.17
10.50	Feb	1995	99.23	99.27—	.4	10.52
7.00	May	1993-98	75.20	76.20—	.4	9.76
3.50	Nov	1998	76.24	77.24	.....	5.40
8.50	May	1994-99	84.11	84.27—	.3	10.33
7.88	Feb	1995-00	79.6	79.14—	.5	10.33
8.38	Aug	1995-00	83.12	83.20—	.4	10.30
8.00	Aug	1996-01	80.7	80.23—	.3	10.24
8.25	May	2000-05	82.3	82.11—	.5	10.21
7.63	Feb	2002-07	77.1	77.9 —	.1	10.10
7.88	Nov	2002-07	82.28	83.12	.....	9.59
8.38	Aug	2003-08	83.9	83.17—	.1	10.16
8.75	Nov	2003-08	86.13	86.21—	.3	10.19
9.13	May	2004-09	89.23	89.31—	.3	10.20
10.38	Nov	2004-09	100.24	100.26—	.3	10.28

n— Treasury notes.
Bid and asked prices quoted in dollars and thirty seconds. Subject to Federal taxes but not to State income taxes.

Bills

Due	Bid	Ask	Yld	Due	Bid	Ask	Yld
-1980-							
1-10	10.79	10.21	0.00	5- 8	11.92	11.78	12.46
1-17	10.69	10.19	10.35	5-15	11.90	11.78	12.49
1-24	10.82	10.36	10.54	5-22	11.90	11.74	12.47
1-31	10.83	10.37	10.58	5-27	11.90	11.70	12.45
2- 5	10.91	10.53	10.76	5-29	11.90	11.76	12.53
2- 7	10.73	10.41	10.64	6- 5	11.88	11.72	12.51
2-14	11.22	10.82	11.08	6-12	11.83	11.69	12.51
2-21	11.44	11.10	11.41	6-19	11.78	11.66	12.50
2-28	11.46	11.18	11.54	6-26	11.77	11.59	12.44
3- 4	11.65	11.37	11.76	06-26	11.81	11.69	12.57
3- 6	11.62	11.40	11.80	7- 3	11.78	11.66	12.56
3-13	11.65	11.43	11.85	7-10	11.75	11.71	12.65
3-20	11.74	11.56	12.02	7-22	11.73	11.73	12.50
3-27	11.76	11.60	12.09	8-19	11.62	11.46	12.40
4- 1	11.80	11.60	12.11	9-16	11.22	11.04	11.96
4- 3	11.82	11.68	12.20	10-14	11.08	10.92	11.88
4-10	11.76	11.72	12.28	11- 6	10.95	10.81	11.81
4-17	11.86	11.68	12.26	12- 4	10.77	10.65	11.69
4-24	11.92	11.76	12.38	-1981-			
4-29	11.86	11.66	12.29	1- 2	10.76	10.72	11.85
5- 1	11.92	11.76	12.41				

Subject to Federal taxes but not State. taxes.

Reprinted, courtesy of the *Chicago Tribune,* January 10, 1980, section 4, page 15.

Figure 2-1. Government Debt Prices (Bonds and Notes)

360 times 11.71 equals) 5.9200. The price would then be $100 minus $5.9200, or 94.08 per $100 bond, or $9,408 for the $10,000 face amount bond. Notice that the prices involve next-day delivery, and the number of days between January 10 and July 10 is 182, the figure used in the calculation. At the end of the 182 days, one would receive the full $10,000, so the interest earned would be $592. The yield calculation shown in the figure is based on this return over 366 days because 1980 is a leap year, and is thus (366 divided by 182 times $592 divided by $9,408 equals) 12.65 percent. Notice that this yield is based on the money actually invested, $9,408, and not the face amount of the bill, $10,000.

Banks and brokers dealing in the U.S. government security market make their profit on the spread between their purchase and sale prices, and there may also be a commission. This price difference is reflected in the bid and ask columns of the table. If one were holding the July 10 Treasury bill and wanted to sell it, a dealer would pay $9,405.97. This provides a $2 profit margin if the dealer buys the Treasury bill and then sells it quickly to someone else.[4]

Notice that the T-bills are a *$10,000 minimum* and are sold at a *discount* from this price. The return is realized when the bill is redeemed for the face amount of $10,000. The Treasury does not explicitly pay interest to a registered owner since these are *bearer* obligations with the name of the owner not listed on the security. There is also no "coupon clipping," as is discussed below for some debt securities, and no subsequent deposit of the coupon in exchange for a cash interest payment. The largest bill is a $1,000,000 denomination.

Certificates of deposit (CDs) are short-term obligations of commercial banks. Legally they are much like a personal savings account except that they pay a higher interest rate and have specific maturity dates. They are usually issued in multiples of $100,000 with maturities ranging from 30 days to one year. As with savings accounts, they are insured by the Federal Deposit Insurance Corporation up to $40,000 per CD holder in each bank. There have been some failures of relatively large banks, the largest of which was Franklin National Bank in 1974. It is very rare for depositors to suffer as a result of such problems, but there is still some risk of default in CDs. Because of this small risk, it is possible to obtain a higher interest rate on CDs than it is on Treasury bills. On January 10, 1980, for example, large banks were paying an interest rate of more than 13 percent on CDs maturing in one month. A second advantage of CDs as a short-term investment security, in addition to their higher interest rate, is that it is possible to obtain a specific maturity date tailored to the length of time desired by the investor so long as the maturity is 30 days or longer. A potential disadvantage of CDs is that they are not as marketable as Treasury bills. It is possible to sell CDs in the secondary market through brokers, but it is not very easy unless it is a CD of one of the largest banks and the amount is relatively large.

Commercial paper is very much like a CD except that it is issued by corporations rather than banks. It is essentially a very short-term bond, often issued for a few days or weeks. Most issuers of commercial paper are large corporations that are considered to have very low risks. However, there have been defaults such as Penn Central, and there is no insurance on this debt. The interest rate on these short-term securities is usually about the same as that available on CDs of large banks. Like these CDs, commercial paper of large corporations can be purchased from dealers and can be sold back to dealers if desired.

Money-market mutual funds are a new development in the financial markets that make it much easier to manage short-term investment portfolios. These mutual funds specialize in such securities as Treasury bills, CDs, and commercial paper. Shares in these money-market funds can be purchased at any time when cash is available, and the minimum purchase of shares is usually very small. When funds are later needed for operating or other purposes, shares of the fund can be sold immediately at their current market value. These funds have risen to about $60 billion in total asset value by 1980, and many offer features such as telephone redemption of shares, check-writing privileges, and the opportunity to switch to other mutual funds managed by the same company at no charge. Thus these funds offer an opportunity to put money to work for exactly the length of time desired, in exactly the right amount. The price paid for this convenience is a management-and-expense fee, typically around 0.4 percent per year, but this fee varies from fund to fund. One of the new money-market funds that has recently come into existence is the Common Fund for Short-Term Investments. Its function is similar to the other money-management funds, but it is unique because it is sponsored by the Common Fund, a mutual fund founded as a cooperative venture of several colleges and universities. This fund is discussed in chapter 3.

Referring again to the four primary characteristics of investments securities, Treasury bills, CDs, and commercial paper all have relatively short maturities. They have little or no default risk and very little risk of fluctuation in their market value because their maturities occur so soon. In most cases these securities are held to maturity after they are purchased so there is essentially no risk of fluctuations in market value. Thus the return of these securities consists almost entirely of their interest yield. The only real risk of these securities is that the rate at which their proceeds can be reinvested is not known. Short-term interest rates rise and fall sharply with changes in monetary conditions; thus the interest received on a short-term portfolio also fluctuates sharply. If funds are to be invested for a longer period of time, some stability in income can be obtained by purchasing an intermediate or long-term bond. In normal times these bonds also provide a higher annual interest rate, but they have much more risk of fluctuation in their market value, as will be discussed in chapter 4.

Intermediate and Long-term Debt Securities

U.S. Treasury notes and bonds are intermediate- and long-term debt obligations of the U.S. government. New notes and bonds are periodically issued by the government with maturities ranging from two to ten years for notes and with maturities out to about thirty years for bonds. Other than differences in maturity, the securities are identical. If purchased through a Federal Reserve Bank at one of the periodic auctions of the securities, the purchaser pays about the par or face value of the bond or note; that is, the purchaser pays $1,000 for a $1,000 bond. Interest is received semiannually, and the holder receives the face value of the security at maturity.

Government bonds and notes are like Treasury bills in that they can be readily purchased or sold in the secondary market through a bank or broker. Consider, for example, the Treasury note in figure 2-1 that is shown on the line beginning "9.00 February 1987." This line refers to the Treasury notes that will mature on February 15, 1987. They have a "coupon" interest rate of 9 percent. One of these notes could be purchased on January 9, 1980, for a price of $92-17/32 per $100 of bond. Notice the figure after the decimal refers to thirty-seconds. Thus a $10,000 note could have been purchased for $9,253.13. Interest would be received on this note at the rate of $900 per year, an amount based on 9 percent of $10,000. Note, however, that the total yield of this bond is 10.52 percent. This yield is above 9 percent because the purchaser receives a capital gain of almost $747 at maturity when the government pays back the full $10,000.

These bonds are usually not registered to the owner. Typically, the owner will cut a small 1- by 3-inch coupon from the security every six months, depositing this coupon with a bank. The bank collects the interest and deposits it to the account of the bond's owner.

In normal times Treasury bonds and notes have a higher yield than bills because of their longer maturity. Like Treasury bills, these securities are considered to be free of default risk, but there is a price paid to achieve the higher yield. This price is the risk of fluctuations in market value. As interest rates rise, the market value of existing bonds falls because individuals would otherwise rather buy the new high-yielding securities. This is illustrated by the line in figure 2-1 for the "3-¼s, 1985" Treasury bond. These bonds have an interest rate of 3-¼ percent and they mature on May 15, 1985. If one of these bonds had been purchased when it was first issued, the holder now would have incurred a substantial capital loss since it had a market value on January 9 of only $76-12/32 per $100 bond. Thus a $10,000 bond purchased when issued would only be worth $7,637.50 on January 9. This point is discussed in more detail in chapter 3.

Corporate bonds is an all-inclusive title for the many different types of long-term bonds corporations issue. Figure 2-2 shows a sample announcement for a $50,000,000 issue of the Gulf Power Company. Interest is payable on these bonds semiannually beginning February 1, 2010. These securities were "underwritten," or sold, by all the investment-banking companies listed in the announcement. These companies were willing to sell the

New Issue

February 22, 1980

$50,000,000

Gulf Power Company

First Mortgage Bonds
15% Series due February 1, 2010

Price 100% plus accrued interest

Copies of the Prospectus describing these securities and the business of the Company may be obtained from any of the undersigned in States in which such underwriters may legally offer these securities. This announcement is neither an offer to sell nor a solicitation of an offer to buy these securities. The offer is made only by the Prospectus.

BACHE HALSEY STUART SHIELDS
INCORPORATED

BLYTH EASTMAN PAINE WEBBER
INCORPORATED

MERRILL LYNCH WHITE WELD CAPITAL MARKETS GROUP
MERRILL LYNCH, PIERCE, FENNER & SMITH INCORPORATED

SALOMON BROTHERS

DREXEL BURNHAM LAMBERT
INCORPORATED

A. G. EDWARDS & SONS, INC.	**LADENBURG, THALMANN & CO. INC.**
PRINTON, KANE & CO.	**ROTAN MOSLE INC.**
PRESCOTT, BALL & TURBEN	**SCHARFF & JONES, INC.**
KORMENDI, BYRD BROTHERS, INC.	**THOMAS & COMPANY, INC.**

Reprinted by permission of A.G. Edwards and Sons, Inc.

Figure 2–2. Bond Issue Announcement

bonds at a price equal to 100 percent of the face value purchased. A minimum purchase would typically be $10,000.

Like government bonds, corporate bonds can be purchased through a broker from the secondary market, and they can be sold back to this market if desired. Corporate bonds differ from government bonds in two important respects. First, there is a larger default risk. Corporations from time to time do have difficulty paying interest and principal. The Penn Central Transportation Company is a prime example but not the only one. Second, they are not as marketable as government bonds so they may be more difficult to sell if funds are needed for other purposes. Because of these differences, corporate bonds pay a higher interest rate than government securities. Figure 2-3 shows the trading activity of bonds traded on the New York Exchange on January 9, 1980. As an example, consider the line that begins with "ATT 8.80s 05." This line refers to bonds issued by American Telephone and Telegraph. These bonds mature in 2005 and have a coupon rate of 8.80 percent, which is paid on a semiannual basis (s). On January 9, 1980, $49,000 worth of these bonds were traded at a price equal to 82 ¼ percent of their face value. Thus it would have been possible to purchase a $10,000 bond for $8,225.00. The *current interest yield* on these notes would be 10.7 percent, a number obtained by dividing 8.80 percent by 0.8225. However, the total *yield to maturity* is about 10.9 percent because at maturity the bond holder would receive from AT&T the full $10,000 rather than the $8,225.00 invested in the bond.

When purchasing corporate bonds, a major concern has to be to the financial strength of the company. It is possible to buy bonds that have some collateral or security. For example, Pan American Airlines has sold bonds that represent mortgages on some Boeing 747s. If Pan Am were to default on these securities, the bondholders would essentially own the airplanes. However, most people look to the financial strength of the company for security rather than the potential ownership of a row of seats on a 747. To assist bond purchasers in making judgments about financial strength of companies, bonds are rated by two major investment companies. Moody's and Standard and Poor's both rate bonds issued according to their quality with ratings ranging from triple-A down to C for bonds not in default.

One final feature of corporate bonds that needs to be watched is the obligation or right of corporations to retire or pay off their bonds early. Sometimes they promise that they will repay the principal of some portion of the bonds each year. This provision, called a *sinking fund,* provides some protection to bondholders since it forces the company to repay some of its debt each year. It can also be a problem, however, because a bondholder might not want to give up a bond that has an attractive interest rate. Some-

Final N.Y. bonds

Wednesday, January 9, 1980

	Yld	Sales ($1000)	High	Low	Close	Net chg.
WORLD BANK						
IntBk 5s85	6.8	6	73.28	73.28	73.28	— 1.20
IntBk 8⅝s95	11.0	4	78.20	78.20	78.20	— 2.4
IntBk 8s81	8.5	2	94.16	94.16	94.16	+ 1.8
CORPORATION BONDS						
ARA 4⅝s96	cv	5	57	57	57	+ ½
ATO 4⅜s87	cv	3	63¾	63¾	63¾	......
AetnCr 9¾86	10.8	2	90	90	90	+ 2½
AetnLf 8⅛07	10.3	8	79	79	79	......
AlaP 9s2000	12.5	3	72½	72	72	+ ⅞
AlaP 8⅞s03	12.5	28	70⅞	70	70⅞	— ⅜
AlaP 9¾s04	12.3	2	79½	79½	79½	+ ½
AlaP 8⅞06	12.6	10	70¼	70¼	70¼	— 1¼
AlaP 8¾07	12.3	5	70⅞	70⅞	70⅞	+ ⅞
AlaP 9¼07	12.2	10	76	76	76	+ 1⅜
AlaP 9⅝08	12.7	1	76	76	76	......
Alexn 5½96	cv	2	49	49	49	......
AllgL 10¾99	12.7	10	84½	84½	84½	+ ½
AllgL 4s81	cv	4	96⅛	96	96	+ 3
Allen 6s87	cv	5	80	80	80	......
Allen 11½94	cv	1	135	135	135	+ 4
Alcoa 5¼s91	cv	78	103½	103	103	+ 3
Alcoa 9.45s00	10.8	6	87½	87½	87½	+ ⅜
AMAX 8s86	9.5	7	84⅛	84⅛	84⅛	......
AMAX 8½84	9.6	4	88½	88½	88½	— ½
AFoP 4.8s87	7.4	14	64½	64½	64½	+ 1
AForP 5s30	10.6	23	47	45½	47	+ 1½
AAirl 4¼92	9.7	50	44¼	43⅛	44	+ ¾
ABrnd 5⅞92	8.8	21	66½	66½	66½	+ 1
ABrnd 8⅛85	9.3	5	87⅝	87⅝	87⅝	+ ¾
AExC 8½s85	10.0	8	86¼	85⅛	85⅛	— 1⅞
AHoist 5½93	cv	15	107	106¼	106¼	+ 4¼
AHosp 5¾99	cv	19	113	112	113	+ 2⅞
AInvl 8¾s09	11.3	5	77¼	77¼	77¼	......
AmMot 6s88	cv	35	85	85	85	+ ½
ASmel 4⅝88	7.7	1	60⅛	60⅛	60⅛	+ ⅛
ASug 5.3s93	8.9	5	59⅞	59⅞	59⅞	+ ⅛
ATT 2¾s80	2.9	12	95	95	95	......
ATT 2¾s82	3.2	20	86	86	86	......
ATT 3¼s84	4.3	35	75⅝	75½	75⅝	+ ½
ATT 4⅜s85	5.8	64	76	75⅝	76	......
ATT 2⅝s86	3.9	10	67¼	67	67	— 1
ATT 3⅞s90	6.3	36	61⅝	61	61⅝	— ¼
ATT 3⅞90r	6.4	5	60½	60½	60½	......
ATT 8¾00	10.5	99	83⅝	82⅝	83¼	+ ¼
ATT 7s01	10.1	62	70¼	69⅝	69⅝	— ⅛
ATT 7⅛s03	10.2	87	70¼	69⅞	70	......
ATT 8.80s05	10.7	49	82¾	82¼	82¼	— ¼
ATT 7¾s82	8.4	30	92½	92½	92½	— ⅝
ATT 8⅝s07	10.6	30	81½	81	81½	+ ½
Ampx 5½94	cv	23	68	67	68	+ 1¼
Anhr 7.95s99	10.6	5	75	75	75	— 5
Anhr 9.9s86	10.3	10	96½	96½	96½	......
AppP 11⅛83	11.7	1	95	95	95	+ 1
AppP 10½84	11.2	1	93½	93½	93½	+ ¼
Arco 8.70s81	9.3	10	94	94	[illegible]	......
Arco 8s82	8.7	8	91⅞	91⅝	91⅞	+ ⅛
Arco 8s84	9.0	35	89⅛	88¾	89⅛	— ⅞
Arco 7¾86	9.0	5	85¾	85¾	85¾	+ ⅜
ArizP 9½s82	10.0	10	95	95	95	— ¼
ArizP 9.8s80	9.9	25	99⅛	99⅛	99⅛	......
ArizP 12⅛09	11.9	51	101⅞	100	101⅞	— ⅛
ArlnRlt 5s86	cv	8	46	46	46	— 2
Armr 5s84	5.6	8	88½	88½	88½	......
AshO 4¾93	cv	11	119½	119	119½	+ ½
AshO 8.8s00	11.2	15	78½	78½	78½	— 1½
AsCp 9¼90	11.6	5	80	79⅝	79⅝	+ ⅛
AsInv 7⅜88	9.7	1	75¾	75¾	75¾	+ ¾
AvcoC 5½93	cv	25	69⅞	68¾	68¾	+ ¾
AvcoC 7½93	11.5	15	65	65	65	......
AvcoF 7⅞89	10.5	2	75	75	75	+ 1¾
AvcoF 11s90	11.3	5	97¾	97¾	97¾	......
AvcoF 10½5	11.6	5	90⅜	90⅜	90⅜	+ ⅜
AvcoF 9¾83	10.5	33	92¾	92¾	92¾	+ ⅛
AvcoF 8⅞91	11.8	9	76	75	75	— 1
Bally 6s98	cv	60	125¼	123½	124	+ 1½
BalGE 10⅛83	10.4	5	97	97	97	+ ⅜
BalGE 8⅜06	11.1	2	75⅝	75⅝	75⅝	+ ⅜
BalGE 9⅜08	11.6	10	82⅛	81	81	— 1¼
BangP 8¼94	cv	15	83	83	83	+ ⅜
BangP 11½98	13.1	44	87¾	87¾	87¾	— ¼
FoMcK 6s94	cv	43	86½	85½	85½	......
FruF 9.15s83	9.9	9	92¼	92	92	+ 1
FruF 8s87	10.1	5	79	79	79	+ 1⅞
Fuqua 9½98	13.2	43	73⅜	72	72⅛	— 1⅜
Fuqua 9⅞97	12.9	12	76½	76½	76½	+ ½
Gamb 10s89	11.9	11	84	84	84	......
GambC 9⅜86	11.8	8	79½	79½	79½	+ 1
GnATr 5¾99	cv	10	72½	72½	72½	......
GCig 5½87	8.0	1	69⅛	69⅛	69⅛	+ ½
GnEl 7½96	9.6	5	78	78	78	— ½
GnEl 8½04	10.1	2	84	84	84	+ 1
GElCr 8.6s85	9.8	10	88	88	88	+ 1½
GElC 8.65s84	9.7	10	89	89	89	......
GElCr 8¼86	9.6	10	86	85⅞	86	......
GElCr 9⅛84	9.9	5	92½	92½	92½	+ 1
GElCr 9¾87	10.7	141	91¼	91	91⅛	— ¼
GFood 8⅞90	10.3	4	86⅝	86½	86½	+ ½
GHost 7s94	12.3	3	56¾	56¾	56¾	+ 1⅝
GnInst 4¼85	cv	1	195½	195½	195½	+15½
GMA 5s80	5.3	10	94¾	94¾	94¾	—1/32
GMA 5s81r	5.4	10	92½	92½	92½	......
GMA 4⅝82	5.4	3	85⅛	85⅛	85⅛	+ ⅛
GMA 4½85	6.2	10	73	73	73	+ ¼
GMA 4⅝86	6.4	9	72	72	72	+ ⅞
GMA 4⅞87	7.1	10	69	69	69	......
GMA 6¼88	8.4	16	74	73⅜	74	+ ⅝
GMA 7⅛90	9.5	4	74⅝	74⅝	74⅝	+ ⅝
GMA 8s93	10.1	7	79	79	79	+ ½
GMA 8⅞99	11.0	25	81	80⅛	81	......
GMA 8.70s83	9.4	10	93	92⅞	93	+ 2
GMA 8⅝s85	9.9	10	87¼	87⅛	87¼	+ ⅝
GMA 8⅛s84	9.2	10	89½	88½	88½	+ ½
GMA 8⅛86A	9.7	51	84	83	84	+ ⅝
GMA 8⅛86J	9.6	5	84⅜	84¼	84¼	+ ¼
GMA 8⅛96	10.6	10	77	76½	76½	+ ⅜
GMA 7.35s87	9.0	10	81¼	81¼	81¼	+ ⅜
GMA 8s02	10.8	10	74	73⅝	74	......
GMA 8⅜88	10.3	9	84	84	84	+ 1⅞
GMA 8⅞85	10.0	25	89¾	89⅛	89⅛	— ½
GMA 9s84	9.7	6	92½	92½	92½	+ 1⅛
GMA 9⅝89	10.4	87	93	92⅛	92⅜	......
GMA 9.4s04	11.2	15	84⅛	84⅛	84⅛	— ¾
GM 8.05s85	9.0	5	89	89	89	+ ⅛
GTE 4s90	cv	6	60½	60½	60½	+ ⅛
GTE 6¼91	7.4	5	85	85	85	+ ¼
GTE 5s92	cv	17	65⅛	64½	64½	......
GTE 9¾95	10.9	9	89⅛	89⅛	89⅛	— ⅞
GTE 6¼96	cv	1	81½	81½	81½	+ ½
GTE 9⅜99	11.7	5	80	80	80	— 1⅝
Gene 10⅜84	12.1	1	85½	85½	85½	+ 1
GaPac 5¼96	cv	153	90	89	89½	+ 1½
GaPac 6⅞82	7.7	18	89⅛	89⅛	89⅛	+ ⅛
GaPac 7¼85	8.7	28	84	83¾	83¾	— ⅜
GaPac 12s87	12.4	25	96¾	96	96¾	+ ¾
GaPw 8⅞00	12.2	10	73	72½	72½	— ⅜
GaPw 7⅜01	12.1	35	61⅛	61	61⅛	+ ⅛
GaPw 8⅛01	12.5	22	66	65	65	+ ⅝
GaPw 7⅝01	11.9	16	64	64	64	+ 2
GaPw 7½02J	11.8	1	63⅜	63⅜	63⅜	+ 1⅞
GaPw 7½02D	12.1	2	62⅛	62⅛	62⅛	— ¼
GaPw 8⅝04	12.3	10	70¼	70¼	70¼	+ ⅛
GaPw 11⅝00	12.6	5	93⅞	92⅛	92⅛	+ ⅛
GaPw 11¾05	12.7	10	92⅞	92⅞	92⅞	— ⅛
GaPw 9⅝08	12.5	2	77⅛	77⅛	77⅛	+ 1⅜
GaPw 10½09	12.5	7	84	84	84	+ ½
GaPw 11s09	12.5	72	88	87¾	88	......
GldLw 4⅝87	cv	1	101	101	101	......
GloMar 12⅜98	13.5	10	91½	91½	91½	+ ¼
Grace 6½96	cv	83	135¼	132	135¼	+ 3¼
Greyh 6½90	cv	44	83¾	83	83¾	+ ¼
GreyF 9¼92	12.0	10	77	77	77	......
GthRt 6¾82	8.4	1	80	80	80	+ 1⅞
Grum 4¼92	cv	105	77	76¼	77	— ⅞
Grum 8s99	cv	69	140	137	139	— 4
GlfWn 6s88	8.8	8	67⅞	67⅞	67⅞	......
GlfWn 5½93	cv	96	91¼	89⅞	90	+ 1½
GlfWn 7s03A	12.2	58	57½	56⅞	57½	+ ⅝
GlfWn 7s03B	12.5	30	57½	56	56	— ½
GlfMo 5s56f	....	1	32½	32½	32½	......
GlfRes 10⅞97	12.8	8	85	85	85	......
Hellr 8.1s87	10.1	10	80	79⅞	80	+ 1⅝
Hercul 6½99	cv	11	79	78⅝	79	+ ½
Heubn 4½97	cv	9	58⅛	58	58	+ ⅛
[illegible]	[illegible]	[illegible]	[illegible]	[illegible]	[illegible]	[illegible]
PhilEl 7⅜01	11.5	43	63⅞	63⅞	63⅞	+ ⅞
PhilEl 8½04	11.8	10	72	72	72	+ 1
PhilEl 12¾81	12.8	49	99¾	99½	99⅝	— ⅛
PhilEl 9⅛06	11.9	18	77½	77	77	......
PhilEl 9⅛08	12.3	7	75	74	74	— 2
PhilEl 12½05	12.6	12	99¾	99½	99½	+ ⅜
PhilM 8½85	9.6	15	89	89	89	+ 1
PhilM 9⅛03	10.7	23	85¼	85¼	85¼	......
PhilM 8.65s84	9.6	15	90½	90½	90½	— ⅜
PhilM 9.55s86	10.2	5	93½	93½	93½	......
PhilP 8⅞00	10.8	5	82½	82½	82½	— 1⅜
Pittstn 4s97	cv	35	49½	49¼	49¼	— ¾
PorG 10½80	10.8	6	97½	97½	97½	+15/16
PorG 10s82	10.8	5	93	93	93	+ ¼
PorG 11⅝05	12.3	5	94¾	94¾	94¾	......
PotEl 8⅜09	11.2	35	74⅞	73	74⅞	— ⅜
PrimeC 6¾98	cv	37	132	128	128	+ 3
ProcG 8¼05	10.1	5	82	82	82	+ ½
PSInd 7⅝01	10.9	10	70	68¼	70	+ ½
PSNH 12s99	13.3	47	90¼	90	90	— ⅛
PSEG 9s95	11.1	23	81⅝	80¼	81⅛	+ 1⅛
PSEG 8¾06	11.3	73	77¼	77¼	77¼	......
PSEG 9¾09N	9.7	25	100⅛	100⅛	100⅛	— ⅜
Pugt 10¾83	11.2	4	96½	96⅛	96⅛	— ⅜
RCA 9¼s90	10.2	6	91	89¾	91	— ⅛
RainB 9½85	10.5	10	92⅛	90⅛	90⅛	— 2½
RalsP 5¾00	cv	29	80⅝	80½	80½	+ ¼
RamIn 10s00	cv	44	117	115	117	+ 4
RamIn 10s93	13.6	5	74	73½	73½	......
RapA72 7s94	13.3	54	52½	52	52½	+ ⅝
RapA69 7s94	13.3	21	52¾	52⅛	52¾	......
RapA 7½s85	10.0	28	75	74½	75	+ 1
RapA 6s88	10.1	14	60	59½	59½	— ⅞
RapA 10¾03	14.6	87	73⅞	73¾	73⅞	+ ⅝
RapA 12s99	14.8	18	84	81	81	— 3
RapA 10¾04	14.5	24	74⅜	73⅝	74⅜	+ 1¼
RdgB 5½s88	cv	21	186½	185½	186½	+ 7
RepTx 9⅜01	11.3	22	83	83	83	......
RevrC 5½92	cv	15	64	63	64	+ 1⅝
Revl 8.45s85	9.4	31	89½	89½	89½	+ 1
ReyM 4½91	cv	36	69	68½	69	+ 1⅝
ReyTb 7⅞94	10.1	5	78	78	78	+ ⅛
Riegel 5s93	cv	10	71¼	71¼	71¼	+ 1¼
RocIn 4¼91	cv	28	118	117	118	+ 4
RohmH 9s85	10.0	5	90¼	90¼	90¼	— 1⅛
Rohr 5¼86	cv	16	85½	84	84	— 1
Ryder 9¾82	10.5	9	92¾	91	92¾	+ 2⅜
Ryder 12¼86	12.5	5	98	98	98	— ⅜
SCM 5½s88	cv	24	74¼	74¼	74¼	......
Sabin 6½99	cv	7	150	150	150	......
StLSaF 4s97	8.9	35	45	45	45	......
SanD 10.782	11.1	10	96⅜	96⅜	96⅜	— ⅛
Sandrs 5s92	cv	10	73	73	73	+ 5
SFeIn 6¼98	cv	23	153	151⅝	153	......
SavEl 12½81	12.8	22	100	98	98	— 2
SeaCnt 10¼98	12.9	10	79¼	79¼	79¼	+ ⅜
Seafst 9¼01	11.4	5	81	81	81	......
Sears 4¾83	5.8	15	82⅝	82½	82½	......
Sears 8⅝95	10.1	15	85⅜	84¾	85⅜	+ 2⅜
SearA 8⅜86	10.2	18	83½	82¼	82¼	+ ¼
Seatrin 6s94	cv	38	53½	53	53⅛	— ¾
SecP 7.7s82	8.4	15	91¾	91¾	91¾	+ ¼
SecP 8.8s85	10.1	1	87¼	87¼	87¼	— 1
SLR 10¾03	13.0	10	83	83	83	+ ½
ShellO 5.3s92	7.8	6	68⅜	68⅜	68⅜	+ ⅞
ShellO 8s07	10.5	5	76½	76½	76½	+ ⅜
Signl 8.85s94	10.8	5	82	82	82	— 3
Sinclr 4⅜86	cv	10	227	227	227	+13⅜
Singer 8s99	12.7	4	63	62⅛	63	+ 1
SmK 8.15s84	9.2	4	89	88¼	88¼	— ¾
SohioB 8⅝83	9.3	25	92½	92½	92½	+ 1⅞
SohioP 8¾01	11.1	5	78½	78½	78½	— ⅝
SoCBl 10s14	11.1	5	90	90	90	— 1⅞
SoCBl 9.2s10	11.1	35	83	83	83	— ¼
SoCBl 8.2s83	9.1	50	90¼	90⅛	90⅛	— 1¾
SoCBl 8¼15	11.0	5	75¼	75¼	75¼	— 1¼
SoCBl 9⅝19	11.0	20	87¾	87⅜	87¾	+ ¼
SoCBl 9⅞18	11.1	115	88⅝	88	88⅜	+ 1¼
SoestB 10s83	10.7	5	93½	93½	93½	......
SoBIT 2⅞87	4.4	2	65½	65½	65½	— ⅛
SoBIT 7.6s08	10.7	1	70¾	70¾	70¾	......
SoBIT 7⅜10	10.7	13	69	69	69	......
SoBIT 7⅝13	10.7	56	71¼	71	71⅛	— ⅛
SoBIT 8s14	10.8	5	74¼	74¼	74¼	+ 2¼
SoBIT 8¼16	10.7	21	77	76⅞	77	+ 1
SoBIT 8⅝18	10.7	1	80½	80½	80½	......
SoBIT 10.9s19	11.2	102	97⅝	97¼	97¼	— ⅜
SCE 3⅛80	cv	10	95¼	95¼	95¼	......
SoCG 8¾s96	11.6	10	75⅜	75⅜	75⅜	— 1⅛
SoCG 12¾99	12.4	5	103⅛	103⅛	103⅛	......
SNET 8⅛08	11.2	8	72½	72½	72½	+ ⅜

Reprinted, courtesy of the *Chicago Tribune*, January 10, 1980, section 4, page 12.

Figure 2-3. Bond Market Prices

times corporations will pay off their debt by simply buying bonds in the secondary market from individuals that want to sell. They can also have the right to "call" bonds at specific prices. They might, for example, have to pay $1,020 for a $1,000 bond, but if they do call a bond, one has to sell it back to them at this price.

Municipal bonds are like corporate bonds except that they are issued by state- and local-government authorities. Their unique feature is that federal income tax does not need to be paid on the interest received by the bondholder. As a result, the stated interest rate is relatively low, and municipal authorities therefore can pay much less interest than they would have to pay if the bonds were not tax free. These bonds are purchased primarily by commercial banks, casualty insurance companies, and wealthy individuals, all of whom desire to reduce their federal income taxes. They are not of much interest to colleges and universities since the tax-free privilege has little value to an institution that does not pay taxes. However, some institutions issue these securities either directly or through a state agency since they are often the least expensive way to borrow long-term funds for construction and other improvements.

Stocks and Convertible Securities

Stocks and convertible securities have long been considered the most glamorous and inflation-proof of the available securities. Their image has been considerably tarnished in recent years, however, with the substantial decline in the stock market and with high interest rates available on long-term debt securities. There are several types of these securities, each of which will be discussed below.

Common stock represents ownership or equity in a corporation. If a company has 100 shares outstanding, each share represents 1 percent of the company's profits or losses after its expenses and other legal obligations. Over the past several decades, common stocks have provided an average return of about 9 percent. About one third of this return has come from dividends with the other two thirds coming from gains in the value of the stock. This return is certainly not guaranteed since yearly fluctuations in market value provide a significant risk. The range of returns for purchasing a typical portfolio at various times in the last twenty years will be discussed in chapters 4 and 5.

Dividends on common stock provide a much more stable return than does capital appreciation. The Coca-Cola Company common stock provides an interesting example. As shown in figure 2–4, Coca-Cola common stock sold for $35.375 at the close of business on January 9, 1980. Its expected dividend for 1980 is $1.96 per share, based on previous quarterly payments, providing a dividend yield of about 5.5 percent. This stock is more highly valued than many others as indicated by its "P-E ratio" of 11. This number means that investors are willing to pay a price for one share of common stock that is equal to 11 times the annual earnings of Coca-Cola. This relatively high value comes in part from the fact that Coca-Cola dividends have increased significantly each year. The dividends were 66 cents per share in 1969, and they have risen to an expected $1.96 in 1980. In spite of this stable and growing dividend, however, the market value of Coca-Cola stock has fluctuated substantially. This stock sold for $32 ½ per share in 1969. It then rose to a maximum price of $75 in the first half of 1973, but subsequently fell to a low of $22 ¼ in 1974. As of January 1, 1980, the price had increased from its low of $22 ¼, but it was still well below the peak price of $75 per share.

Preferred stock is like common stock in that it represents legal ownership of a company. It is different in that the dividend to be paid by the company is stated on the stock certificate, much like the interest rate is stated on a bond. Therefore it is a fixed rate. The advantage of this type of instrument is that the dividends on preferred stock must be paid before dividends can be paid to common stockholders. Thus the dividend is assured so long as the company has sufficient profits to pay the preferred dividends. These dividends are not a legal obligation of the corporation as are interest payments. In many cases the preferred dividends are *cumulative;* that is, if one or more dividends are skipped, the obligation of the company accumulates. Common-stockholders then cannot receive any dividends until all unpaid preferred dividends are paid. While the preferred dividend is more likely to be paid than the common dividend, the disadvantage is that these dividends do not grow over time as most people expect common-stock dividends to do. One result of this characteristic is that preferred stocks trade almost as if they were long-term bonds. When interest rates and dividends are greater on *new* issues of bonds and preferred stocks, the value of *old* preferred stocks and bonds falls. Thus there is market-value risk in preferred stock.

Convertible securities may be either bonds or preferred stock that are convertible under specified terms into common stock of a company. The idea behind these securities is that they offer a bondholder or preferred stockholder the opportunity of trading these securities for common stock of the company. This is an advantage if the common stock goes up in price. Because of this advantage to the security holder, companies can issue convertible bonds and convertible preferred stock at lower interest rates and dividend yields than they could if a conversion privilege were not attached to the security.

NYSE composite prices

Wednesday, January 9, 1980

52-Week High Low	Stock	Div.	P.E. ratio	Sales (hds.)	High	Low	Close	Net Chg.	52-Week High Low	Stock	Div.	P.E. ratio	Sales (hds.)	High	Low	Close	Net Chg.

A

39¾ 29½	ACF	2.24	7	178	37	36⅜	36¾	+ ¾
18⅜ 14¾	AMF	1.24	6	396	15⅜	15	15¼	....
25 12½	AM Intl	.28	119	479	18½	17¾	17⅞	− ⅜
12¼ 9½	APL	1.00	45	58	10½	9¾	9¾	− ⅛
42 32	ARA	1.82	6	313	34¾	33¼	33⅞	....
47¼ 22⅝	ASA	2.40e	..	1475	43½	40⅝	43⅛	+ ⅞
12¾ 8⅛	ATO	.56	4	116	10½	10¼	10¼	+ ⅛
28¼ 17	AVX s	.25	15	218	28½	27⅝	27¾	+ ¾
43⅞ 29½	AbbtLb	1.00	15	1177	42½	41¼	41⅜	+ ⅜
27¾ 17½	AcmeC	1.20	6	38	28	27½	28	+ 1
4⅞ 3¼	AdmDg	.04	6	3	3⅞	3⅞	3⅞	....
13½ 10¾	AdaEx	1.32e	..	97	13½	13¼	13½	+ ¼
6⅛ 4⅛	AdmMl	.20e	46	41	4⅝	4½	4⅝	....
39⅞ 30½	AMD n		14	868	40¼	37½	38	− 1⅜
36⅜ 28⅝	AetnLf s	1.80	5	1457	34⅛	33¼	33¾	+ ¼
28¼ 19½	Ahmans	1.20	4	156	21½	21	21	− ½
3¼ 2⅛	Aileen			45	3	2⅞	2⅞	....
37¼ 24⅜	AirPrd	.80	11	394	37¼	36¾	37⅛	+ ¼
28¼ 17⅜	AirbFrt	1.20	10	41	25⅜	25	25¼	+ ¼
17½ 11⅜	Akzona	.80	7	234	13	12¾	12¾	+ ¼
8¾ 6½	AlaP dpf	.87	..	8	6⅞	6⅞	6⅞	+ ⅛
87½ 67	AlaP pf	9.00	..	z10	68½	68½	68½	+ 1
105 86½	AlaP pf	11.00	..	z10	88	88	88	− 1
80 62	AlaP pf	8.16	..	z100	63⅜	63⅜	63⅜	− ⅛
80 62½	AlaP pf	8.28	..	z20	64	63	63	....
15⅞ 13⅜	Alagsco	1.48	7	2	13½	13½	13½	− ⅛
42¼ 15⅜	AlaskIn	.80	28	176	39¾	39¼	39¾	+ ½
36 27	Albany s	1.00	9	122	32	31½	31¾	+ ¼
8⅜ 6⅞	Alberto	.36	9	7	7¼	7	7	....
45 34¼	Albrtsn	1.20	8	23	40	39¾	40	+ ⅞
50⅞ 32⅝	AlcanA	2.40	6	4220	55¼	52¾	52¾	+ 2⅛
37¼ 22⅜	AlcoStd	1.40a	6	34	32¾	32¼	32¼	− ⅛
9⅜ 6	Alexdr	.40	6	105	6⅞	6¼	6⅞	+ ⅛
34⅜ 20	AllgCp	1.08a	6	13	26⅞	26¼	26¾	− ¼
32⅞ 15⅞	AlgLud	1.40	5	389	33	32¼	32½	− ¼
48 31¼	AlgLd pf	3.00	..	87	49¼	48¼	48¼	+ ½
22½ 18⅝	AlgLd pf	2.19	..	14	19½	19½	19½	− ¼
18 14⅜	AllgPw	1.80	7	252	15⅝	15½	15⅝	....
17¼ 13⅜	AllenGp s	1.00	6	44	15¼	14⅞	15⅛	....
57½ 24	Allergan	.60	20	427	57½	56¾	56¾	+ ¼
49½ 28½	AlldCh	2.20	..	988	49½	48⅞	49¼	+ 1¼
13½ 11⅛	AildMnt	.86	7	45	13	12⅜	12¾	+ ¼
22¼ 11½	AlldPd	.60	10	55	19⅜	19¼	19½	+ ⅜
27½ 20⅞	AlldStr	1.60	5	484	24	23½	23½	− ¼
38⅝ 29⅜	AllisCh	2.00	5	475	33¾	32¾	32¾	− ¼
18⅜ 12	AllrAu	.64b	8	1	14⅞	14⅞	14⅞	....
21⅜ 14⅜	AlphPr	.72a	6	47	16	15¼	16	+ ⅛
60½ 47⅜	Alcoa	2.80	4	5188	57⅜	56½	57⅜	+ ⅞
29 16	AmiSug	1.00	9	12	26¾	26¼	26½	+ ⅛
49¼ 35½	Amax s	2.40	8	1516	49¼	47⅝	48¼	+ ¼
63⅞ 45½	Amax pf	3.00	..	314	64¼	62½	63⅛	+ ¼
32¼ 17¼	Amrce	1.32	5	42	23¾	22⅞	23	....
52 32¼	Amrc pf	2.60	..	3	38½	38½	38½	+ ½
49¾ 25⅛	AHess	1.40b	5	1206	49¼	47	47¼	− ½
109⅝ 56¾	AHes pf	3.50	..	8	107¼	104	104½	+ 2
14⅜ 9¼	AmAir	.40	3	1185	11	10½	10¾	+ ⅛
6⅛ 3⅛	AmAir wt		..	128	4⅜	4	4⅛	− ⅛
20⅞ 16	AAir pf	2.18	..	93	16⅞	16⅜	16¾	+ ¼
18¾ 12	ABakr	1.20	8	151	17⅞	17¼	17¾	+ ½
68¼ 47⅝	ABrnds	5.50	6	211	68	67⅜	67¾	+ ¼
33½ 28¼	ABrd pf	2.75	..	14	26¾	26¾	26¾	....
35⅛ 28¼	ABrd pf	2.67	..	7	34½	34⅜	34⅜	....
47⅜ 32⅝	ABdcst	1.60	6	1288	38½	36½	36½	− 1½
16 13	ABldM	.78	6	33	14½	14¼	14½	....
41⅛ 33¾	AmCan	2.90	6	78	36⅜	36	36½	....
22¼ 16¾	ACan pf	1.75	..	2	17¾	17¾	17¾	+ ¼
7¼ 3	ACentry		28	28	5½	5½	5½	+ ½
36½ 24⅜	ACyan	1.60	9	1722	35¾	32½	32½	− 1
18½ 9⅞	AmDistl		75	126	18¼	18	18	− ¼
26¾ 17¼	ADT	1.16	8	230	20¼	19¾	19¾	− ½
23½ 17½	AEIPw	2.22	8	867	19	18½	18¾	+ ⅛
36¾ 27¾	AmExp	1.80	7	1041	32½	31¾	31¾	− ¼
14½ 9½	AFamil	.60b	4	249	10¾	10¼	10¾	....
22½ 17⅝	AGIBd	2.00e	..	35	18¾	18¼	18½	+ ¼
21¾ 16½	AGnCv	1.44	..	56	21½	21	21	+ ¾
38⅜ 25¾	AGnIns	1.00	6	333	37	36	36½	+ ½
16½ 10⅛	AHeritLf	.48	8	11	13¾	13½	13¾	....

24½ 14¼	AmHoist	1.12	6	160	21¾	21½	21½	+ ⅜
29½ 24⅜	AHome	1.60	11	2628	28	27¼	27¼	+ ⅛
131 110½	AHome pf	2.00	..	2	125	123½	125	+ 4⅜
35¼ 23⅝	AmHosp	.80	12	781	32¾	32¼	32½	+ 1
11½ 8	AmInvt	.40	6	111	9¼	9	9	− ⅛
33½ 24½	AMI s	.80	12	1267	33	32½	32½	+ 1
9¼ 5½	AmMotrs	.07e	4	1874	8¼	7⅞	8	+ ⅛
48¼ 36	ANatR	3.20	11	x789	47¼	46½	46½	....
31½ 19½	ASLFl n	.80b	4	x17	24¼	23¾	23¾	+ ½
19⅜ 11⅞	AShip	.80	33	351	16⅞	15½	16½	+ 1
58¼ 39½	AStand	3.60	6	125	54¼	53½	53¾	+ ¾
10¾ 6⅜	ASteril	.32	9	205	9¼	9	9	− ⅛
34½ 23½	AmStr	.80	4	1455	26¾	26	26¼	+ ⅛
64¾ 51⅜	ATT	5.00	7	4165	52¾	52	52¼	− ⅛
67⅜ 53¾	ATT pf	4.00	..	12	55¼	54¾	54¾	+ ½
47⅝ 38⅞	ATT pf	3.64	..	106	39½	39½	39½	+ ¼
14⅞ 11	AWatWk	.92	4	8	12¾	12¾	12¾	+ ⅜
19 15⅜	AWat pf	1.43	..	z20	17¼	17¼	17¼	+ ⅜
13 10	AWat pf	1.25	..	z100	10½	10½	10½	....
13¾ 10½	AWa 5pf	1.25	..	z50	11¾	11¾	11¾	+ ¾
21 16	Ameron	1.20	5	86	18¾	18	18¾	+ ⅜
15¼ 11¼	AmesD	.40b	5	29	15¼	15	15¼	+ ⅜
26 20¾	Ametek s	1.00	12	228	26½	25½	25½	+ ⅛
27⅜ 17½	Amfac	1.20	6	1087	27¾	27¼	27½	+ ¼
41 29½	AMPInc	.76	12	742	39½	39	39¼	+ ¼
24⅞ 13½	Ampco	.60a	11	74	25¾	25	25¾	+ ¾
20¾ 14¼	Ampex	.20	11	653	21	20¼	20¾	+ ⅛
7½ 3½	AmrepCp		12	47	6½	6⅛	6½	+ ⅛
24⅜ 14⅜	Amstar	1.35	8	226	20¾	20½	20½	+ ¾
7¾ 6	Amst pf	.68	..	5	6¼	6¼	6¼	....

C

40 27	CBI Ind s	1.00a	15	434	41½	40	41⅛	+ 1⅜
56¾ 44⅞	CBS	2.80	8	436	53¼	52¼	52¾	+ ½
10¼ 6	CCI		6	1137	10¼	9⅝	9¾	− ¼
60½ 31⅛	CIT	2.60	7	254	52¼	51¾	51½	+ ¾
12¾ 7⅝	CLC		32	6	9¼	8⅞	8¾	− ⅛
18¾ 10⅛	CNA Fn		4	68	18¼	17½	17½	− ¼
22¾ 15¼	CNA pf	1.10	..	15	22½	21¾	21¾	− 1⅜
11⅞ 9½	CNAI	1.14	..	12	10½	10	10½	....
65 48½	CPC	3.00	8	590	63	62⅛	62⅞	....
17 14½	CP Nat	1.88	10	29	16¼	16	16	....
28½ 16¼	CTS	.80	8	655	20¾	19⅞	20⅛	− ¼
50 32	CabotC	1.60	7	236	48½	47¼	48¼	+ ½
21¾ 9¾	Cadence		7	48	18¼	17¾		

28½ 26⅜	CartHw pf	2.00	..	8	28	28	28	....
8¾ 6½	CartWal	.40	9	398	8½	7⅞	7⅞	− ⅛
13⅜ 7⅛	CascNG	.92	6	68	12¼	12	12	+ ½
19 13	CastlCk	.80b	8	94	14½	14	14½	+ ½
62⅞ 49⅛	CatrpT	2.10	8	1077	55¼	54½	55¼	+ 1½
17¾ 11¼	CecoCp	.75	4	122	13½	13⅛	13⅛	....
48¾ 39¾	Celanse	3.20	5	714	47¼	46½	46⅜	− ⅞
8¼ 3⅜	Cenco		7	371	7¾	7½	7⅜	....
38¼ 18¼	Centex	.25	13	188	36½	34¾	34⅞	− ⅛
16½ 12¾	CenSoW	1.42	6	877	14½	14	14½	+ ⅛
20¾ 18	CenHud	2.16	6	15	18½	18½	18½	+ ⅛
17½ 14⅜	CenIlLt	1.70	6	50	15½	15	15	....
28⅜ 24	CnILt pf	.80	..	z270	25	25	25	....
27 20½	CnILt pf	2.62	..	z100	21¼	21¼	21¼	+ ¼
14½ 11½	CenIlPS	1.36	6	66	12½	12¼	12½	+ ¼
50 20⅞	CenLaE	1.68	10	125	50¾	49½	50	....
16 12¼	CeMPw	.64	6	41	13¼	13	13¾	+ ¼
15¼ 11	CenSoya	.84	7	200	14½	13½	13⅞	− ⅜
28¼ 23¾	CenTel	2.00	8	671	25¾	25¼	25¾	....
54⅜ 29⅝	CentrDat	1.00b	14	207	47⅞	46¼	46¼	− 1⅜
8⅞ 6¾	CntryTel		8	68	8½	7⅞	7⅞	+ ⅛
19¼ 13¾	Crt-teed	.90	11	25	14¾	14¾	14¾	+ ⅛
24¾ 15¼	CessAir	.80b	10	795	24¾	24	24¾	+ 1¼
28½ 20⅝	Chmpln	1.40	5	1971	24	23½	23½	+ ¼
28¾ 20¾	Chml pf	1.20	..	12	23	22¾	22¾	....
13¾ 9	ChamSp	.80	7	146	10¾	10¾	10½	− ⅛

Reprinted, courtesy of the *Chicago Tribune,* January 10, 1980, section 4, page 14.

Figure 2–4. Stock Market Prices

52-Week High	52-Week Low	Stock	Div.	P.E. ratio	Sales (hds.)	High	Low	Close	Net Chg.
50	5⅛	ChartCo	.60a	4	695	36¾	34⅞	35⅞	+ 1¼
45¾	1⅜	ChartCo wt		..	485	28⅝	27	27⅞	+ 1⅛
25½	17¼	ChartCo pf		..	224	19⅜	18⅞	19	+ ⅛
11	8¼	ChasFd	.80e	..	x42	10⅝	10¼	10½	+ ⅛
43⅞	28⅝	ChasM	2.40	5	1402	41	39¾	40	......
14½	9¼	Chelsea	.60b	3	46	10	9⅞	9⅞	......
44¾	34	ChmNY	3.16	5	141	38	37¼	37¼	− ⅜
22¾	17½	ChNY pf	1.87	..	x59	19⅝	19	19⅝	+ ⅜
24¾	18½	ChesVa s	.84	9	25	23	22¼	22¼	......
25⅝	20⅞	ChesPn	1.08	9	560	22	21⅝	21⅝	+ ⅛
34½	25	Chessie	2.32	5	772	29⅜	28⅞	29⅛	+ ⅜
19⅞	8¼	ChiMlw		14	49	15¼	14⅞	14⅞	− ¼
29⅜	22½	ChiPneT	2.00	5	55	25⅞	25¼	25¼	− ⅛
5½	3⅜	ChkFull	.10e	7	89	4⅜	4⅛	4¼	+ ⅛
21⅛	10⅛	ChrisCft	.52t	8	226	17¾	17⅛	17⅜	......
9¾	8⅝	ChCft pf	1.00	..	1	9	9	9	+ ¼
9⅝	5½	Christn	.40e	6	87	9⅜	9⅛	9⅛	......
24¾	17	Chroma	1.10	6	209	23⅝	22⅝	23	− ¼
95	66⅛	Chroma pf	5.00	..	2	90	89	90	− 2
11⅜	5½	Chrysler		..	4114	8½	7⅞	8⅛	− ⅛
4½	2	Chrys wt		..	331	3¼	3	3⅛	+ ⅛
22⅜	8⅛	Chrys pf		..	257	10⅝	10	10⅜	+ ⅛
28⅞	20⅛	ChurCh	.60	9	176	26	24½	25	+ ¾
30¾	27½	CinBell	2.52	5	10	28	27¾	27¾	......
21⅛	16½	CinGE	1.96	6	x131	17	16⅞	16⅞	+ ⅛
43	33	CinG pf	4.00	..	z100	35	35	35	− 1
103¼	77½	CinG pf	9.30	..	z30	81	81	81	− 1
81½	63	CinG pf	7.44	..	z30	65	65	65	......

52-Week High	52-Week Low	Stock	Div.	P.E. ratio	Sales (hds.)	High	Low	Close	Net Chg.
102½	77	CinG pf	9.28	..	z20	77	77	77	......
29⅛	18	CinMil s	.80	9	126u	29¾	29⅛	29⅝	+ ⅝
26⅝	20¼	Citicrp	1.30	6	3314	26¼	24¼	24¼	......
90¼	53	CitiesSv	3.60	11	204	87½	86	86	− ¼
2½	1¼	CitzSoRt		1	260	1⅝	1½	1½	......
22	14	CityInv	1.20	4	1126	18¼	17⅞	17⅞	+ ⅛
2¾	1	CityInv wt		..	44	1⅞	1¾	1¾	− ⅛
34	23	CityIn pf	2.00	..	55	27¾	27½	27¾	+ ¼
45	35	ClarkE	2.20	5	716	38¼	36½	36¾	− 1⅛
32⅜	15½	ClarkOil	.80a	5	370	30⅛	29⅝	29¾	+ ⅜
37¼	27	ClvClf	1.40a	9	138	34⅜	34	34¼	+ ¾
19⅝	15½	ClevEl	2.00	7	438	17⅝	17¼	17¼	+ ⅛
78¼	60	ClvEl pf	7.40	..	z20	63¾	63¾	63¾	......
11⅜	6⅞	Clevepk	.60	17	84	8¼	8	8	− ⅛
13¾	9½	Clorox	.76	6	493	10⅜	10	10⅛	− ⅛
12½	8½	CluettPe	.68	5	71	9½	9¼	9⅜	......
11¾	9	CluettP pf	1.00	..	6	9¾	9⅝	9⅝	− ¼
10	4⅝	Coachm		..	96	6	5⅝	5⅞	+ ¼
25½	20¼	CoastCp		..	1741	24⅜	23⅝	24	+ ⅜
33	17¼	CstlCp pf	1.19	..	4	25¾	25¾	25¾	+ ½
33	18¼	CstlCp pf	1.83	..	1	28	28	28	+ 1⅜
7⅜	5½	CocaBtl	.44	8	182	6⅛	5⅞	5⅞	− ¼
36⅛	31½	CocaCl	1.96	11	2410	35¾	35	35⅝	+ ¼
23	13⅝	CldWBk s	.88	7	9	21⅜	21	21¼	+ ¾
16⅜	10½	ColeNt	.72	6	47	14¼	13½	14¼	+ 1
5½	3	Coleco		..	160	4⅜	4⅛	4⅛	+ ⅛
19⅝	13¾	ColgPal	1.08	7	1098	14⅞	14¼	14½	+ ¼
45	35	ColgP pf	3.50	..	z100	36½	36½	36½	+ 1½

Figure 2–4 continued

Some people feel that convertible securities offer the best of both worlds to holders of these securities. The interest rate on a convertible bond, for example, provides some guaranteed return to the bondholder regardless of the future value of the stock. On the other hand, if the stock price does go up, the bondholder can take advantage of this gain by converting the bonds into shares of stock at a price lower than the current market value. The company also benefits because it pays a relatively low interest rate while the bonds are being held, and it is able to postpone sale of stock until the bondholder converts. Unfortunately, the depressed stock market of recent times has taken away some of the popularity of convertible securities. When the price of the company's stock falls, bondholders see the value of their bonds also falling and wish that they had taken advantage of a regular bond at a higher interest rate. The company also wishes that it had sold regular common stock rather than the convertible bonds since it missed a chance to sell stock at a higher price. In addition, if interest rates in general rise, the floor support for the value of the convertible security will drop substantially, meaning that the insurance many purchasers of the security thought they had was not very useful. This point is discussed further in chapter 3.

Mutual funds of common stocks are one way of obtaining a diversified portfolio of stocks without managing the portfolio oneself. By purchasing a share in a mutual fund, one in effect is purchasing a share in the portfolio of stocks held by the fund. One such fund is the Common Fund, specifically designed for the investment of endowment funds of colleges and universities. As a cooperative venture of several schools, it is in a position to manage its portfolio with the tax-exempt status of educational institutions in mind. This fund holds a mix of bonds and stocks considered to be appropriate for endowment-fund portfolios. It will be further discussed in chapter 3.

Options

In recent years many investors have used the options market to generate profits, and sometimes rather substantial losses. For years, investors have borrowed money to purchase securities, a process known as "buying on margin." Because investors have to pay interest on funds they borrow to finance purchase of securities bought on margin, they expect the rise in the security price to more than offset the charge for interest. If margin requirements are set by the Federal Reserve at 50 percent, an investor could borrow, for example, $1,000, invest $1,000 of his own, and buy $2,000 worth of securities. Assume he buys 100 shares of a $20 stock. If the stock doubles, he would have doubled his money had he invested $2,000 of his own. Instead, by borrowing $1,000, he has tripled his own $1,000 investment, ignoring the interest on the borrowed funds. He sells the 100 shares for $4,000, repays the $1,000 loan, and personally has wealth of $3,000 versus his original $1,000. This process is called *leverage*. The English call it "gearing" which more aptly describes the process. One should recall that gears operate in both directions. Thus if the stock drops to $10, the investor has lost everything, for the lender will require that the $1,000 in remaining value of the $10 shares be used to repay the loan. In fact, margin requirements are usually such that the margin position must be maintained with a declining stock price. In this case, if the value of the securities pledged for the loan failed to exceed the value of the loan by, for example, 1.6 times, the lender would require the investor-borrower to place enough additional money in the account so that the loan amount was once again no more than 50 percent of the (decreased) value of the investment.[5]

The American traded-options market allows the investor specifically to purchase options for the right to buy (call) or to sell (put) certain securities at specified prices any time over a particular period. Usually this period is less than nine months. This option is a separate security and may permit even greater gearing than the margin purchase noted previously. Thus an investor might be able to pay $300 for the right to call 100 shares of that same $20 stock at a price of $22 anytime in the next 90 days. Twenty-two dollars is the *exercise* price or *strike* price of the option. Notice that if the stock fails to rise above $25, there is no profit for the investor. Below that figure, there will be a loss in the 90-day period for the option is not exercised. Above that figure there is a profit when the option is exercised. For example, if at some time the price of the stock moves to $28, the investor may call the 100 shares from the seller of the option, implicitly paying $22 per share. The shares may immediately be sold at $28 per share. There is a $600 profit on the 100 shares, and the investor paid $300 to purchase the call originally. Notice that he has doubled his money even though the stock price has not doubled nor even risen as much as in the previous example. This example shows the magic of the option market. As shown in table 2–1, options allow one to magnify gains *and* losses, and this magnification can be equally dramatic in both directions. One should always remember that gears operate in both directions.

There are differences in the traded-option and in the margin situation. Margin arrangements can be used with any security, assuming a lender can be found, and most brokerage houses make available margin accounts to customers. For several years the offering of new marketable options for trading on the various option exchanges was under a moratorium, limiting trading in marketable options to existing securities on which new options can be written. This moratorium was lifted in early 1980. The option has a fixed time period; everything is lost if the stock fails to move in the desired direction. Moreover, very complicated combinations of purchaser and sales of options and underlying securities permit the investor to develop involved strategies that provide a payoff at some point under a range of price changes for the underlying stocks.[6]

Some college financial managers have entered this area in a particular way. The managers of endowments for these colleges sold (*wrote*) untraded options, giving a purchaser the right to call a stock away from the college endowment. The college manager was betting that, on the average, the money received from selling options would exceed the opportunity cost of losing the profits from stock holdings that rose sharply in value. This benefit of course rests on (1) the premium paid for the call and the duration of the call, (2) the strike price at which the option is "in the money"—is it near the current market price or far away?, (3) the volatility of the stock (the historic stock price variation or the variation of the market as a whole may not be relevant in predicting the future), and (4) the administrative and brokerage costs involved in writing options.

Table 2–1
Option versus Stock Returns

Market Value of Stock	Holder of Stock with No Option		Holder of Option		Holder of Stock Who Sells Option on Stock	
$18	Cost: original investment [$20 × 100]	$2,000	Cost: original investment [price of option contract]	$300	Cost: original investment [$20 × 100 − $300]	$1,700
	Proceeds: market value of stock [$18 × 100]	$1,800	Proceeds: [option is not exercised]	0	Proceeds: market value of stock [option is not exercised]	$1,800
	Gain/(loss)	($200)	Gain/(loss)	($300)	Gain/(loss)	$100
	% Return on original investment [($200)/$2,000]	(10%)	% Return on original investment [($300)/$300]	(100%)	% Return on original investment [$100/$1,700]	5.9%
$22	Cost: original investment	$2,000	Cost: original investment	$300	Cost: original investment	$1,700
	Proceeds: market value of stock [$22 × 100]	$2,200	Proceeds: [option is not exercised]	0	Proceeds: market value of stock [option is not exercised]	$2,200
	Gain/(loss)	$ 200	Gain/(loss)	($300)	Gain/(loss)	$ 500
	% Return on original investment [$200/$2,000]	10%	% Return on original investment [($300)/$300]	(100%)	% Return on original investment [$500/$1,700]	29%

$25

Cost:			Cost:			Cost:	
original investment	$2,000		original investment	$300		original investment	$1,700
Proceeds:			Proceeds:			Proceeds:	
market value of stock [$25 × 100]	$2,500		market value of stock less: exercise price [$22 + 100] [option is exercised]	$2,500 $2,200 $ 300		exercise price [option is exercised]	$2,200
Gain/(loss)	$ 500		Gain/(loss)	0		Gain/(loss)	$ 500
% Return on original investment [$500/$2,000]	25%		% Return on original investment [0/$300]	0%		% Return on original investment [$500/$1,700]	29%

$28

Cost:			Cost:			Cost:	
original investment	$2,000		original investment	$300		original investment	$1,700
Proceeds:			Proceeds:			Proceeds:	
market value of stock [$28 + 100]	$2,800		market value of stock less: exercise price [option is exercised]	$2,800 $2,200 $ 600		exercise price [option is exercised]	$2,200
Gain/(loss)	$ 800		Gain/(loss)	$ 300		Gain/(loss)	$ 500
% Return on original investment [$800/$2,000]	40%		% Return on original investment [$300/$300]	100%		%Return on original investment [$500/$1,700]	29%

Most schools owned the stock; a broker then negotiated with people who wished to purchase options at various prices and for various maturities. In some cases individuals would approach the broker about an option. The broker would then talk to the college officials, and if the option price offered seemed reasonable, the officials would authorize purchase of securities against which the option would be written. Some firms and some colleges wrote "naked" options: They sold options on securities they did not own, assuming that they would pay whatever small amount might be owed to the option holder in the rare event the stock's price change made the option valuable. This policy is a more risky one, as some people and brokerage firms learned in the stock-market surge of early 1978.

The benefit to the option writers came in the form of the premiums that option purchasers were willing to pay and the relatively limited numbers of option writers. In recent years insurance companies, pension funds, and wealthy individuals have entered the area of writing covered options, and premiums have declined. Brokers tend to like options because the commissions earned per dollar traded are relatively high compared to many other types of securities. Writers of options see them as a way to increase the average return of their portfolios. Although they miss the sharp increase in value of some securities or maybe the increase in a whole portfolio during a broad market rise, their view is that the long-run extra return from premium income and the income from their portfolio in normal times will exceed the income of the portfolio excluding option writing. Historically, there is mixed or negative evidence to support their view; the great problem is predicting whether option writing for the educational institution will prove profitable in the future, especially if more writers enter the market.[7] For the option purchaser, of course, the option usually represents a low-cost means by which to purchase a stock whose price is expected to increase in the near future, with spectacular profits if the judgment is correct.

A survey of pension-fund managers in early 1979 showed that more than 90 percent were not involved in an options program and had no plans to consider it. If they were to use options, the involvement would typically mean writing calls on underlying positions. Most of the managers disliked the options market because of high commission rates on the options, uncertainty about outcomes on booming stock markets, and the relevance of considering short-term returns (from option income) for long-term-oriented pension funds. The last point seems misguided in one sense, if the options are continuing programs, but one cannot tell whether this is a problem with the survey interpretation for the respondent.[8] We return to this issue in chapter 6.

Option prices are quoted. Although the major stock exchanges have moved into trading listed options, the Chicago Board Options Exchange (CBOE) still represents the major volume leader. As an example, figure 2–5 indicates the value of some traded options. Option quotations for 100 shares are typically given for the current month, three months, and six months ahead when quoted in the financial pages. Options expire on the third Saturday of the month. In the case of the Disney options market, the option price is $40 per share, and the financial column shows Disney closed that day on a major exchange at $44 ¼. For the Disney option expiring on the third Saturday in April, options were traded on January 9, 1980, at a price per share of $6-3/8. Thus each option traded at $637.50. This is a premium over the market price ($44 ¼) strike price ($40) spread of $4 ¼.[9]

The prices in these reports are merely suggestive in that they reflect the last option trade of the day; hence severe disequilibrium from the underlying security closing price does not necessarily indicate that trades could be made simultaneously at the "last" price for both the option and the stock at the price quoted.

Summary

There is a wide range of equity and debt issues that are available in the various financial markets, and most of them will be useful to the financial manager of a college or university. In this chapter the institutional characteristics of some of these securities have been briefly summarized. The next chapter discusses the economics of short-term asset management, suggesting how these instruments and some basic financial knowledge can be used to improve the cash management of the college.

Notes

1. When a company is reorganized, often the bondholders surrender some of their claims, leaving new preferred stock or debt to the other claimants. They do this so that the company will, it is hoped, somehow survive, rather than terminate, with presumably less value to the debtholders.

2. This section of the chapter draws heavily on notes prepared by Professor Dwight B. Crane of Harvard University. Readers familiar with basic characteristics of some financial instruments discussed here should proceed to chapter 3.

3. If bonds are sold before maturity, the yield may be more or less than the yield maturity. Some bonds may be *callable,* meaning that the issuer will redeem them before maturity. Usually the corporate-bond issuer has the option inserted in the bond indenture when bonds are issued in a time of high interest rates. If interest rates decline, the firm will *call* the bonds at an established price over the face amount (for example, $1,030 for five years

Option trading

Wednesday, January 9, 1980

Chicago

	Strike price	JAN	APR	JUL	Stock close
Alcoa	50	7 3/8	9 1/4	10	57 3/8
Alcoa	60	1/2	3 1/8	5 1/8	57 3/8
Am Exp	30	1 15/16	2 3/4	a	31 3/4
Am Exp	35	1/16	1 1/8	1 7/8	31 3/4
Am Tel	50	2 1/4	3 1/4	4	52 1/8
Am Tel	.55	1/16	3/4	1 1/4	52 1/8
Am Tel	60	a	1/16	b	52 1/8
Atl R	60	20 5/8	21 3/4	b	80 7/8
Atl R	70	10 3/4	12 1/2	14 1/2	80 7/8
Atl R	80	1 3/8	4 7/8	6 3/4	80 7/8
Avon	35	b	6 1/2	7	39 3/8
Avon p	35	b	7/8	1 1/2	39 3/8
Avon	40	5/8	2 11/16	3 3/4	39 3/8
Avon p	40	1	2 3/4	3 1/4	39 3/8
Avon	45	1/16	3/4	1 7/8	39 3/8
Avon p	45-	5 5/8	5 1/4	a	39 3/8
Avon	50	1/16	3/16	3/4	39 3/8
Avon p	50	9 5/8	a	a	39 3/8
BankAm	25	2 1/4	3	3 3/4	27 1/8
BankAm	30	1/16	11/16	1 7/16	27 1/8
Beth S	20	4	4 1/2	5 1/4	24 1/4
Beth S	25	3/8	1 3/16	1 3/4	24 1/4
Burl N	45	12 1/2	a	a	57 1/2
Burl N	50	7 1/4	9 1/4	10 3/4	57 1/2
Burl N	60	5/16	2 7/8	4 1/4	57 1/2
Burl N	70	1/16	13/16	b	57 1/2
Burrgh	60	21 1/2	a	a	81 3/8
Burrgh	70	11 1/8	a	a	81 3/8
Burrgh	80	1 3/4	6	a	81 3/8
Citicp	20	4 1/2	4 3/4	5 1/8	24 1/2
Citicp	25	1/4	1 1/8	1 13/16	24 1/2
Delta	35	4 3/8	5 1/4	a	38 1/2
Delta	40	3/8	2 3/8	3 5/8	38 1/2
Delta	45	a	1	b	38 1/2
Dig Eq	50	a	21	a	68 1/2
Dig Eq	60	8 1/2	a	a	68 1/2
Dig Eq	70	1	4 3/4	a	68 1/2
Disney	40	4 3/4	6 3/8	7 1/4	44 1/4
Disney	45	b	2 7/16	a	44 1/4
duPnt o	43 3/8	3/16	b	b	40 1/2
du Pnt	35	a	7 1/4	a	40 1/2
du Pnt	40	1	3 1/4	4 1/2	40 1/2
du Pnt	45	1/16	1 1/4	2 1/2	40 1/2
Eas Kd	45	2 1/2	5	6 1/2	47 1/8
Eas Kd p	45	5/16	1 7/8	2 1/2	47 1/8
Eas Kd	50	5/16	2 1/2	3 3/4	47 1/8
Eas Kd p	50	3 1/2	4 1/8	4 3/4	47 1/8
Eas Kd	60	1/16	3/8	1 3/16	47 1/8
Skylin	15	1/16	9/16	7/8	12
Southn	10	a	2 3/8	2 5/8	12 1/4
Southn	15	a	3/16	1/4	12 1/4
St Ind	50	27 1/2	b	b	76 3/4
St Ind	60	18 1/2	19 1/2	b	76 3/4
St Ind	70	8	10 5/8	a	76 3/4
St Ind	80	1 1/4	4	5 3/4	76 3/4
St Ind	90	3/16	1 1/2	2 7/8	76 3/4
Tx Glf	25	16 1/2	17 3/8	17 1/2	41 1/2
Tx Glf	30	11 5/8	12 3/4	14 1/4	41 1/2
Tx Glf	35	6 3/4	9	9 1/2	41 1/2
Tx Glf	40	b	5 5/8	6 7/8	41 1/2
U A L	20	3 7/8	4 3/4	5 3/4	23 5/8
U A L	25	11/16	1 7/8	2 11/16	23 5/8
U A L	30	1/16	1/2	b	23 5/8
U Tech	35	14 1/8	a	a	48 3/8
U Tech	40	8 5/8	9 7/8	10 1/2	48 3/8
U Tech	45	4 3/8	6	7 1/2	48 3/8
U Tech	50	b	3 1/2	4 3/8	48 3/8
J Walt	25	a	6	a	30
J Walt	30	1 1/4	2 1/4	a	30
Willms	20	10 1/2	10 5/8	a	30 5/8
Willms	25	5 1/2	6 1/2	7 1/8	30 5/8
Willms	30	2 1/8	3 3/4	4 3/4	30 5/8

		MAR	JUN	SEP	
Bruns	10	3 3/8	3 3/4	4	13 1/8
Bruns	15	3/8	13/16	13/16	13 1/8
Dow Ch	25	8	8 1/2	b	33
Dow Ch	30	4 1/4	5	6 1/4	33
Dow Ch	35	1 1/4	2 3/8	3 3/8	33
Dow Ch	40	1/8	7/8	b	33
Ford	30	3 1/8	4 1/8	4 3/4	32 1/4
Ford	35	15/16	1 11/16	2 13/16	32 1/4
Ford	40	1/8	5/8	b	32 1/4
Gen El	45	9 1/4	10 1/2	a	54
Gen El	50	5 1/8	6	7 3/8	54
Gen El	55	2	3 1/4	4	54
Gen El	60	1/2	b	b	54
G M	45	7 3/4	9 1/8	10	52 1/8
G M p	45	3/4	1 9/16	2 1/16	52 1/8
G M	50	4	5 1/8	6 1/8	52 1/8
G M p	50	2 3/16	3 1/8	3 7/8	52 1/8
G M	60	7/16	1 7/16	2 5/16	52 1/8
G M p	60	8 5/8	9	8 3/4	52 1/8
G M	70	1/16	5/16	b	52 1/8
Glf Wn	10	8 3/8	b	b	18 1/8
Glf Wn	15	3 3/8	3 7/8	4 3/4	18 1/8
Glf Wn	20	3/4	1 1/2	2	18 1/8
I T T	25	2 1/2	3	3 1/2	26 3/4
I T T	30	1/2	15/16	1 3/8	26 3/4
I T T	35	1/16	b	b	26 3/4
K mart	20	a	5 1/8	a	24
K mart	25	1	1 7/8	2 7/16	24
K mart	30	a	1/2	b	24
Kenn C	20	14 1/4	b	b	34
Kenn C	25	9 3/8	10 1/8	10 3/4	34
Kenn C	30	5 1/4	6 3/4	8	34
Kenn C	35	2 9/16	4 3/8	5 5/8	34

Reprinted, courtesy of the *Chicago Tribune*, January 10, 1980, section 4, page 12.

Figure 2–5. Option Market Prices

after issuance or $1,020 for the next three years), typically paying for these bonds by a new issue of debt at the lower interest rate. Bond price quotes in the financial papers usually list the *lower* of the yield to call or the yield to maturity unless otherwise stated.

4. Again, as noted in footnote 3, sale before maturity may provide a higher or lower return than holding the security to maturity. This issue is discussed in chapter 3 as part of the exercise of "riding the yield curve."

5. These "margin calls" may result in the holding's being sold if the owner fails to deposit additional funds in a timely manner. In times of a declining stock market, this sale further depresses security prices. Such potential financial instability is one reason the Federal Reserve Board sets margin requirements as part of its monitoring of the U.S. economy. Margin requirements can and do differ among types of securities (bonds versus stock), for example, and individual brokerage houses differ among themselves and, in some cases, among customers although by law they will not lend more than allowed by the Federal Reserve Board.

6. As an example, see pp. 347–387 of William F. Sharpe, *Investments* (Englewood Cliffs, N.J.: Prentice-Hall, 1978). There is a variety of hedge strategies that are designed to provide a range of probabilistic outcomes based on the security and option prices involved and the subsequent price of the security. These discussions are beyond the scope of this book and are well summarized in Sharpe, *Investments,* pp. 362–363. Thus people may sell a put option and buy a stock, sell a stock short and buy a call, buy a put and a call of the same strike price and same expiration date (a straddle), or buy two puts and one call (strip) or one put and two calls (strap).

7. One report of the estimated risk reduction from holding a well-diversified portfolio on which the institution writes call options (as discussed in chapter 2) is found in R. Corwin Grube, Don B. Panton, and J. Michael Terrell, "Risks and Rewards in Covered Call Positions," *Journal of Portfolio Management,* winter 1979, pp. 64–68. They generally found that total portfolio risk and return were reduced by this portfolio strategy, as would be predicted from efficient market assumptions. However, the transaction costs (mainly brokerage commissions) reduced the return to a level *below* the return of a similarly risky portfolio involving T-bills as the risk-free security. Hence the covered-option writing strategy would be inferior to the policy of holding a well-diversified portfolio of common stock in common with a risk-free security balance, as discussed in chapter 6.

8. See "A Yellow Light for Options," *Institutional Investor,* February 1979, pp. 83–85.

9. A small *a* in the report means there was no trade in that price option for that maturity; a small *b* means that maturity option is not offered. The Options Clearing Corporation operates the option record keeping for the

most part by computer and stands behind the options that people buy and sell. The option holder who "exercises" an option typically does not want the stock but simply asks the cash difference between the strike price and the current market price. The Options Clearing Corporation randomly selects an option seller and calls for settlement. If settlement is not made, the OCC pays the holder of the option.

3 Short-term Cash Management

Introduction

Short-term is an arbitrary classification for funds management, and for our purposes we may classify it as "transactions with a life span of one year or less." For example, a school may plan a new gymnasium or the refurbishing of a classroom building. To that end, it may sell revenue bonds to the public or to local lending institutions. These bonds are long-term obligations of the college, but the interim investment of the money as funds that are disbursed over one or two years requires an idea of the short-term investment possibilities. There will presumably be distributions of cash every three to six months as the contractor submits bills for the completed portions of the work. This obligation is different from the fund management required for the investment of tuition inflows. For a semester-financing system, funds come in two large blocks during the academic year. They must be invested somewhere for an average of two months, with disbursements from these balances made weekly and monthly. Notice that this problem is a periodic one, arising every four months or so, with comparable amounts from period to period; the construction project involves a longer period, with infrequent and varied amounts paid throughout the construction of the project. Also related to the short-term cash-management area is the problem of purchase management. How large a stock of textbooks, pencils, office typewriters, and the like should be ordered at one time? In a related area, are there alternatives with different economic costs for managing the disbursements of cash for such purposes as payroll, pension funding, and payments to suppliers? All these topics are discussed as part of this chapter.

In reviewing the issues of short-term financial decisions, we look at both the *costs* and the *revenues* of various decisions. In the area of cost, examples reveal how one may quantify some nonfinancial data and how seemingly nonfinancial decisions have a financial impact. We discuss the variables that a manager may study and offer some obvious and not-so-obvious examples of financial decision making in the short term.

These examples include the taking of discounts on accounts payable, the consideration of volume discounts for the purchase of supplies, the granting of various forms of financial aid to students, and the issue of reciprocity in purchasing goods and services. In this area of cost, we also review the *sources of funding* that may be available to cover the short-run seasonal

51

needs of schools. In considering the issue of a *central treasury function* for handling the short-term cash management of many different parts of a college, we discuss the concept of *cash-balance analysis*: How large a cash balance should a college keep on hand? How is the balance changed in a centralized treasury versus decentralized disbursement of funds?

By considering the income from the various types of investment securities reviewed in chapter 2, one can see how revenues affect the short-term cash-management decision of the college financial manager. How do interest rate changes alter revenues? We review both the *maturity schedule* of a bond portfolio and the *yield curve*. Finally, *leverage* can be a part of the financial-management process in any college, and we discuss the decision to borrow additional money in the hope of investing for a greater return than the cost of the loan.

These examples are presented to blend the decision environment of the college manager with the institutional-security material of chapter 2 (types of securities available and their characteristics) with some of the basic economic concepts of chapter 1. By seeing the techniques of analysis combined with the characteristics of various financial instruments as applied to some problems of college financial managers, one can begin to recognize the elements of financial decision making.

Managing College Operations

Several factors directly related to the funds-management function affect the cost of specific choices for short-term cash management. First, staff personnel and office space must be made available; in the long run, both of these elements are variable costs. Second, in the short or long run, banks usually have charges associated with transactions. Sometimes these charges are per check. At other times the institution is expected to keep a certain minimum amount on deposit in the school's checking account instead. The loss of interest income that the school could earn by investing this minimum deposit elsewhere represents an opportunity cost to the school and is a cost incurred in return for the bank's providing financial services to the school.

Other costs are more difficult to determine. Ideally, any firm, individual, or school would like to match cash inflows and outflows. If the people who provide infusions of cash were well coordinated with the people who require cash from the school, there would be no cash-management problem with associated costs. In fact, that is not the way the world works. Some people and institutions provide financing: Suppliers who give credit for 10 to 60 days and employees who are paid at the end of the month rather than daily or weekly are two good examples. Even the federal government and the Social Security Administration permit some bundling together of income and FICA taxes withheld on employees until a later date, giving the school the use of that money for some time after it is withheld from the employees' paychecks. On the other hand, the school supports other people. Late room-and-board payments are one example since the school must pay the suppliers of goods students use before the students pay the school. This situation means that the school is financing them in the interval. Late tuition payments are even more glaring as a source of financing that the institution provides. Cash advances to employees are another example of financing.

These situations serve to illustrate the problem of determining the costs associated with a particular policy that seemingly may have little to do with short-term financing decisions. An explicit interest charge must be stated in each financing situation. However, many costs are *indirect* in the extreme and are sometimes not even recognized by the party providing the financing. In many cases the actual costs cannot be determined until after the transaction is completed. Even then the costs of other alternatives for solving the particular issue at hand may never be known, so a comparative evaluation is hard. In all these situations, however, for a manager to make a reasonable judgment about the alternative economics, some estimate must be made.

Management of Accounts Payable

Often suppliers will quote terms such as "2/10, net 30." This phrase means there will be a 2-percent discount for payment of the account within 10 days, but the net amount is due in 30 days. After 30 days there may be no interest charges until the sixtieth day, but there will often be strained relations with the supplier. What do these figures suggest? A supplier willing to provide 10 days' financing for 2 percent seems to be very strange, but that is *not* what is happening. A better way to view this problem is to say that the cost of the goods is X, which is owed in 30 days. Alternatively, if you pay in 10 days or less, you may receive a discount. Assuming the school would pay the supplier on the tenth day as opposed to paying on the thirtieth day, then the 2-percent discount is really payment for surrendering 20 days' financing. Since there are 18 periods of 20 days in a year on an annual basis, this *cost* of financing is $360/20 = 18 \times 2\% = 36\%$.

Stated in other terms, if the school can raise money at *less* than 36 percent per annum interest, foregoing the discount by paying at the end of 30 days instead of paying at the end of 10 days is not a very economic decision.

Several other points are worth noting. First, there is no purpose in paying *before* the tenth day, for use of the money is then lost for no reason. The supplier is willing to support the school for 10 days. Second, if the 30-day-net really is fictitious and the supplier is quite willing to wait for 60 days for final payment, then the opportunity cost of not taking the discount is far lower. In this case, the school has 50 days' use of the money (60 − 10), and the annual interest equivalent is 360/50 = 7.2 × 2% = 14.4%, which is a lower figure. Perhaps for the right to avoid negotiating with banks in times of tight money, the college financial administrator will find this a reasonable source of financing. Note though that in periods of tight money, the suppliers are probably less likely to tolerate lagged payment of bills; they face the same scarcity of funds with a concomitant high price for those funds. Third, about the most foolish thing to do is to pay the bill on the eleventh day. Then the cost is 2-percent discount foregone for one day's use of the money, or a 720 percent per annum interest charge. Thus one either pays on the last day the discount can be taken or the last day for reasonable payment of the bill without supplier ill-will; the decision depends on the discount terms and the school's cost of money. Although indirect, in this situation there is a reasonably easy way to calculate the implicit interest cost of a purchase discount.

Management of Orders

The costs are more subtle (and hence harder to determine) in the case of *volume discount for large purchases.* If there are regular purchases and use of a given commodity, then there may be discounts for large-volume purchases. The manufacturer or supplier of services gains some economies of scale: one large box instead of many smaller boxes, early receipt of funds for a large order, and so forth. Some of these savings to the manufacturer are passed on to the buyer as an incentive for customers to have infrequent larger orders instead of more frequent smaller orders. For the buyers there are other costs. The primary expense is that the unused goods received must be physically moved to storage, and space must be available. Over time those goods must be moved again to their ultimate usage area; prior to a move they must often be guarded from theft and temperature extremes. These are called *holding costs* and are often expressed as cost per period (for example, a month) per unit stored. There may be order charges that are invariant with a given order, regardless of the size of the order.

Although some statistical tools allow many formulations of this "inventory" problem, one common solution is known as the *square-root-inventory* model. The economic (optimum) order quantity is:

$$Q = \sqrt{\frac{2RC}{i}}$$

where i = the actual per-annum interest cost
Q = the optimum order size in dollars
R = the amount spent per year on the good in question
C = the cost per order, a fixed charge

Suppose a college uses 500,000 exam booklets per year. Operating on the quarter system, midterms and finals approximately produce reasonably level demand for booklets over nine months. The cost of money and the cost of storing books are directly related to the number of books stored and are assumed to be 21 percent of the cost per year, or 16 percent for nine months. The internal order-processing and handling costs are assumed to be $10 per order.

Ordering all booklets at once would provide an annual cost of

$$\$10 + \frac{500,000 \times \$0.10}{2} \times 0.16 = \$4,010$$

assuming the booklets cost $0.10 a piece and the average inventory is one half the beginning inventory of 500,000 booklets and the ending inventory of no booklets. Under formula, the economic order quantity (EOQ) is $2,500.

$$\sqrt{\frac{2 \times 500,000 \times \$0.10 \times \$10}{0.16}} = \$2,500$$

The annual cost would then reflect 500,000/25,000 or 20 orders per year, inventory of 25,000/2, and would be $20 \times \$10 + [(25,000/2) \times \$0.10] \times (0.16) = \$400$, about one tenth the single-order choice.

If a volume discount of 1 percent on total cost of at least 100,000 booklets are ordered, then we know that at best the manager should order just this minimum because it is more than the optimum order quantity computed. There would be 500,000/100,000 or 5 orders per year, and average inventory would be 100,000/2 or 50,000. Accordingly, total annual cost would be

$$5 \times \$10 + \left(\frac{100,000}{2} \times \$0.099\right)(0.16) = \$842.$$

Thus because this cost is higher than the EOQ-calculated total cost, the manager would not take the volume discount.

Notice this formula assumes that cost are the same *per unit* and that usage is reasonably level over the period. The formula mathematically finds the economic (that is, lowest cost) order size. To minimize the costs of ordering (*c*), a single order per year is preferable. To minimize the cost of funds involved in inventory financing, it would be better to stock only a minimum inventory, preferably zero. Yet these goals conflict. The formula finds the proper trade-off between those extreme solutions.

Because this formulation assumes that costs per unit are identical, it does not take into account available volume discounts. For that solution, the problem must be reformulated using different unit costs. Comparing the total costs to the school under different optimum order sizes as the price per unit purchased declines with unit order size will provide the lowest cost to the school. Notice that the person using this model has to assume some direct interest cost or value of money per annum to the institution.

Financial Aid to Students

An economic analysis that introduces the portfolio theory about which we will say more later is appropriate to the idea of student-aid financing. If we provide additional tuition financing to students in a given year, permitting payment of tuition on a monthly basis rather than at the start of the semester, there is a cost. The obvious additional cost is the administrative one of receiving and depositing payments each month, with a normal bottleneck each period as the majority of students pay their bills on the first of every month. (An alternative, which we might also analyze in economic terms, is a rotated staggered payment by students thoughout the month.) Another cost is the loss of interest to the institution, which could have invested that money during the period, or alternatively, the additional interest the institution may have to pay for money to pay the faculty and staff pending receipt of student tuition money.

But there are two additional costs that are more indirect, which may change over time, and which may never be known with much certainty. First, although the effects on any given student may not be determinable, there may be an additional demand for enrollment.[1] More students may come to the school, and fewer students may withdraw under this plan. To the extent that extra students and fewer drop-outs represent marginal income to the school, this extra income could be netted against the cost when evaluating this program of tuition payments throughout the semester. Second, there may be sharply different probabilities for nonpayment of bills under the two plans. Late-paying students cost money in collection. Some students must be gently reminded. Others may be forcibly reminded, sometimes by the school's accepting only $0.50 per dollar due by turning the charge over to a collection agency. There may be ill-will, but there also may be a salutary effect on other nonpayers. To the extent that fewer students default under this monthly system than under the other system and their average bad debt is lower, then the expected bad-debt loss of the school may be reduced. This saving too represents a subtraction from the direct financing cost of the monthly tuition program.

Reciprocity Agreements

A final example of the subtlety of costs is the issue of *reciprocity.* In the academic area, this may be seen in the case of free tuition for spouses or children of faculty of other schools where the same privilege is extended to one's own faculty. What is this service worth? Again, what is gained and what is lost? To the extent that faculty will work for lower salaries in exchange for this tuition plan, and that many will never collect on the tuition plan because they will leave the school, their children will want to go elsewhere or cannot meet the school's normal admission standards, or the like, then there may be a net saving to the school. In the short-term cash-management area, buying a particular good from a local supplier who agrees to send her employees to one course per evening is a form of reciprocity. Again, what is the extra tuition income, what are the extra costs the institution may have to bear to provide the instruction for the employees, and what is the extra cost of the goods purchased from this supplier, if any?

These examples are merely illustrations, and many others are possible. What they provide is a way of thinking economically about what are seemingly noneconomic problems. We have usually assumed a cost of funds to the institution. In the end, that cost will be an amalgam of many financing sources the school may use.

Borrowing Short-term Funds

Banks and local savings institutions often lend money at a particular interest rate for a particular purpose over a given period of time. Often the bank will suggest a compensating balance of X percent of the loan. The foregone interest that the school might earn on this money is a way of compensating the financial institution beyond the normal interest charges. For example, the bank may be willing to lend $100,000 for one year at 9 percent, but require a 20-percent compensating balance. Only $80,000 will be available to the schools, yet the interest charge will be based on the full amount: $9,000 divided by $80,000 equals 11.25 percent. Yet is this the real cost? To the extent that the school needs additional liquid funds in a noninterest-bearing checking account, this segregation may not be as costly as suggested. Then the school can reduce the amount of money not available, and the effective cost of the loan will be less. As an example, assume the school keeps $40,000 in a non-interest-bearing checking account as a buffer for daily fluctuations in cash receipts and disbursements. Perhaps $30,000 can be earmarked as the compensating-balance account, with the understanding that daily outlays beyond daily receipts are first charged against the general $10,000 account and then against the $30,000 compensating account. As long as the *average* daily balance per month in the compensating account is above $20,000, then the bank's requirement is usually met. (Analysis of historic daily fluctuations could provide evidence on how large a balance is needed to give reasonable certainty that the $20,000 average will be met.) Then one may argue that the full $100,000 is available, and the cost of the loan really is 9 percent. There may be other costs for the loan, in the form of associated charges for check processing and the like. Sometimes there are savings from a large block of financing because the bank realizes some scale economies from lending larger amounts of money to a number of well-researched borrowers about whose financial condition the bank is reasonably comfortable rather than to several small borrowers each of whom must be investigated.[2]

As discussed in chapter 2, the term structure of interest rates may cause a bank to have various interest rates for loans of different maturities. If short-term rates are relatively high, then the bank may have a lower rate for a longer term loan. This outcome occurs because the bank assumes that its cost of money will decline over the years, and it can still make a profitable loan. Usually this loan would have a prepayment penalty so that the school cannot effectively have a short-term loan borrowed at long-term rates by repaying after one year! Usually, though, longer term loans have more restrictive terms and higher interest rates than shorter term loans. No bank wants to become involved in running the affairs of its borrowers, whether they be individuals, corporations, or colleges. The bank wants to lend money profitably. To the extent that there is more time for things to go wrong, for unexpected events to arise and for current conditions to change radically, the long-term lender wants compensation for this greater risk, and the compensation takes the form of a higher interest rate.

State financing authorities also exist to aid public and private universities. Often these financing authorities exist for specific public institutions and/or for specific public purposes (for example, dormitory construction). In such cases, long-term financing by the school allows it to "piggyback" on a large (public) financing body. The money raised, however, then will be invested in short-term instruments until the need for its spending occurs.

These examples indicate the pluralistic sources and uses associated with short-term cash in the school. Funds received from long-term sources are not perfectly matched with their uses, and the funds must be invested in the interim. Other sources are short-term in nature and must be invested for a few days or weeks until the associated outflow occurs. Some lenders will require segregation of their funds, whereas others will permit the economics of comingled funds as long as the institution does not ultimately use the money for other than the intended purposes.

Many administrators will wish to take advantage of the Common Fund for short-term securities. This is a mutual fund owned by a number of colleges and universities that provides short-term investment of cash balances. Funds can be transferred easily into and out of the fund, and it provides professional management of cash balances for the smaller college or university. The address is given in the bibliography at the end of the book.

Investing Short-term Funds

The inventory model noted earlier suggests that there are possibilities for setting different thresholds at which cash is transferred from higher earning, short-term uses to lower earning accounts. Thus cash above $100,000 might be kept in a savings account or a Treasury bill; smaller amounts of cash needed for a few days or a week may be kept in a checking account from which disbursement is easier. Most individuals know that they could earn interest on funds if the funds were transferred to a checking account only when they expected a check to be presented for payment; on the other hand, the nuisance value and the cost of time prevent such management. Usually individuals transfer funds into and out of their checking account as different "trip limits" are reached. At the lower level, the low balance will require more funds; at the higher level, some funds are transferred to earning accounts.

Daily-income funds and NOW accounts (available at some New England savings-and-loan offices) allow corporate or individual users to have insurance privileges on their funds and to earn interest until the check is presented for payment. (The NOW "checks" are called Negotiable Orders of Withdrawal, part of the legal fiction that NOW accounts are not really checking accounts!) In the case of the short-term money-market funds, however, usually there is a minimum of perhaps $1,000 before a check will be honored. Thus the school will again have a need for a regular checking account for smaller amounts.[3]

It is because of this transfer problem and the balance between convenience and earning assets, that many schools will have a *central disbursing agency*. This means that the cash balances for the school are bundled together in one area. Otherwise each separate disbursing authority will have transaction balances kept idle for needs that may arise only occasionally. By centralizing this cashing authority, the idle balances can be reduced. In addition, centralization provides a control function; some individual can be responsible for verifying that the disbursement is authorized.

Against the greater interest income possible and the control function encouraged by the central treasury are several arguments. First, there may be extra communication and paperwork. For example, individuals who can authorize payment fill in forms that request that the disbursement be made. Second, there can be a loss of interest unless the localized individual receiving cash can deposit it to the central account and the authority knows the money is on deposit; otherwise, the additional balance will not be recognized until the bank notifies the central treasury that a deposit has been received.

Whether the centralized treasury is economic can be determined by comparing different balances and the resulting income with the alternatives. A middle ground, authorizing localized disbursements of amounts up to a certain level on the central account with notification to the treasury for certain large disbursements also has much to commend it. Notice that this example is not for control purposes alone: Mr. X can authorize up to $1,000 in payment. Rather, the aim is to let the central treasurer have some idea of how much the idle balance will be. Large disbursements reduce the figure considerably and may require a special transfer. Whether all these procedures are economic is, as noted, a question to be settled by studying the actual data. An example of this calculation follows.

Costs of Cash-balance Analysis

On the most basic level, assume that the treasury can centralize cash balances, and that historically the average balance in the school's accounts has been $250,000 in total. By centralizing this function, the average balance can be kept at $100,000. If one assumes that the extra $150,000 is worth at least 8 percent per annum, earned either by placing it on deposit or by reducing the loans owed by the school for operating purposes, then the question is: Are the extra communication and human-relations costs from this centralized treasury worth $12,000 per year?

The concept of probabilities is also important. At any time, there will be a random inflow of cash and various outflows. By computing probabilities (or, easier, developing a simple computer-simulation model), the financial manager of a school can study the different effect on earnings from idle cash produced by various policies. There may be a lower minimum balance, which increases the probability that a particular check may not clear, or a discount will be lost. What are the trade-offs? More interest is earned from having more cash in the earning account, yet ill-will, long-distance phone charges, and insufficient-funds charges will rise. Another policy may have much larger levels at which the transfer from the cash account is made to the earning account. What are the costs? Less interest is earned because the average balance of the nonearning checking account is higher and the balance of the earning account is lower. On the other hand, less time is spent transferring funds to the account for interest, and less time is wasted in the occasional transfers from the earning account back to the nonearning account. Again by studying the probabilities in a computer model, one can see what the earnings will be under various assumptions about the world, and decide the degree of risk of a cash inadequacy that is optimal.

Many revenues are simply opportunity costs in another sense, and many of the costs we have reviewed under several hypothetical situations represent revenues in a sense. The obvious revenue of interest from various securities can be thought of in terms of the discussion in chapter 2.

First, savings accounts, Treasury bills, government and agency bonds, certificates of deposit, and the like have different degrees of interest rate risk and other risks. Yields have tended to be lower on less risky items as shown in table 3-1. The fact that some investments have insurance and others do not is an issue, but the problem with insurance is that, even if the debt-issuing institution goes through liquidation and the depositors are fully insured, there may be a round-robin in which each depositor receives $1,000, and the next installment is made only after the other depositors have

Table 3-1
Average Yield Expected on Various Types of Securities

Security	Range of Yield to Maturity 1970–January 1980 (Percentages)	Yield January 1, 1980
90-day Treasury bill (bid-discount)	3.32–12.20	12.20%
5-year government notes	5.04–10.59	10.59
20-year government bonds	5.59–10.27	10.27
90-day certificates of deposit	3.75–13.35	13.35
90-day commercial paper	3.75–12.00	12.00
New Aa utility bonds	7.00–12.75	12.75
New Aa industrial bonds	6.90–11.75	11.75
20-year "prime" municipal bonds (tax free)	4.65– 6.75	6.70
New Aa preferred stock	6.75–10.60	10.60

Based on data from A.G. Edwards and Sons, Inc.

received their $1,000. (In fact, in most cases of difficulty of financial institutions, the banking authorities in the federal or state government seek a merger with a stronger institution, and the depositors are in no way inconvenienced.)

The inventory model discussed earlier and the hypothetical computer simulation presented offer some insights for financial management of short-term cash flows in the college. In addition, from time to time financial managers may see other ways to increase revenues from short-term idle cash balances, and it is worth discussing the risks of these options.

Maturity Balancing: Forecasting Interest Rates

Sometimes treasurers will look at a figure of interest rate yields on comparably risky securities (for example, government bonds) as shown in figure 3-1 as the *term structure* of interest rates. Seeing that five-year rates are higher than one-year rates, they will invest in long-term money, planning to sell in one year. As we discussed in chapter 2, this leaves the institution vulnerable to swings in interest rates, for a rise in rates means that the value of the five-year security will fall, in order for a purchaser of the five-year security one year hence to earn the new four-year rate of interest. For example, a five-year issue with a 6-percent coupon selling at $1,000 will fall to $966 in price if four-year interest rates a year from now are 7 percent. This result is seen by recalling the present-value analysis in chapter 1. Thus $966 invested now in order to receive $60 per year at the end of each of the next three years and $1,060 at the end of the fourth year does represent a 7-percent return. Thus the person who purchased it and who sells it in one year will have received $60 in interest and a $34 loss of principal, for a total yield of $26, or 2.6 percent.

The dotted line in figure 3-1 is a forecast of future interest yields. If the treasurer of the institution feels that the dotted yield schedule will prevail in one month, then he or she may prefer to keep the balances idle, or invest in savings accounts for one month. At that time, one month hence, the money will be transferred to an 11-month maturity. The net earnings, of course, are the 1-month interest on the savings account (for example, 5 percent) and the 11-month interest on the government bond (for example, 7 percent) less the transfer costs and the loss of income from investing in a 12-month bond initially at the yield of, for example, 6.2 percent. Of course, this example assumes certainty; the possibility that interest rates do not rise to 7 percent means that the treasurer will remain invested at the lower savings rate for a period or will transfer the money after so many months to the government bonds yielding whatever they are at that time. Perhaps the rate will be lower than today's 6.2 percent, and there will have been a loss from attempting to

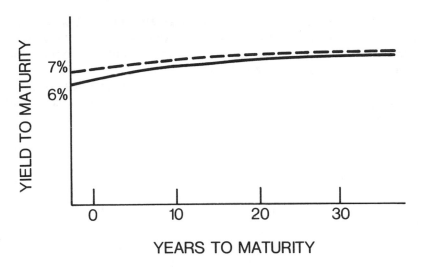

YIELD TO MATURITY

7%

6%

0   10   20   30

YEARS TO MATURITY

Figure 3–1. The Term Structure of Interest Rates

forecast the change in interest rates. As an example, assume that one is considering how to invest $100,000 for no more than one year, that the alternatives include a savings account at 5 percent which is not expected to change yields, a 12-month government bond at 6.2 percent, and a short-term, 11-month bond a month from today. Assume that there is a .4 chance of no change in yields and that the 11-month bond can be bought in one month at the same rate as today, 6.2 percent. There is a .4 chance of rates rising to 7 percent, and a .2 chance of government-bond rates for 11-month issues falling to 6 percent. There is a $5 charge for transferring funds, an internal administrative cost. The yield from investing the $100,000 at today's 6.2 percent is $6,200.

The certain yield and cost from a 1-month savings deposit at 5 percent and the $5 transfer cost from the savings deposit to the government bond is $100,000 times 0.05 divided by 12 minus $5, or $412. The income from the government bond is a function of the probabilities, and the expected value is

$$.4 \times 0.062 \times \frac{11}{12} \times \$100,000$$

$$+ .4 \times 0.07 \ \times \frac{11}{12} \times \$100,000$$

$$+ .2 \times 0.06 \ \times \frac{11}{12} \times \$100,000, \text{ or } \underline{\$5,940}$$

The expected value of this strategy is then $5,940 plus $412 which equals $6,352, or $152 higher than the $6,200 yield from the strategy of investing in the government bond today. Although this example is simple, more complex examples build on the same ideas.

The fact that the expected value of this forecasting strategy is positive does not necessarily mean that the manager will follow it. Both the manager and the institution as a whole may have a set of values that says that a bad outcome is far worse than a good one, worse still than indicated by the dollars involved. A gamble offered to an individual such as winning $1,000,000 with .9 probability (9 out of 10 odds) and a loss of $6,000,000 with a .1 probability (1 chance out of 10), may be obviously biased to provide a win. By "bias," I mean the *expected value* or average outcome of this gamble is a win of $300,000; 9 times out of 10 one would win $1,000,000 and 1 out of 10 trials would result in a loss of $6,000,000. Thus on the average of 10, 20, or 30 trials, the *mean* return would be .9 times $1,000,000 plus .1 times −$6,000,000, or $300,000. On the other hand, most of us simply cannot afford to lose $6,000,000, and will not accept this gamble, even if we were charged nothing to take the wager. However, for small amounts of cash relative to the total amount of the institution's wealth and income, such as the short-term cash-management decision is likely to involve, most institutions can safely rely on maximizing the expected value of their income.

Riding the Yield Curve

Notice that the solid line in figure 3–2 has a sharp curve around 2½ years. By using algebra, some treasurers attempt to take advantage of the nature of shifts in interest rate curves. A security with a fixed coupon of 8 percent will have to have a sharp increase in price in these few months around the 2½-year point in order for the return to a holder of that security for these few months to be fairly high. For example, assume that a three-year security yields 8 percent if held to maturity, and a two-year security yields only 7.5 percent if held to maturity. A one-year security yields 7.2 percent. Here the choice is *not* holding the three-year security and then selling it at par after one year, but noting that the sale will be above par, providing extra gain. An 8-percent coupon, three-year bond will sell at $1,000. One year later, given the figure shown here, it will sell to yield 7.5 percent, and the price will have risen to $1,009. Thus the person who held it for this period will have the coupon income of $80, plus a rise in the value of the bond of $9, for a total return of $80 plus $9 divided by $1,000, or 8.9 percent, versus the 7.2-percent yield on a one-year security of comparable risk. This procedure is called *riding the yield curve*. Notice that the critical assumption is *not* that

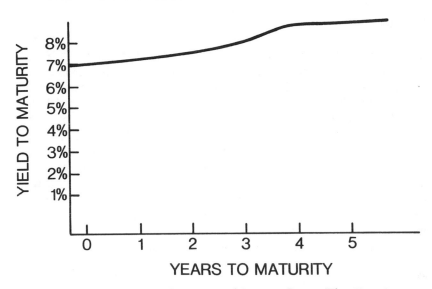

Figure 3-2. The Term Structure of Interest Rates (Five Years)

interest rates will change (as was the preceding case) but that the *yield curve* will not change, or at least will not change too unfavorably. If the two-year rates move to 8 percent, there is no gain; if they move to 8.3 percent, then there will be a loss from the early sale of the three-year security. Again probabilities can help determine the desirability of this strategy; the point is simply that it is not a riskless strategy.

Leverage

Under any of the strategies suggested previously, there is always the magnification possible by borrowing. The manager may gamble on the change in interest rates by lending money for the appropriate period but may use the investable $100,000 of the examples to collateralize a purchase of, for example, $500,000 in bonds. In this case, a correct guess on interest rates or a fortuitous operation of a yield-curve ride can pay a very high return. The reasons are simple magnification of the gains or losses, as indicated in chapter 2 under the discussion of options. As a well-publicized case at the University of Houston illustrated, this procedure can have economic (and legal) pitfalls. The dollar outcomes are magnified, and losses are increased by the amount of the interest paid to the lender of the borrowed $400,000 in the example.[4]

Summary

This chapter presented some of the concepts of short-term cash management and interest rate forecasting in the context of the college financial officer's receipts and disbursements problems. Higher yielding securities may carry higher risk, and longer term securities have higher risk of both default and changes in interest rates, risks that will cause the present value of the principal to fluctuate. Purchasing long-term issues in the hope of selling prior to maturity, especially using borrowed funds to finance part of the purchase, can provide very high returns or quite large losses. The costs and revenues associated with a centralized treasury function and with the cash-inventory models outlined here are more determinable and more certain than the outcomes associated with highly uncertain money and bond markets. The money- and bond-market forecast may be a profitable exercise, but neither the financial manager of the school nor his or her superiors should think it is novel or certain.

By recognizing that money is a mobile asset that is not free (because it can earn income), a college manager will review a number of problems or opportunities in a different light. Payment of accounts and ordering of goods are subjectible to several forms of economic analysis that can produce nonintuitive guidelines for payment. In addition, by handling the firm's cash balance with regard to the variety of, and possible changes in, interest rates, the manager may use cash in a constructive, profitable manner. The "profits" can be used either to reduce the funds tied up in short-term low-yielding assets or to provide additional cash in later periods for other purposes in the college.

Notes

1. In the long run, of course, if all competing schools move to this monthly program, then all that is accomplished is to raise the financing costs for all schools. The pattern of retail credit from department stores is similar: free credit or free delivery may stimulate sales of a given store in the absence of competition. Once other stores match the services, there may be no additional sales for all stores collectively, and the consumer is paying for a service that may or may not be wanted.

2. Economics of scale were discussed in chapter 1. Banks depend on many other items such as the ability to secure the loan with assets of the borrower. These issues are discussed in chapter 4 in the case of Prairie State University.

3. Although efforts to secure federal legislation permitting NOW accounts throughout the nation have not been successful to date, individ-

uals and institutions are able to have accounts that allow the transfer of funds from savings to checking when there are insufficient funds in the checking account. Many banks offer this service. Usually there is a transfer fee, and transfers must typically be in $100 multiples.

4. For a summary of the issues and a discussion of the jail sentences, see the *Wall Street Journal*, October 24, 1978, p. 6. Earlier extensive articles on the case appeared in the *Wall Street Journal,* December 22, 1977, p. 1, and April 10, 1978, p. 6. For an update see the *Wall Street Journal,* February 14, 1980, p. 4.

4

Project Financing: Building a Dormitory

Introduction

Over the long run, a college has revenues from several major sources. Typically these revenues come from the sale of certain services (for example, dormitory space and education) and the income from certain monetary assets (for example, foundation income and endowment income). Indeed, even the income from services may be considered as income from an asset: the faculty (a capital asset) and the reputation of the school (called "goodwill" in a private business). On the other side of the accounts are expense outflows such as salaries, wages, repairs, and the cost of purchased goods.

The next two chapters will look at two categories of projects that a school often considers. One is a revenue-producing project (often called an auxiliary service) such as a dormitory. The other project is revenue-consuming: student-aid financing.

It is sometimes very short-sighted to view any one project in isolation: There are always financial and educational interactions among projects, and the whole of a school is often more (or less) than the sum of a variety of projects, cost centers, or revenue centers. However, the issue of project interactions is most easily introduced as part of investment-program evaluation, a topic covered in chapter 6.

The case situation in this chapter describes a dormitory building plan of a small liberal arts college in the Midwest. For the reader, a careful study of the case followed by some consideration of what he or she would do with the financial implications of the situation is in order. After this important thought process, it would be appropriate to read the subsequent comments on long-term project financing relating specifically to this case. Following those comments are some general remarks regarding project financing.

This procedure of analyzing a case is useful in the other cases included in this volume, for the case is a way to show the specifics of a situation in a typical environment and to demonstrate how one draws financial conclusions from a variety of (seemingly) nonfinancial data. Again it is important that the reader consider the situation prior to reading the discussion that follows the case text.

Before reading the dormitory case, most readers will find it useful to review a more complete discussion of the long-term debt-financing sources available to a school.

Long-term Debt Financing

Bond financing has become important to public schools (selling bonds through their state taxing authority) and to some private colleges (who also can often join together under a public authority to also sell bonds for specific purposes). These bonds are sometimes *general obligation* (G.O.) issues involving the "full faith and credit" of the borrower. In other situations, the bonds are *revenue issues:* Interest and principal are paid from revenue from the building financed whether the building is a dormitory, a stadium, or some other unit. Sometimes institutions borrow directly (a private placement) from financial institutions such as banks or insurance companies. Again repayment may be a general obligation of the school or a revenue issue. These direct borrowings can also take the form of a mortgage where the building serves as collateral for the loan.

In the case of the revenue debt, if the revenues are insufficient, there is often an implicit assumption that the institution will repay the debt. Failure to repay such debt constitutes a long-term loss of credit worthiness that will be reflected in future inability to borrow, or certainly future borrowings at a much higher rate. For example, as a result of the financial panic of 1837, the state of Mississippi failed to meet some interest and principal payments on its outstanding debts. Even now, the financial ratings may reflect this action, and, as a result, the state must pay a slightly higher interest rate than would otherwise have been the case.

In most situations, funds raised through a revenue issue are not interchangeable: Money borrowed for one purpose must be used for that purpose. On the other hand, repayment of these debts can be made from a general pool of funds. As we shall see, this portfolio effect is important when evaluating a school's financing capacity.

Prairie State University [a]

Introduction

In the late summer of 1972, David Wesley, financial vice-president of Prairie State University, was pondering a recommendation that he would have to make to the university's board of trustees. Recently considerable pressure had been growing for the replacement of a number of older campus housing units for married students, and now a specific proposal had been put forth

---

[a] This case was written under the direction of Professor Samuel L. Hayes III and revised in 1977 by E. Eugene Carter. Copyright 1977 by the Trustees of the Institute for Education Management. Reprinted by permission.

for the construction of 144 new units to be ready for the academic year 1973–1974.

While Wesley could understand the need for new housing, he was concerned about the financing priorities that the university faced and was well aware that there were no funds currently available to finance the approximate $2-million cost. Among several financing alternatives, the most detailed involved a revenue-bond proposal, but Wesley wondered whether it was wise to assume the financial obligation that this entailed. He therefore decided that a careful review of this project and its impact on the financial resources of the university were in order.

The financial needs of Prairie State University were met largely by appropriation by the state legislature, supplemented by student fees and federal funds. The unrestricted Education and General revenues for fiscal year 1971–1972 were derived from the following sources:

State-appropriated funds	$9,211,000
Student fees and collections	2,823,000
Federal funds	207,000
Endowment income (land-grant income)	129,000
Organized activities	568,000
Other sources	30,000
Total	$12,968,000

Other revenues (mainly research grants and programs) exceeded $10 million in 1971–1972.

If the university built the married-student housing, it would have to be financed by gifts and/or by long-term debt that would be repaid from the housing revenues. Instructional buildings such as the $3.8-million Life Science Building and the $575,000 Nursing Building now under construction, were financed by bonds sold by the state under its long-range building program. Other facilities, however, had to pay their own way. For example, bond issues supported by student fees were sold by Prairie State University to finance the current construction of a $3.8-million Creative Arts Complex and a $2.4-million Health and Physical Education Center Building and a football stadium. Private donations also helped finance the physical-education facilities.

Need for Married-student Housing Facilities

On-campus married-student housing had in recent years been inadequate to meet demands, and the average occupancy rate had been 95 percent during 1971–1972. Moreover, the housing office was forced to turn away 43 applications for the newer units for the autumn quarter of the current year. At present there were 620 housing units at the university, 156 of which were substandard World War II frame structures donated by the U.S. government. (Of these substandard units, 40 would be phased out under the proposal, leaving 116.) Some married students found private housing in town, although it was expensive in comparison to university housing. Other students found housing in the burgeoning trailer courts in the area. General enrollment forecasts are shown in table 4–1.

Estimates placed the total cost of the projected additional married-student housing units at just over $2 million. The proposed housing complex would comprise six separate buildings consisting of 24 two-bedroom units. Each unit would contain approximately 650 square feet and would be completely furnished including a refrigerator, stove, washer, dryer, and all other furniture except linen and cutlery.

Financing Alternatives

As Wesley reviewed the alternatives, it appeared to him that there were several possibilities for financing the project in the event that the university decided to proceed. One set of options involved finding the resources by which the university could assume full ownership of the housing units itself. Because there were no funds on hand within the university for the project, this obviously involved obtaining $2 million in either loans or gifts from outsiders. Since there were no prospective donors, he first examined the possibility of a bank loan. There were several banks located near the school that were capable of extending the necessary mortgage, but initial inquiries with their lending officers had drawn cautious responses. The bankers expressed concern that the revenue projections might be overoptimistic and that in the event of a default the lenders would find themselves with hard-to-dispose-of property. In addition, Wesley knew that the Department of Housing and Urban Development (HUD), under a 1968 act, had available an annual subsidy for certain types of capital projects undertaken by schools such as Prairie State. While he felt confident that the subsidy could be obtained for a public-bond offering, he was not sure that it would apply to a privately negotiated bank loan.

Initially some attention had been given to the idea of issuing full faith-and-credit bonds with the state as guarantor. This possibility had to be rejected, however, because such a state guarantee could be given only to raise funds for institutional buildings, not housing units. In view of this limitation, Wesley next turned to the revenue bond as an alternative.

Prairie State University had used revenue bonds for a number of past financing projects and by 1972 had approximately $24 million of outstand-

Table 4–1
Student Body Composition

Enrollment Projected for 1972–1973

By Sex		By resident status	
Male	4,714	State residents	6,365
Female	3,143	Nonresidents	1,492
Total	7,857	Total	7,857

By Class		By College	
Freshmen	2,570	Agriculture	891
Sophomore	1,773	Engineering	1,101
Junior	1,414	Letters and sciences	2,047
Senior	1,536	Professional school	2,454
Graduate	442	Education	614
Nondegree	122	General studies	750
Total	7,857	Total	7,857

Enrollment Trends

Year	Men	Women	Total	Married [a]
1972–73	4,714	3,143	7,857	1,374
1971–72	4,966	3,147	8,113	1,440
1970–71	5,145	3,042	8,187	1,708
1969–70	4,909	2,809	7,718	1,492
1968–69	4,647	2,627	7,274	1,488
1967–68	4,384	2,384	6,768	1,335
1966–67	4,096	2,172	6,268	1,111

Enrollment Estimate (Net)

Year	Estimated Enrollment [b]	Married Students [c]
1973–74	8,453	1,648
1974–75	8,480	1,654
1975–76	8,496	1,657
1976–77	8,522	1,662
1977–78	8,612	1,679
1978–79	8,638	1,684
1979–80	8,627	1,682

[a] Included in total.

[b] These projections were made by the office of the executive secretary of the State University System in mid-1972. Consideration is given to high school enrollments, trends of enrollment, and retention factors.

[c] Estimated at 19½ percent of estimated enrollment.

ing indebtedness, not including the proposed $2-million offering to finance the current housing project under review. Of this total, $16 million had been issued under a 1954 indenture that specified that additional bonds for new facilities could be issued as long as certain conditions were met. (The *inden-*

ture is the formal agreement between the issuer of the bond and the bond-holders.) The most important of these covenants was that the coverage of fixed charges on the indebtedness (that is, the revenues generated to cover interest and principal repayment) would be at least 1.4 to 1. Income to pay these bonds issued under the 1954 indenture came primarily from the net revenues of the pledged facilities and secondarily from certain student fees, land-grant income, and investment income. Table 4-2 presents an historical calculation of the funds-flow picture for the university as it related to the coverage of debt service for the years 1969–1972.

Wesley was particularly concerned about the impact that the new indebtedness would have on the coverage of these financial commitments by virtue of the new principal that would now be added. Projected net revenues that would be realized annually from the proposed 144 new married-student apartments, plus 104 established units to be pledged to these bonds, and less 40 units to be retired, was estimated to be $181,242 (see table 4-3). In addition, he had been told that HUD would approve a subsidy of $47,050 per year to help pay the principal and interest on the proposed bond issue. Under the terms of this grant, payment would be made each year until the bonds in this series were retired. Debt-service coverage would be 1.67 for a typical year (table 4-4).

An entirely different approach would have the university forego owner-ship of the housing units and seek a private group that would finance and own the units themselves. Wesley knew that there were certain tax benefits

Table 4-2
Income and Debt Service Coverage

		1972	1971	1970	1969
	Gross revenue from income facilities	$3,688,898	$3,254,960	$3,057,382	$2,756,919
	Pledged student fees	243,633	250,268	231,599	221,133
	Land-grant income	36,417	30,318	36,497	37,462
	Investment income	109,656	157,360	231,355	143,468
	Total revenues	$4,078,604	$3,692,906	$3,556,833	$3,158,982
	Current expenses	$2,415,792	12,107,073	$1,792,948	$1,531,136
(A)	Net revenues available for debt service	$1,662,812	$1,585,833	$1,763,885	$1,627,846
(B)	Debt service for the indicated year [a]	$1,045,285	$1,049,723	$ 984,877	$1,025,189
(A/B)	Debt-service coverage	1.59X	1.51X	1.79X	1.59X

[a]Service for $16 million of debt under the 1954 indenture agreement. Principal and interest payments for this debt would average about $1 million per year for the next 30 years, with a maximum of $1,084,241 in 1991.

Table 4–3
Estimated Net Revenues of Proposed Married-student Housing

1. Net enrollment will increase from 8,113 for autumn 1971 to 8,425 for autumn 1981; married students will be 19.5 percent of total students each year through 1981.
2. Utilization of housing for married students and faculty for the past 3 years has been 86 percent in 1969–1970, 93 percent in 1970–1971 and 95 percent in 1971–1972. Utilization of added "new" units will be estimated as follows:

In first year of use	70%
In second year of use	75%
In third year of use	80%
In fourth year of use	85%
In fifth year of use	90%
Sixth year and after	92%

3. Rental rates currently in effect are $122 per month for two-bedroom units of the type planned. The existing student houses to be pledged for the first time to this indenture rent for $70–$80 per month; faculty houses pledged for the first-time rent for $85–$100 per month.
4. Additional gross revenue to be realized from the 144 new units is estimated to be $1,834,101 over the next 10 years, or an average of $183,410 per year.
5. Additional gross revenue to be realized from the 104 existing units to be pledged to this indenture and the retirement of 40 units is estimated to be $68,392 per year.
6. Estimated operating costs for 144 new units at $388 per year is $55,872. Estimated operating cost for 104 existing units at $242 per year is $25,168. Decreased operating costs due to retirement of 40 units at $262 per year is $10,480. Total added operating cost from all net additions is $70,560.
7. The board of regents may adjust rental rates whenever necessary.
8. Projected annual *net* revenues from all additions and retirements are as follows:

Gross revenues	$251,802
Expenses	70,560
Net revenues from operation	$181,242
HUD subsidy	47,050
Total net revenues	$228,292

9. Using a 6½ percent annual interest rate, annual debt-service charges for the $2 million issue for 30 years will be $153,155. Thus a more complete version of table 1A–6 would show a 30-year discount factor for an annual receipt of $1 at 6.5 percent to be 13.0587. Then the annual payment of interest plus principal on a 6.5-percent, $2-million debt would be $2,000,000 divided by 13.0587, or $153,155.

that could be utilized by individual investors that would be of no value to a nonprofit institution like Prairie State. It was quite possible therefore that such a private group could be attracted to this kind of investment opportunity and thus spare the university any of the financial burden involved in the mortgage loan or bond offering.

Wesley was aware, however, that several of the university's trustees had expressed reservations about private ownership for such housing units. Their concern centered around the consequent loss of control and the administrative headaches that might result.

Table 4–4
Projected Net Revenues and Debt Service

Average annual net revenues available for debt service (July 1, 1969, through June 30, 1972)	$1,670,894
Projected annual net revenues from facilities operated partially from July 1, 1969, through June 30, 1972	23,405
Projected annual net revenues from facilities financed by this issue and from the pledging of 104 added housing units and the proposed retirement of 40 old units including $47,050 HUD debt-service subsidy (item 8, table 4–3)	228,292
Total estimated annual net revenues	$1,922,591
Estimated debt-service for fiscal year ending June 30, 1974 based on average service charge of $1 million for the old issue and $153,155 for the new issue of debt (notes to tables 4–2 and table 4–3)	$1,153,155
Estimated debt-service coverage for fiscal year ending June 30, 1974	1.67

In reviewing the material on this question, Wesely realized that there was a variety of shorter term and longer term questions that would have to be dealt with in this decision. He therefore resolved to lay out his recommendation with a detailed consideration of the major implications involved.

Prairie State University: Analysis

The figures in table 4–5 are useful in analyzing the capability of this project to finance itself. The first column reflects anticipated first-year cash flows, and the second column shows the average for, for example, 10 years using data from the case. The major difference is the occupancy ratio, which is presumed to be 70 percent for the first year and to average 87 percent for the following 10 years.

By combining the number of units, the revenue per month, and the expenses per month, we may compute the income after expenses prior to the subsidy ($91,699 for the first year and $127,583 for the 10-year average). Adding the subsidy provides a net revenue of $138,749 in the first year and $174,588 per annum over 10 years. Notice that this calculation presumes that most of the maintenance costs such as heating and cleaning will continue even if the units are not fully occupied. For the first year this assumption may be unusually conservative: If only 70 percent of the anticipated 10-year average maintenance is spent in the first year, reflecting lower initial occupancy, then the total operating expense would decline to $39,110 from the $55,872 shown here.

The typical debt-service cost, as mentioned in the case, will be $153,155

Table 4–5
Evaluation of Revenue and Expenses: Prairie State Dormitory

144 New Units	First Year	10-year Average
Usage ratio	.70	.87
Units	144	144
(times)		
Months	12	12
(times)		
Rent per unit	$122	$122
(equals)		
Revenues ($210,816 at 100%)	$147,571	$183,410
Expenses (144 × $388)	55,872	55,872
Net revenue before subsidy	$91,699	127,538
HUD subsidy	47,050	47,050
Net revenue: new units	$138,749	$174,588
Gross revenue from 104 existing less		
40 retirements	$68,392	$68,382
Operating cost of 64 units [a]	− 14,688	− 14,688
	$192,453	$228,292
	÷ 153,155	÷ 153,155
Coverage ratio	= 1.26	1.49

[a]By the text of the case the operating cost of 104 units is $25,168, and the cost of the 40 units to be retired is $10,480. Hence the operating costs of the 64 remaining units is the difference in these two figures, $14,688.

for a $2-million loan over 30 years at 6 ½ percent interest. Thus the buildings will not generate sufficient free cash in the first year to cover the loan; even over the 10-year average, the $174,588 of net revenue barely covers the payments required each year.

The lenders of course are aware of this problem, and it is for this reason they ask that revenues from the existing buildings also be pledged to cover the debt obligation. These calculations are shown on the next lines of the table: the gross revenues to be pledged minus the associated operating cost of all 104 units plus the savings from not operating the 40 units to be retired. The third line shows the revised net-income figure. The result shows that the total cash generated ($192,453) divided by the debt payment of $153,155 provides a *coverage ratio* of 1.26 in the first year. Stated another way, there is cash generated that is 126 percent of the required debt-service charges. For the 10-year average, of course, there is a higher figure for net revenues from the new buildings, and the total revenues pledged for new and old buildings provide a 1.49 coverage ratio.

Several additional points are worth noting: construction financing, cost of financing, probabilities of the figures' being accurate, and implications of the coverage ratio.

Construction Financing. Usually construction financing loans for 18 to 24 months are made by a lender, with "take-out" permanent financing agreed upon in advance, probably from a different lender. This latter loan is usually larger than the construction loan by the amount of interest on the construction loan. Implicitly this arrangement is assumed here, and the loan represents the permanent financing. If this is not the pattern, notice that for the first 12 to 24 months of the loan, during construction, there is no income from the new units to make loan payments!

Financing Costs. It is useful to study the present value of the project under alternative assumptions such as a shorter life or even a slightly higher interest rate that could change this analysis. For example, using the 25 years in table 1A-6 (page 21), note that the present-value factor for 9 percent is 9.8226. Dividing the loan today, $2 million, by this factor provides the amount of the mortgage payment that will cost the borrower (and pay the lender) 9 percent per annum plus repay the total loan over the 25 years. This figure, $2 million divided by 9.8226, is $203,612. Using this number for computing the coverage in the first year, we find a ratio of only .94. Over 10 years the figure is $228,292 divided by $203,612, or 1.12. More importantly, notice that this $203,612 figure is about 20 percent above the amount of uncommitted cash associated with the 10-year average net income from the new dormitories. Although we shall return to this topic later, the calculation of a slightly shorter mortgage life and a marginally higher interest rate shows the importance of these two assumptions in the financial profile of the entire project. (The reader may want to calculate what a 12 percent interest assumption would do to the calculations!)

Accuracy of Projections. There is a projection of about 92 percent utilization, which will require about 100 additional married students. Including the capacity of the new units and the (156 minus 40) 116 substandard units, then the total capacity as shown in table 4-5 is 724 units. Current usage based on available space is 580 + 40 old units. A 95-percent occupancy, with 43 students turned away, represents 633 units. This represents a presumed demand of (633 divided by 724) 87 percent of capacity as shown in the 10-year average. If we assume that the 95-percent demand for capacity utilization represents demand for the 580 good units, plus 43 turned away, then current demand is for 595 units, or 82 percent of the proposed capacity. From the projections shown here, it is clear that the amount of income from the new units will *not* be sufficient to cover the $153,155 annual financing charge until the units are about 78 percent full; if they fail to meet this occupancy rate or if the maintenance figures are wrong, the dormitories will be a drain on the remainder of the school's financial resources.

The hope, of course, is that the attractiveness of the new units will encourage students to return to the campus, and may actually attract new students to the school.

Coverage Ratios. These ratios indicate a margin of safety to the borrower. They suggest to the school how much additional revenue may have to be diverted. Here the portfolio issue becomes apparent; while it is true that the other dormitories can be pledged, they *could* be pledged for other purposes. Thus this project is *not* self-supporting in the sense that it is reducing today's borrowing capacity of the school. Over time some assets are always being used to support other assets. Once the "machine" is set in motion, this is the way it operates.

On the other hand, there is the issue of what other areas need financing. In this case faculty salaries come from state appropriations, and classroom buildings are financed from a state building fund. Thus two obvious alternative needs are not competing for money. Furthermore, the HUD subsidy and the fact that these bond proceeds can be used only for this purpose mean that this money will be lost otherwise.

Thus there is no other obvious way to attract this money, and the revenues pledged from the other buildings may not be needed elsewhere. This outcome from both the source of the loan and the lack of need to divert the other revenue to other worthy projects is often not the situation in a university.

Finally, it should be emphasized that coverage ratios and other indicators of ability to repay the loan are of more than casual interest, for lenders can and do foreclose, even on colleges. Windham College in Vermont owed the Vermont National Bank $225,000, and the trustees showed no ability to repay the debt. Finally, the bank held an auction, successfully selling items such as the college banner and fully equipped FM radio station in order to recover the money due the bank. The auction was haulted after a few days when sufficient funds were raised, preventing the sale of campus buildings.

Policy Analysis

Although many other marginal comparisons and assumptions are possible, the preceding calculations and comments serve to indicate the economic appraisal of this project, including the margin of safety for covering debt-service charges. There also are several other issues: Should the school be concerned about housing at all? If so, are there more economic alternatives to meet the need? Even if Prairie State decides to build its own dorms, what are the alternatives?

Housing as a Concern. The more conservative assumptions are that the school is in the business of education and not housing, that such a project entails risk to the financial solvency of a school, and that if there is sufficient demand, a private developer will provide housing. Against this argument is the whole-environment view, in which student housing is seen as an important part of the college experience for which the school bears some responsibility. A marketing argument is that housing provides an attractive feature with which to attract students, especially graduate students in physical sciences who wish to be near the school laboratories. Finally, there is an argument that the townspeople are likely to resent both trailer camps and rising rents charged existing tenant residents as students bid up local housing costs. The validity of these arguments on both sides is beyond the scope of the financial case analysis per se, but it is important in reaching a decision.

What Is the Most Economic Way to Provide Housing? There are many competing demands for services and funds, and a strong tax argument to suggest that a private developer should be encouraged to provide housing. Because of the specifics of real-estate taxation policies (chiefly, rapid depreciation of the real-estate and various federal subsidies), there may be individuals known to the school who would be pleased to own this housing.

Against the lower cost of private ownership of the housing is the feeling that the school would lose control over quality. For example, the developer may design the housing toward general-purpose apartments that would attract nonstudents, as protection for the investors. Also the developer might require some guarantee from Prairie State either to provide certain occupancy or not to compete. These various choices represent a way for the school to increase its borrowing power.[1]

Optimum Way to Finance Housing. Granting the nonobvious assumption that housing is the responsibility of the school and that the school should own the housing, there is the question of whether this financing is the best. It may be possible to obtain a private mortgage from alumni or other lenders that has a longer maturity and/or a lower interest rate. Although the local banks are small and the buildings are worth little as collateral (who else would buy them in bankruptcy or foreclosure, and for what purpose?), perhaps a bank mortgage from the local lenders could be arranged. Again what are the terms and conditions associated with this financing choice? More important, would the HUD subsidy continue? A final choice involves the school's selling its own revenue bonds, as we have analyzed previously. The difficulties involve reduced enrollment, and the fact that the trend in married students' demanding campus housing is downward even though the number of married students has remained stable at around 1,500. The arguments for the housing with revenue-bond financing are that the lender cannot really foreclose and that the buildings from the World War II vintage will have to be replaced at some point anyway.

Conclusions: Project Financing

Although the points regarding the accuracy of projections and the need to study *sensitivity analyses* around various "likely" figures have been made previously, they are only the beginning of the evaluation. There is always a question of other opportunities, both for achieving the goal in question and for using the funds. For example, having the dormitory built privately might permit one scarce asset (money or borrowing capacity) to be used more effectively in other areas where other sources of funding are not available (for example, a special library collection or recruitment of distinguished faculty).

Given the qualification of what the school should be doing and how it should be doing it as noted previously, then this chapter still offers guidance on how one computes a coverage ratio for long-run financing. I have implicitly and explicitly suggested possibilities for improving the coverage ratio such as adding revenues from sources that cannot otherwise be applied to financing decisions, writing a loan agreement that permits additional building as long as certain ratios continue to be met, delaying the maturity of a bond agreement to improve the rating, pledging general revenues, and the like. In addition to showing the application of marginal concepts from economic analysis, I hope also to have shown that the impact of subsidies can do a considerable amount to distort internal-resource allocation. Subsidies allow lenders to favor one type of project sharply over another. With a dictum of spending whatever one can finance, college financial managers often have a temptation to overallocate funds to particular projects (for example, buildings), not recognizing that such internal reallocation unfavorably affects the ability of the school to finance other items that are not subsidized.

Finally, the cash-flow analysis from any particular project is derived from some philosophical consensus of what a school ought to be doing and what are reasonable alternatives for approaching those missions. The cash flow, of course, merely highlights that money is a restricted resource, that there are comparative costs for using it in different time periods (interest and present-value analysis), and that different alternatives involve different risks to the school.

In spite of these qualifications, quantitative or judgmental issues are relevant as a *supplement* to financial analysis and not as a *substitute* for it! Unless a manager or board has an idea of the magnitude of funds involved and the financial characteristics of a decision, polemics and emotion often can result in an unfavorable outcome.

Some guidelines, then, are:

1. Determine the relevant cash flows for each period for any (broadly defined) project using college resources.
2. Confirm that the required cash investment in the project *after* the first year can be supplied.
3. Evaluate the externalities of a project. (*Externalities* are benefits or costs indirectly involved as a result of accepting or rejecting a project.) Where are funds jointly required in conjunction with other college commitments? Where might additional benefits accrue to the college from the project under consideration? If the project is accepted, are changes requiring or producing funds in other programs likely to have additional impact on the college?
4. Recognize the time value of money and alternative uses for cash. The manager will compute the present value of a project on many occasions. If the net present value (NPV) is negative, are the nonquantifiable benefits sufficient to offset the loss? If the NPV is positive, are there negative qualitative issues that are relatively larger in some sense?
5. Finally, what other alternatives are available for meeting some or all of the objectives of this project? What is the cost and the NPV of the alternatives?

Prior to discussion of the portfolio effects of investments of endowment funds, we turn to another project that is often not viewed in project-financing terms: the issue of student-aid financing.

Notes

1. There may be a subtle difference in cost to the institution and cost to society that can be lost. Suppose the public school already had land on which the housing can be built. In one sense, if the tax incentives mentioned favor private development, then the land should be sold to a private developer who operates as described. The funds realized can be used for other university purposes. But suppose the land cannot be sold easily and that the state legislature would use income from that sale (if allowed) only to reduce given appropriations. Then the university administrators have a greater incentive to build the housing themselves since the total cost (ignoring the land) would probably be lower than having an outside contractor build the housing. If the land could not be legally sold (as may be the case for a public or independent college in a number of situations), then a long-term lease of

the land to the developer may be an appropriate route. Most of the tax incentives involve accelerated depreciation, and land cannot be depreciated in any case. However, restrictions on leasing may prevent this action as well. Notice that the lowest cost to the state (private development as assumed) will not be realized if there is no incentive for the school officials to consider the cost of the land in their analysis.

5 Project Financing: Tuition and Student Aid

The economics of higher education has been reviewed by many people, usually with an outlook of gloom. Spiraling inflation in the United States, coupled with the declining inclination of students to attend college and combined with a declining traditional enrollment age pool, causes consternation in the minds of many educational officers. In this chapter, we explore some elements involved in setting tuition policy from the standpoint of economic analysis, suggesting the variables that need to be considered, even when the specific values of those variables are not always clear. Then we comment on cost allocation among programs, suggesting how this information may relate to tuition policy. Finally, we review various public and private plans that affect the student-aid program. Although the issue of tuition and student aid is primarily a concern of private schools, setting tuition policies for public colleges is a problem that is increasingly affecting educators and legislators alike, and thus this analysis will be of interest to both.

Tuition Policy: Introduction

Several issues are directly involved in setting tuition policy. One aspect of analysis is the revenue side: What will be the market's reaction? What will competing schools do? What will students do? A second consideration is the costs of the institution: If tuition bears some relation to costs, how should the cost be allocated? Given the allocation, how should differential tuition be charged among fields or programs? A third factor relates to the long-run implications of any tuition policy: Over time what will be the reactions of faculty, students, and the public at large? How costly could these reactions be to the college?

Breakeven Analysis

One of the most basic elements to consider is the response of enrollment to the contemplated change in fees. For example, if there are 2,000 students now paying $3,200, how many students will there have to be for a $200 tuition increase to result in at least the same revenue? Notice that the conclusion that a $200 increase times 2,000 students will generate an extra $400,000 is wrong if one assumes that at least some students will discontinue *this* progran in *this* school at *this* time and that they cannot be replaced in the long run from the enrollment pool.

To answer the question, first observe that total income is now 2,000 times $3,200, or $6.4 million. Dividing $6.4 million by the new tuition, $3,400, we find that 1,882 students are needed. Thus the breakeven drop in students is 5.9 percent [(2,000 minus 1882) divided by 2,000]. If less than this percentage of students is lost, then the tuition increase will result in more revenue than the old tuition level.

Various studies have been made of the response of enrollment to tuition increases. One 1967 study found that a $100 increase reduced enrollment between 3 percent and 6 percent depending on family income of the student. A later study suggested that a $100 increase reduced enrollment from 0.13 percent to 2.6 percent, depending on the specific college within the university. Still another suggested about a 2.5-percent decline in enrollment for a $100 increase.[1]

Such studies are interesting but hardly definitive. Are students like the ones they studied apt to react the same way today? Are those students typical of another college's students? Finally, $100 as a percentage of college costs was much higher then than it is today; so perhaps one is more interested in the effect of a percentage increase in costs than of an arbitrary $100, and although it can be imputed from the dates and schools involved, the studies do not give us that information. On the other hand, one may also want to look at tuition and other college costs as a percentage of family income; if it is an increasing percentage of the typical student's income (or, at least, larger than it was 10 or 15 years ago), then the student may be more sensitive to any increase in an already large portion of his or her total expenditures.[2]

A variation to consider is the net effect of a tuition increase on paying students if scholarship students are to face exactly the same net costs as before. In the example given, if half the students receive tuition scholarships that are indexed to tuition, then only the nonscholarship students are bearing the cost of the increase. Thus if 1,000 students pay full tuition, then the same figures and percentages apply, but to a smaller pool. If 5.9 percent of the 1,000 students leave, the tuition income under the new policy will be the same as under the old policy (941 times $3,400 equals 1,000 times $3,200 equals $3.2 million).

A more interesting variant to consider is the breakeven point if the scholarship students receive only partial reimbursement for any tuition increase and, hence actually pay some of the increase. Here there are two unknowns: the percentage of full-paying students who leave and the percentage of scholarship students who leave. We can solve the example for several different combinations of losses by trial and error. First, assume that this small surcharge induces none of the scholarship students to leave. Then the formula for the number of full-paying students R that must stay in the school so that the revenue is the same $6.4 million is

$$(\$3,400 \times R) + [\$3,300 \times (1,000 - O)] = \$6.4 \text{ million}$$

Here we are assuming that the scholarship students will pay only $100 of a $200 tuition increase, and we are ignoring how the previous scholarship aid developed; presumably, it will continue at the same level. If we previously had 1,000 full-paying students and 1,000 scholarship students, then the new R in the preceding equation will be 912, employing a maximum decline of 8.8 percent [(1,000 minus 912) divided by 1,000]. Alternatively, if we replace the $(1,000 - O)$ term with S for scholarship students, then we can set S at, for instance, 950, assuming a 5 percent loss in those students, and find that the maximum drop in R that will leave total revenues at $6.4 million is 40 students, or 4 percent. This analysis can be completed for any number of combinations.

Notice that breakeven analysis does not imply any likelihood about the outcome being above or below that level. One can use probabilities for various changes in enrollments to estimate the *expected* revenue from any tuition increase. Thus there is some small chance of no enrollment change and some small chance of a 15-percent drop, for example, and there are higher probabilities of outcomes somewhere between these two extremes. By assigning probabilities to these various outcomes, the college official can study the likely revenue increase from a tuition change.

Tuition and Enrollment Strategy

Notice that the college has several options in using tuition as a "weapon" for recruiting students.[3] As shown in table 5-1, we might call these strategies A through E, using a simple tripartite division of tuition, financial aid, and admission standards. An A strategy implies few low-income students and a smaller program—an elitist program for well or ill if the strategy works. Strategy B will have a more segmented student body as there will be fewer middle-class students and more from the other income classes, and this strategy will probably generate more total revenue than A. In effect, the school is redistributing income from higher income students (attracted by lower admission rankings at the margin) to lower income students who meet higher admission standards. Strategy C is a "volume" strategy but may not work if public institutions with implicit "tax-supported scholarships" to all students are geographically and programmatically competitive. Strategy D

Table 5-1
Undergraduate Strategy Options

Strategy Descriptions	Strategy	Tuition	Financial Aid	Admissions Standards
Elitist	A	Raise	Hold	Hold
Segmented	B	Raise	Raise	Hold
Volume	C	Hold	Hold	Lower
Cost cutting	D	Hold	Hold	Hold
Large volume	E	Lower	Lower	Lower

is a cost-cutting program requiring reduced programs and cost controls. Finally, strategy *E* reaches for the middle class and large volume, and seems to be the policy followed by more and more institutions these days. It directly competes with the mission of many public colleges and universities.

Part of revenue strategy is the idea of selecting a *market niche*. Professors have aspirations, and figures such as the research productivity of the faculty and percentage of graduate students to total enrollment become important; it is hoped that the apocryphal story of the Noble laureate who remarked that the sight of any student made him ill and a freshman's appearance brought on convulsions illustrates this attitude. On the other hand, when considering tuition charges, there are several guidelines for a small private college.

1. Avoid the state school's strongest programs; on the basis of economics alone, this competititon will be hard to face.
2. Look for areas where student demand will grow or is already large.
3. Consider graduate programs both for prestige for the undergraduate programs and for recruitment of faculty. Also, note the possibilities of using graduate students as teaching assistants in undergraduate courses.

Some of these issues will be examined in more detail as part of the Wichita State University discussion in chapter 8.

Tuition and Cost

As part of any tuition analysis, it is useful to see where the costly programs develop. Some programs have a small number of majors but provide a large service function: Mathematics and economics are often in this category. Other programs have few majors and few service students: declining interest in education, classics, literature, and history often has placed these programs in this role in recent years. Some departments may have historically accidental concentration of senior, high-paid faculty, with resulting higher costs per student hour. Some programs or departments have greater requirements for specialized equipment or laboratory sessions such as engineering and some of the sciences. Finally, graduate- versus undergraduate-student mixes also result in different costs.

One argument is equal access to education without regard to cost and, hence equal tuition. This policy offers a social view that is not without merit. It suffers, however, from two practical short-run problems in today's world and a third, longer run, problem. First, it somehow assumes that social costs are irrelevant, that the student should not bear the cost of providing value to him or her. One can argue that all students should be subsidized X dollars, but that argument implies different tuition charges. Equal tuition implies that students receive varying subsidies depending on their major, an argument that seems weak on a social-equity basis. If medical education costs $15,000 per year per student and graduate history education costs $4,000, a $3,000-per-year, per-student subsidy implies medical tuition of $12,000 and history tuition of $1,000. Charging medical and history students alike $2,000 per year means the medical student receives an extra $11,000 subsidy. Second, when competing schools charge different tuitions, then it is likely that any one school with flat tuition charges will have an excess of students seeking admission to the high (social) cost, subsidized programs (for example, medicine), with fewer students in the low-cost, high-tuition programs (for example, large lecture programs such as history). Such a policy may permit the program in high demand to raise admissions standards, but that outcome ought to be adopted in its own right and not simply received as the result of some accidental tuition behavior of competing institutions.

In the long run, flat tuition ignores scarce resources from donors and the public or students, resources that are needed for expansion and replacement. The high-cost programs whose costs are forced up by equipment and other charges tend to be a severe disadvantage unless one assumes a solid link between high-cost programs and generous alumni. Otherwise, if $1 million is available for expansion, why should it go to support 30 undergraduate nuclear engineering students per year rather than 150 English Master of Arts in Teaching students? To the extent that the engineering students' undergraduate tuition might pay more of their own costs under a differential tuition policy, then the funding is probably less controversial; there is less subsidy from the rest of the university.

When one analyzes costs, there are always difficulties. Furthermore, there is no good solution. On the other hand, accepting the status quo provides no basis for future expansion and implies a judgment that somehow today is "right" or "equitable." Thus while the economist cannot say that one MAT graduate is worth five nuclear engineering graduates, one can ask: At this time in this place, should this college spend five times the amount of money per nuclear engineering graduate that it does per English MAT graduate?

Perhaps it should. Operating solely on the basis of lowest cost per student implies that large-lecture, undergraduate programs would be highly desirable, but few academics would justify that outcome. The problem is that ignorance about cost is hardly the only alternative to a factory-production standard, as some critics might call such a cost analysis.

Student Aid: Introduction

Student financing is intertwined with tuition policy per se, yet it also has a life of its own. Even in public universities with relatively low tuition charges, the need to finance students from particular economic groups exists. Any financial-aid program involves questions of economics, social equity, and legality. In addition, some financial-aid programs that initially seem to be of limited cost eventually create immense financial drains on the college.

Student Need

Traditionally, financial aid to students has been used overtly as an equity- or income-redistribution tool and covertly as a recruiting device. By some mixing of family income and need (as reported by the family and supported by a tax return) and family wealth (as reported, with little ability on the part of any scholarship service to verify it), the family's ability to support a student is broadly determined. Total costs for the child to attend the college are estimated, and the difference represents financial aid required by the student. Today this aid will typically be a package, involving in part a loan, in part a grant (or "scholarship" as the term is used here), and in part employment. Both the total amount of the package and the mixture can be varied depending on the college's interest in that student; this is the recruiting element of the financial-aid picture.

Some writers have noted that merely considering only family income or wealth may create a very incomplete picture of a student's ability to pay. The family may have large holdings of low-yielding assets such as farm land. Moreover, the student may have a sharply enhanced earning ability as a result of the desired academic training; from that incremental future income the student could pay a large portion of the true cost of education.

Funding: The Pattern of College Cash Flows

The Ford Fundation called for a variety of programs to be available for financing higher education, and one of the most innovative responses was the Yale plan. This program was from the first school to approach formally the idea of an Educational Opportunity Bank. Students were allowed to repay their educational obligations under a program linked to their income, with certain graduating-class and personal-income overrides. The initial Yale program was based on the opportunity for a student who was a U.S. citizen to enter the program. Although loan-ceiling standards varied, essentially a student could borrow up to $1,000 at the beginning of an academic year. Upon graduation, he or she was grouped with the graduating class as a cohort. Thereafter, the student repaid $2.90 per $100 deferred if his or her income was under $7,250. If it was over that amount, then the student paid 0.04 percent of *income*. When the student paid 150 percent of the cost of the loan, compound interest, and the cost of insurance on the unpaid balance to repay Yale if the student died, then the loan was ended. In addition, when the cohort of the graduating class repaid all its obligations with compound interest and administration costs, then the whole class was exempted from further payments, with some exceptions.[5]

The actual participation in 1971–1972 and projections for later years revealed several interesting features. Slightly more men than women participated in the program the first year, and freshmen participated more than graduating seniors. For the seven years ending in 1976–1977, the original projections called for new loans to total the following amounts each year:

1971–1972	$1,185,000
1972–1973	2,050,000
1973–1974	3,081,000
1974–1975	4,363,000
1075–1976	4,524,000
1976–1977	4,603,000
	$19,806,000

More important, over these 6 years, the total amount loaned by the university would rise to $32 million, well above the $19.8 million in the preceding figures, simply because earlier years' participants would not be repaying sufficient amounts to cover the rising interest burden.

Part of the difficulty with such an educational bank is that the amount invested by the school keeps rising even if no more loans are made, at least in the earlier years when repayment does not cover interest. Also there may be some problems with state usury laws, which prohibit exorbitant interest rates; Yale had received an agreement from the Internal Revenue Service that all amounts above the loan amount would be deductible interest to the repaying participant for tax purposes. As the plan originally was conceived, the whole plan required the Yale endowment to be pledged because the agreements of the students were not acceptable collateral.

The most serious drawback to the plan is the problem of actuarial qualities. The soundness (on which the lenders would rest their case) is simply whether the participation of students in the program would provide a reasonably large cross-section of Yale graduates whose income could be projected, justifying the assumption that somehow a market interest rate would be earned on the whole program. This concern is related to the economist's principle of *adverse selection:* People who can benefit from a program place themselves in the program, and, more important, people who will not benefit remain outside. The best examples may be retirement programs for large groups, automobile-insurance programs with state-controlled rates, or the like. Here the concern is that students who on the average will have higher incomes after graduating in professions such as law or medicine, would not participate in the program, preferring to finance their education from traditional sources. Those with lower income expectations such as budding classicists or divinity students, would enter the program, secure in the knowledge that they will probably never pay as much as a commercial loan would require. From the data provided by Yale, there was evidence that in the early years the law and medical students participated as much as others in the program.

Duke and Harvard College, among others, have initiated complex programs that permit students to repay from income, subject in varying cases to minimum interest charges, a maximum payout period, and some protection against low income. These programs vary, but all are based on the premise that a college education can be repaid, probably by allocating some of the incremental income from future years. Even if education does not "pay," there is the argument that, as a consumption good, it is reasonable to provide a deferred-payment plan, and the plan can be linked to income. Many of these programs were subsequently terminated or modified to place more of the financing emphasis on various federal government arrangements.

Federal Loan Programs

Although there are a variety of proposed government programs for educational banks that may or may not have income-redistributional aspects to them, the current federal programs include a number of grants to students qualifying under work-study and similar programs. Total federal involvement in the direct financing of students is immense. For the 1979–1980 academic year, $540 million was awarded for work-study grants, $305 million was allocated for loans to graduate and undergraduate students, and $333 million was spent for low-income student grants.

For loan programs directly involving colleges, the Guaranteed Student Loan (GSL) program involves the student's borrowing directly from a lending institution, with the government's subsidizing the interest rate and guaranteeing repayment. Under the National Direct Student Loan (NDSL) program, the government provides funding to the college for lending to students. Under the GSL program, many colleges have established their own lending departments, qualifying as a GSL lender. From an economics standpoint, most college administrators will find the GSL program of interest. Even after being forced to decide on whom should get a loan and whom should not ("acting like a bank"), facing collection costs and servicing costs, negotiating with the government and its regulatory enforcers, there may be benefits to the college. First, the college, rather than the bank, can decide who receives loans and can combine them with a financial-aid program. Second, some servicing costs can be turned over to an outside collection group. Third, and most important, the nature of the insurance means that there will likely be outside funding by a bank or other financial institution. This aspect of the issue is what permits many colleges to use this program; there is additional cash available to a particular portion of the college's operations (student aid) that is secured by the student and by recourse to the federal government, not by the college's endowment.

Sallie Mae

A related program is Sallie Mae, the Student Loan Marketing Association. This program is owned by many colleges and universities and is designed to provide through federal status a government imprimatur to the secondary market for student loans. One difficulty with a student loan is that the lender is trapped by the repayment pattern of the borrower. If the lender needs funds, then the question is, who will provide the after-market. In the case of Sallie Mae, that institution guarantees a warehousing service. Thus existing loans may be turned over to Sallie Mae for cash, with Sallie Mae's making a discount for collection costs. There may be fixed- or variable-rate new loans but with a guarantee that the variable rate set by Sallie Mae will be at least 0.5 percent less than the earnings of the school on new loans made from the proceeds of the warehousing arrangement. In this system, the school loans money to students and the student note acknowledging the indebtedness is collateral for *additional* funds. Under the conditions of the Sallie Mae program, the proceeds from the warehousing arrangement must be reinvested in new student loans within no more than 3 years. Here again a financial institution seen in a related area of the economy such as Fannie Mae, which remarkets household mortgages, has application in the area of education.

Student Financing: Policy Prescriptions

In one sense student financing is a marketing tool, and schools may use it to attract other students. What is often ignored, however, is that the cash involved can accumulate to huge amounts, even though the program is financially sound. It is this cash-flow problem, rather than the lack of interest "earnings" or excessive default (both of which indeed may be serious) that poses serious danger to the college.

The cash burden can be offset by a substantial nest egg from alumni—but one must observe that the money could well be raised for other purposes and hence represents a drain from college needs in other areas. It has an opportunity cost. Alternatively, bank financing may be available, but such a program usually means the school is ultimately a guarantor of the loan, meaning that the loan capacity of the school is reduced, as discussed in chapter 4. Federal programs such as the GSL program and the pseudo-private Sallie Mae offer an external source of funding that removes some of the financial vulnerabilities of the school. However, this is done at the expense of having a narrowed program that is predefined along some dimensions, record keeping, and other administrative requirements that may be more onerous than some other alternatives, and the loss of the option to have a "unique" program that has substantial innovative marketing appeal and attraction to potential students. To the extent that the last option has limited applicability, then the external funding expansion possible with a federal program seems beneficial to most schools. There are serious problems, but, as once was said about some financial offerings to private investors, it may be the only game in town.

Under the bill passed in late 1979 by the House of Representatives, federal aid to colleges was to expand by 50 percent in 5 years. In dealing with the Education Amendments of 1980, the Senate was expected to focus on the GSL and NDSL programs. Although the default problem with these loans has been reduced through a new federal agency, the Middle Income Student Assistance Act of 1978 vastly expanded the number of students who were eligible under the programs. Many critics contended that the public-support programs should not be so generous in aid to high-income individuals.

There is a serious societal issue, the question of how students can be protected against low-income, and/or not be coerced into high-income jobs solely due to mandated fixed-payment loan commitments. One can seek to limit total debt, to provide low-interest rates, and to have a long payment period that increases total interest charges but means low annual payments. Ultimately, either other students or the society at large, to use two extremes, are going to have to subsidize needy students, for the money is not free. Alumni and other friends of the students may provide some funds, but the economics of the situation force some redistributional elements to any sort of income-contingent, loan-financing plan.

Notes

1. See Gregory A. Jackson and George B. Weathersby "Individual Demand for Higher Education," *Journal of Higher Education,* November/December, 1975, pp. 623–652; S. Hoenack, "Private Demand for Higher Education in California," mimeographed from the Office of Analytical Studies, University of California, 1967, or S. Hoenack, W. Weiler, and C. Orvis, "Cost-related Tuition Policies and University Enrollments," mimeographed from the Management Information Division, University of Minnesota, 1973. The latter two studies are reviewed in the Jackson and Weathersby paper. A study that found relatively inelastic demand for higher education is reported in Moheb Ghali, Walter Miklius, and Richard Wada, "The Demand for Higher Education Facing an Individual Institution," *Higher Education,* November, 1977, pp. 477–487. Since the institution studied is the University of Hawaii, the conclusion of inelastic demand may not apply to other public universities that face different competitive environments. Many students will not see the opportunity to attend a major public university in another state as economically feasible, given the transportation and logistics problems.

2. Consider the following data for private four-year universities:

	1967–74F	*1974–78F*	*1978F*
Tuition increase	7.5%	8.7%	10.4%
Total increase; tuition room and board	6.1	7.7	8.1
Consumer price index increase	5.4	7.3	7.4
Disposable per-capita personal income (U.S., calender year, current dollars): Rate of change	7.8	9.3	10.5

Data based on June 30 fiscal years and fixed 1967 enrollment weights. June 1978 CPI is based on all urban consumers. The figures for 1967–1974 and 1974–1978 are compounded annual rates of increase. Table derived from data presented in U.S. Office of Education, *Higher Education Prices and Price Indexes,* 1979, and U.S. Department of Commerce, *Survey of Current Business,* various issues.

See also Mary A. Golloday, ed., *The Condition of Education,* National Center for Education Statistics, Washington, D.C., 1976, p. 230, and the *Economic Report of the President,* 1979, statistical tables.

3. Dwight Crane has conceived these general categories, and I thank him for his insights.

4. Economists have long been involved in analyzing the returns both to the individual and to society from an individual who elects to pursue a college education. For an analysis of the human-capital literature, the arguments concerning public and private goods, the evidence on how lower income families tend to finance higher (public) education for middle-income families because of the system of taxation involved in college financing, the evidence regarding substitutability resulting from the tuition gap between public and private schools, and the difficulty of productivity increases in the service sector of the economy, see chap. 13 in M.D. Orwig, ed., *Financing Higher Education: Alternatives for the Federal Government,* The American College Testing Program, Iowa City, Iowa, 1971. A good survey of the economic aspects of higher education, the results of various empirical studies of the private returns to investment in higher education, and the social issues involved in education may be found in Gordon K. Douglass, "Economic Returns on Investments in Higher Education," chap. 12 in Howard R. Bowen, *Investment in Learning,* Jossey-Bass, San Francisco, 1977, pp. 359–387. Also see William G. Bowen, *Economic Aspects of Education* (Princeton, N.J.: Princeton University, 1964), pp. 37–38 and 53–56. He calls for a fee system for public students in which they pay half the costs of their education. For a discussion of the quality issues within the context of economics, see pp. 70–83.

The same call for 50-percent funding of costs by students for both public and private instructions was made in 1973 by the Committee for Economic Development in its publication, *The Management and Financing of Colleges* (New York: CED, 1973). As befits its general orientation toward the values of the corporate executive, the CED also stressed that those with managerial responsibility should have decision-making authority: "Those who are held accountable must have the power of action." However, the committee did stress that faculties should perform a major role in the governance of colleges and universities and should have a predominant voice in admission and retention standards, introduction of programs and courses, graduation requirements, and recruitment of faculty and students. The committee also called for a 50-percent tenure ratio as a guideline.

5. If the participant was married, then the greater of one half the joint income or the participant's own income was the base for computing repayments due Yale. When a group termination occurred, any participant with unpaid obligations from back years still owed them. Furthermore, all participants had to repay their debt plus simple interest regardless of the class's performance. Upon death, unpaid balances owed to Yale were paid by the insurance program, and the participant's estate had no obligation to the system. It was estimated that the average class could "pay out" in 25 years, with 35 years the maximum time allowed for a class or an individual.

6 Endowment Management

Many books have been written on the field of endowment management for nonprofit institutions. One chapter cannot completely cover the relevant issues in this field; however, this chapter and the next one will review several topics that are central to the economic analysis of endowment management. Whether the endowment is a multimillion-dollar fund that provides a large portion of a college's operating and capital budget or a fund of a few thousand dollars to purchase books in a memorial library, similar issues exist:

> How should the funds be invested? How diversified should the portfolio be? What types of securities should be considered?
>
> How should the manager of the endowment be appraised? What is the manager's responsibility?
>
> How should the money be spent? Should the manager ever spend the principal? Should the value of the endowment be averaged over several years when determining the amount to spend?

We have discussed some of the instruments of investment in chapter 2 and will review those findings again here. In addition, since the stimulus to a reappraisal of many college-endowment policies was the Ford Foundation report in the late 1960s, it is useful to study those comments with the perspective of 15 years. Finance and economic theory have offered new ways of appraising a portfolio in recent years, and blending those insights with historical data on the risk and return of various portfolio strategies brings new light to the subject of endowment management. So we will outline the implications of the Ford study and modern capital-market theory for considering the risk of portfolios. After reviewing some of the conflicting goals of college- and university-endowment policy, we introduce an actual case of endowment-management appraisal by a major private school, Georgetown University. Finally, discussing the Georgetown system, we introduce the topic of spending rules: How much should the school spend, should the amount be averaged over several years, and should a "smoothing" pool of idle cash be set aside to ease transitions from one endowment valuation date to the next? These three questions will be examined in more detail in the next chapter.

Managing Educational Endowments: The Report to the
Ford Foundation

From a committee formed in 1967 to evaluate college-endowment management, this report emerged to criticize sharply the historical policies of educational institutions with regard to managing their endowments.[1] Essentially, the report offered rebukes for past management and urged college administrators to move in the direction of the (then) modern mutual-fund managers, who seemingly were achieving superior returns from their aggressive portfolio management. With hindsight, the decline in the stock market and the Ford Foundation's own endowment could not have come at a worse time for the sake of anyone listening to the report. Much of the thrust of the report was an encouragement of more aggressive risk taking by educational-fund managers. The rapid and severe decline in the value of some of the riskier investments (for example, growth stocks) and of the Ford endowment caused most trustees to regard the whole report with circumspection. However, many of the Ford findings are still relevant, although one may take strong exception to some of the policy prescriptions, as noted below.

One could summarize the criticisms and policy recommendations as follows:

1. Past performance had been mediocre. College endowments had performed poorly in comparison with the market and other endowments.

2. In large part, this poor performance resulted from the lack of *any* objective except preservation of capital. Arguing that the crash of 1929 was probably no longer relevant, the Ford report chastised university administrators for ignoring their opportunity costs: How many years of conservative management resulted in a loss of income that equaled half the endowment? Recall that the previous 25 years generally had been years of rising stock markets: Bond portfolios were bound to have poor returns in this period relative to the alternative of investing in almost *any* stock portfolio.

3. The responsibility for appraising the manager and for establishing general policy was diffused over too many people. Essentially, one small group of trustees or administrators should be responsible for appraising the portfolio manager. Too many supervisors had resulted in an overly conservative policy and a subsequent lack of action.

4. One or more portfolio managers should be given a long-term commitment of funds. The money should be managed for long-term total income (yield plus appreciation). As an example, the Ford report suggested dividing the fund into several parcels, with each fund manager given responsibility for five-year horizon planning for a separate pool of money. Then at some point the managers would be appraised.

5. Managers should invest in fewer stocks and bonds, concentrating their investments in "good" stocks rather than simply diversifying so broadly as to match the market. There was somehow a vision that a large enough endowment mandated the hiring of a superior investment advisor who would consistently outpace the market. (This implicit assumption is the one most challenged by most of the theoretical and empirical work in investment finance in recent years).

6. Managers should be given several years' trial, and the fluctuations of the market in those intervals should be considered in the long-run appraisal of the managers.

7. In the meantime, the school should remove for spending 5 percent per year from the annual ending value of the endowment. If growth stocks in which the fund invested yield less than this amount, some capital (appreciation) would be sold to make up the difference. If in 1 year the income from securities exceeded this 5-percent figure, the balance would be added to capital.

As an example, if a $100 stock position rose to $108 by the end of the year and paid $2 in dividends during the year, the 5-percent spending rule says $5 (0.05 times $100) should be removed from the portfolio for spending that year. The $2 dividend means $3 is drawn from the security's ending value. Hence 2.8 percent of the *ending* portfolio ($3 divided by $108) would be sold and added to the dividend to provide the $5. Although a single stock is often "lumpy" (one does not typically sell 2.8 percent of a share), this process is easily handled with a large portfolio of, for instance, $100,000, especially when there are additions during the year. One donor's gift of $5,000 may be invested in part. (The *unit system,* discussed shortly, still credits that donor's designated fund or department with the full $5,000 worth of units.)

The report avoided discussion of many investment vehicles: race tracks, encyclopedias, commercial or farm real estate, and the like. In part, these are specialized investments requiring particular managerial skills. Few universities are involved in such ventures. When given a business or some such nonstandard investment, the usual inclination of a university is to sell to some buyer, using the proceeds to add to a securities portfolio. The rest of this chapter will follow on this assumption, which is recommended as good general policy.

Comments on this Ford Foundation report will be presented in the remainder of this chapter and in the next one. However, several points are worth noting here. First, the report emphasized the importance of a *unit system* of investment appraisal. An example of this approach is part of the Georgetown case, but a word of explanation is appropriate here. When different people add the same amount of money to a portfolio at different points in time, it is very difficult to determine who should get what share of the future income and profits from a pooled fund unless there is a unit system. Thus if Mr. *A* (a donor, or a department) contributes $100 to the university's endowment pool in January and Ms. *B* contributes $100 in July when Mr. *A*'s $100 gift has declined to $80 because of market movements, how should they share in future income? Under the unit system, any time a contribution is made, the value of a unit is calculated, and so many new units are added. Thus if a unit were arbitrarily set at $10, Mr. *A* bought 10 units. In July, each unit is worth only $8. After Ms. *B*'s purchase of ($100 divided by $8) 12.5 units, there are now 22.5 units outstanding, each worth $8. Thus in the future, if no additions or subtractions are made, Mr. *A*'s money will generate 10 divided by 22.5 of the income and Ms. *B*'s money 12.5 divided by 22.5.

Second, the recommendation to sell a portion of the endowment to meet the spending-rule requirement reflects the nature of the U.S. federal tax code, which induces corporations to retain earnings in the business instead of distributing them as dividends. In part, this outcome occurs because a growing business will need equity capital. If a firm needs $100 but pays instead $100 in extra dividends, the owner pays income tax and then reinvests the after-tax money in the firm. Since the firm still needs $100, it must either ask for more money from the investors as a group than it paid them, or it must seek other investors. If other investors buy the additional stock that is issued, then the old investors have reduced their proportionate interest in the firm and in its future dividends. Furthermore, if the firm grows and prospers, then the individual investor can sell his common stock in the firm over time in small amounts or all at once, receiving a long-term capital gain instead of ordinary dividend income. A long-term capital gain is taxed usually at a reduced rate, often 40 percent of the tax rate applied to dividend income. Thus even a nontaxpaying institution such as a college should recognize that the incentive for many investors is either not to receive dividends at all, or to receive them in the form of capital appreciation in the stock, a few shares of which are sold annually in lieu of the dividends foregone. Given this environment, any institution that restricts itself to dividends and interest alone as sources of income may be unfairly limiting its income. It is not that the stock market must rise but only that the nature of the tax laws favor reinvestment of earnings, with higher dividends and stock prices in the future.

Third, the problems of turnover (buying and selling securities for the portfolio) and diversification are far more complex than the report implies. This issue is one that we will discuss later. It is important to note that one significant portfolio the report cited for good management would flunk a modern appraisal in terms of good management: the University of Rochester. By concentrating the endowment in the stock of several local firms, one of which became outstandingly successful (Xerox), the university portfolio did indicate "superior" returns. The problem with such a concentration is that returns can easily go the wrong way. Furthermore, the nature of the investment (founders and company directors on the Board of Trustees), coupled with the large size of the block, may make divestment difficult even if it is prudent. Subsequently, Xerox stock did decline sharply, with concomitant underperformance on the part of the Rochester portfolio.

Historical Security Returns

As chapter 2 discussed, any security falls into a general category. Averages describing the characteristics of those categories over a four-year period are provided in the study of Ibbotson and Sinquefield for the period 1926–1978. Table 6–1 summarizes the findings of this study.

Table 6–1
Basic and Component Series: Total Annual Returns, 1926–1978

Series	Geometric Mean (%)	Arithmetic Mean (%)	Standard Deviation (%)
Basic Series			
1. Common stocks	8.9	11.2	22.2
2. Long-term corporate bonds	4.0	4.1	5.6
3. Long-term government bonds	3.2	3.4	5.7
4. U.S. Treasury bills	2.5	2.5	2.2
5. Consumer price index (inflation)	2.5	2.6	4.8
Component Series			
6. Real interest rates (bills-inflation)	0.0	0.0	4.6
7. Equity risk premium (stocks-bills)	6.4	8.7	22.3
8. Default premiums (corporates-governments)	0.8	0.7	3.2
9. Maturity premiums (governments-bills)	0.7	0.9	6.0

Source: Roger G. Ibbotson and Rex A. Sinquefield, "Stocks, Bonds, Bills and Inflation: Update," *Financial Analysts Journal,* July–August, 1979, p. 43. For sources of data, see original article. Reprinted by permission.

Note: Casual inspection suggests that the behavior of real interest rates before and after the Treasury Accord was very different. The arithmetic mean and standard deviation for the subperiod 1926–1951 were −0.64 and 6.47 percent, respectively; for the subperiod 1952–1978 they were 0.41 and 1.46 percent.

Two statistical points are worth noting briefly. First, the standard deviation is a measure of risk. Although subject to some technical limitations, one can say that the mean return plus and minus one standard deviation gives one picture of the typical annual return for the 52 years. For example, for common stocks, one can say that about two thirds of the years had arithmetic returns that fell somewhere in the range of

$$11.2\% - 22.2\% = -11.0\% \quad \text{to} \quad 11.2\% + 22.2\% = 33.4\%$$

About 19 out of 20 annual returns fell in the interval of -2 standard deviations from the mean to $+2$ standard deviations. Second, the geometric mean is the average compounded return over the whole period. Whatever the ups and downs of the market, the starting amount invested, plus all subsequent dividends or interest, plus the selling amount resulted in some gain. The geometric return measures the *compounded* rate of return that would have allowed the initial amount to grow to the accumulated final amount. The geometric return would never be more than the arithmetic mean; the greater the difference, the greater the volatility of annual returns. Thus a person who invests $100, sees it fall to $50 in the first year, and rebound to $100 in the second year has a *geometric* mean return of 0. The *arithmetic* mean return is the average of -50 percent for the first year and $+100$ percent for the second year, or 25 percent. Both returns are useful under various circumstances.[2]

In reviewing table 6–1, notice the difference in annual returns. Riskier investments (common stocks) have a higher annual return over the period than less risky investments (Treasury bills, which have no default risk and very little interest rate risk because of the short time to maturity). The consumer price index (line 5) is a measure of the inflation over this period, and one could recompute the returns for the various securities in relation to inflation. Thus, roughly speaking, the real average arithmetic return of common stocks was 11.2 percent (line 1) minus 2.6 percent (line 5), or 8.6 percent. Table 6–1 indicates that the average return on U.S. Treasury bills has been zero when the return is adjusted for inflation (line 6). For holding equities rather than holding T-bills, investors received an average arithmetic return that was 8.7 percent greater (line 7). The *difference* between long-term government-bond yields and long-term corporate yields represents the aggregate premium paid for the default risk of the corporate issues (line 8). Furthermore, the *difference* between the long-term government-bond and Treasury-bill rates indicates the premium paid for avoiding interest rate risk, here called maturity premium (line 9). Since both are government issues, the default risk is presumably the same, zero. Hence the difference in yields implies that for this period, long-term government-bond holders received slightly less than 1 percent extra per annum, on a geometric basis, for accepting the risk of substantial interest rate shifts. Notice that based on these 52 years of data, the long-term geometric return of common stocks was 6.7 percent more than the return of long-term government bonds, and 5.9 percent more than long-term corporate bonds. For this higher return, however, the holder of the average common-stock portfolio had a standard deviation of return almost four times as large (22.2 percent divided by 5.7 percent or 5.6 percent) as the holder of a government- or corporate-bond portfolio.

Endowment Management: Goals of the College

A familiar adage in finance is that one can eat well or sleep well but not both. As the discussion of spending rules in chapter 7 will indicate, a major difficulty with applying this concept to college-endowment management is that the people who eat well today are not the same ones who could eat well in the future. This is in contrast to the individual investor case in which the individual may plan on investing aggressively today, spending foolishly or conservatively today, or on anything else, with the knowledge that much of the cost or benefit of such a program will accrue to him or her at some later date.

One may choose to invest a new infusion of money in a building or in professors' salaries; that is one decision on how to "eat well." Alternatively, the money may be saved for future spending (eating in the future), and the question is how to split the money between lower risk, fixed-income securities such as corporate bonds, and a common-stock portfolio. Once that division is selected, then there is still the question of how many stocks and what types of stocks are appropriate: some will have higher risks and (one hopes) higher average returns than others.

For purposes of this discussion, assume that the split between income and principal is *not* meaningful; this point was emphasized by the report to the Ford Foundation and has legal backing. Essentially, it argues that some portion of principal may be spent, especially price appreciation; to prohibit such spending means that current yield becomes the dominant consideration and forces the endowment manager to forego what may be many profitable investments. As the discussion of spending rules will indicate, however, there is a need to consider purchasing-power changes. In some cases, people can argue that price appreciation will offset the rising price level, so prohibiting spending appreciation is prudent. We prefer to discuss this issue explicitly later.

Alternative goals arise to guide endowment-management policy:

1. *Maximize the value of the portfolio, for instance, 20 years in the future.* This policy suggests maintaining low annual spending and investing

in higher risk portfolios that are likely to yield higher returns over time. However, the volatility of returns and spending in the short run may disrupt the school financially.

2. *Conserve principal at all costs.* This policy ultimately dictates investment solely in Treasury bills or long-term government bonds. The difficulty is that such a policy may not be truly conservative if one thinks of the purchasing power of the endowment. As the inflation-adjusted data in table 6–1 indicate, for the 52 years studied, common stocks have acted as an inflation hedge more effectively than government bonds. There is an argument that unanticipated inflation is bad for stocks, but, in the long run, for most institutions and individuals, common stocks represent practically the only direct inflation hedge available; 30-year government bonds bought 30 years ago with 3 percent coupons have *not* covered inflation in recent years; in fact, they have dropped in price as yields on newer government-bond issues have risen with increases in inflationary expectations on the part of the buyers.

3. *Maximize income, given prudent principal protection.* This policy would dictate some government bonds coupled with corporate bonds, with slightly more risk; the total portfolio produces a higher current yield than would be available just from government bonds. It eliminates low (current) yield bonds that have price-appreciation potential because they are currently selling at a discount.

4. *Maximize marketability.* This policy dictates no special new issues or thinly traded issues that the endowment manager might face difficulty liquidating, whether the issues are bonds or stocks.

5. *Maximize long-term total return.* This is the maxim suggested by the report to the Ford Foundation and would come closest to looking at the geometric return. In contrast to maximizing the value of the portfolio in year 20, this return would study annual income as well as total price appreciation over the period. It would force the managers to be concerned with income and price appreciation; the former is ignored in goal 1.

6. *Achieve a variety of objectives.* In fact, no single goal dominates individual investment management or college management. There are bound to be pluralistic goal structures, with the importance of certain goals ebbing and flowing as investment trustees and the markets ebb and flow. There may be one goal (for example, maximize long-run total return) subject to various constraints (for example, maintain a certain minimum in short-term securities and a set minimum probability of preserving principal).

Different school administrators might prefer different goals. Some schools may have particular spending patterns in mind or face a need to be venturesome in order to move the endowment to a level that can eventually do some good. Schools with large endowments may be more concerned with protecting what is there already. Goal selection is a critical issue and needs to be settled by trustees prior to giving specific instructions to the fund manager.

Risk and Return in Portfolio Performance

Investment advisors follow different strategies, and the only way to evaluate them fairly is to study their performance over several years. The most important single variable determining an advisor's performance is totally beyond his or her control: the course of the stock market. Market movements swamp investment selection in the short run, as has been repeatedly demonstrated by the various studies of mutual-fund managers compiled by Arthur Lipper and by the annual August 15 *Forbes* magazine tabulations.

What is important is not that some funds are on top in one year and other funds in other years but that the typical fund performance swings violently. Thus the top funds in 1968, the last really big bull market for a number of years, were typically the bottom in subsequent years. Some changed policies, becoming more conservative; often such a change came just as the market seemed to rebound a bit. As an example, Mates Investment Fund had the number 1 performance of 381 funds surveyed by Arthur Lipper Corporation in 1968, with a net asset value of $15.51 per share. For each of the next 5 years, it was never higher than the bottom 20 percent of all funds, and in some years was in the bottom 1 percent. By 1973 its net-asset value had fallen to $1.61. Although more spectacular than most of the other funds, the example is not atypical.[3]

At the time of the report to the Ford Foundation, funds were often gauged only by their annual returns. What has evolved from much of capital-market theory in the last decade is the idea that funds must be appraised on both risk and return. Risk is usefully measured in terms of standard deviation of return. As shown in figure 6–1, investors may invest in lower risk portfolios or in higher risk portfolios, with a declining extra return as the risk increases. For various reasons, the portfolio risk will not be simply the sum of the risks of the individual's securities but will typically be *less;* some of the risks of individual stocks are self-canceling, or at least partially offsetting. Thus a portfolio manager who produces higher-than-market returns in given years may not be selecting superior stocks but may simply be selecting a very risky portfolio, one toward the right in the figure. Even worse, the manager may be selecting a portfolio that has a higher risk and return than the *market* (labeled *M* in the figure) but which is suboptimal. If this is portfolio *A,* notice that portfolio *B* would have a higher expected return and less risk than portfolio *A.* In fact, any portfolio in the area shaded in the figure is dominant to *A;* all portfolios in this area have a

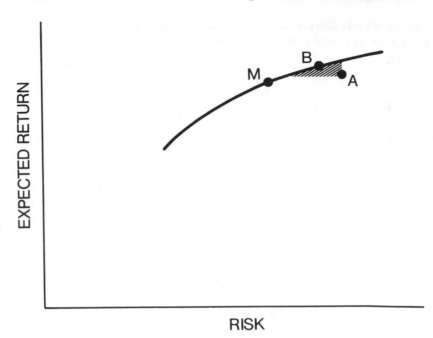

Figure 6-1. Portfolio Risk and Return

higher expected return for no more risk and/or a lower expected risk for at least the same expected return.

Investment specialists often refer to the curve in figure 6-1 as the *efficient frontier* of security portfolios; this is the collection of portfolios that offers the highest expected return for any given level of risk. Portfolios above the curve are desirable—but they do not exist by the definition of the curve!

In recent years finance theorists have pointed out that this analysis is incomplete. At any time investors can place some money in fixed-income securities (lend money at fixed rates) or they can borrow money to invest even more dollars in their portfolios (leveraging or margining their portfolio, as discussed in chapter 2). Since there are nonrisk investments, or at least very-low-risk ones such as short-term government bonds and Treasury bills, then the risk and return from a mixed portfolio falls along a line drawn from the return of this no-risk investment and the tangency of that line with the efficient frontier. Under a number of assumptions, that tangency will occur at the market portfolio, *M* in figure 6-1. However, even if that assumption is not valid, the line will intersect *M* at some point, for any investor can buy the market portfolio. The portfolio may be mixed with loaned funds in any proportion, with the resulting expected risk and return.

Now the task of the portfolio manager becomes more difficult, for given the new frontier open to the investor of being anywhere on that line, the appraisal of the investment manager becomes contingent on the fund's performance *not* in relation to the stock market as a whole (which can be exceeded by the manager's taking very high risks) and not by doing as well (or better) than the efficient frontier of portfolios but by performing as well or better than the possible range of portfolios offered by that line.

How then does the manager perform "well"? One option is to concentrate in stocks that offer subsequent superior performance in relation to their risk, that is, somehow to find securities that are not captured in that efficient frontier. Yet by definition, over the long run, the efficient frontier includes all these portfolios. The other option is timing the market swings: Invest heavily just before the market rises and move to fixed-income securities prior to a market decline. Both of these choices are difficult ones! This does not mean that investment managers are worthless, contrary to some of their critics who have seized on much of the research behind this brief exposition of capital-market analysis. Rather, it only means that they typically cannot select stocks with "superior" returns, defined as returns above the market adjusted for the risk involved. Nor can they typically time market movements. What they can do is efficiently diversify a portfolio and confirm that the risk profile of the portfolio is appropriate for the investor. There also may be some small, unknown securities that these managers can discover prior to their entering into broad market knowledge and hence being priced in line with the efficient portfolio theory outlined. Once that "discovery" is made, however, there is no excess return from high-risk stocks. And given the wide number of analysts and the information available, efficient market theory suggests that there is rather quick and thorough discounting of information.[4]

The Common Fund also provides a mutual fund for the investment of a college's money in a broadly based common-stock account. Colleges may deposit money and withdraw money in varied amounts. Withdrawal may be a set dollar amount per period or a moving average of the fund value over different dates. By using the unit system of accounting mentioned before, purchases and sales by colleges do not affect the ultimate value of the investment of other colleges. The fund is owned by the various colleges that participate in the investment, and it is managed by a professional staff of money managers, as noted in chapter 2.

Georgetown University: Background

The case presented here outlines the sophisticated portfolio-appraisal system used by this university. This appraisal service is available from various brokers and investment advisors, although the specific vendor offering the analysis provided in this case is well known. From this case we can discuss the implications of the figures for appraising the portfolio manager: Did the manager time moves into the market and out of it in a superior fashion? Did the return of the portfolio exceed a risk-adjusted market return? For these purposes, beta (β) is a measure of portfolio riskiness compared to a market riskiness of 1.00. Beta may be thought of as a measure of the excess return over what a security would have returned if the market return had been just as expected. Thus if a fund's beta were 1.4 and the market were expected to return 10 percent in a given year, then consider what would happen if the market earned 6 percent more. In such a case the fund would be expected to earn beta times 6 percent more than was anticipated had the market only returned 10 percent. Similarly, had the market returned, for instance, 4 percent less than expected, the fund would be expected to return beta times -4 percent less than forecast when the market returned 10 percent.

Georgetown University

Founded in 1789, Georgetown is the oldest Catholic institution of higher learning in the United States. Located in Washington, D.C., Georgetown began as a small liberal arts college, with one building, three professors, and five students. The college was raised to university rank by Congress in 1815. The graduate school was established in 1820, offering to the student who would "remain longer and study the higher branches of Mathematics and Philosophy..." the degree of Master of Arts "if success in his examinations entitle him to it."

The development of Georgetown's professional schools began in 1851 with the establishment of the Medical School. The Law Center was opened in 1870. The Georgetown Hospital was founded in 1898. The School of Dentistry was added in 1901. The School of Nursing was begun in 1903.

In 1919 at a time when America was becoming more aware of the responsibilities of world leadership, Georgetown founded the School of Foreign Service for the training of future American diplomats and overseas business executives. It was the first international school of its kind, and it remains the only American institution offering the Bachelor of Science degree in Foreign Service.

The School of Languages and Linguistics, founded in 1949, utilized one of the first language laboratories in the United States. The business-administration curriculum was introduced into the School of Foreign Service in 1936. In 1956 the School of Business Administration was established in its own right.

Georgetown University now comprises five undergraduate schools, a graduate school, a school for summer and continuing education, and three professional schools. The student enrollment, which has increased by 50 percent over the past 10 years, includes about 10,500 men and women from all 50 states and from approximately 90 foreign countries. Georgetown's faculty has grown during the past decade to over 2,000 teachers of many national origins and different religious faiths.

The changes in fund balances that indicate many of the sources and uses of funds for the university in the 1976 fiscal year are shown in table 6-2. Although the endowment was not a major source of income to the university, its management and composition had been a source of recent concern, commencing in 1970 with the appointment of a new treasurer. By June 1976, a common pooled fund of investments had a total value of nearly $34 million. the physical plant had a value of $136 million, and other funds net of funded debt and accounts payable of the university resulted in a total fund balance for the school of $141 million (see table 6-3). However, this current state of the university finances did not tell of the sharp changes in accounting practices and investment management since 1970.

Table 6-2
Changes in Fund Balances, Fiscal 1976
(*Thousands*)

Additions from:		
Students for services	$40,700	
Patients for services	39,900	
Federal grants and contracts	23,700	
Private gifts, grants, and contracts	11,300	
Investment income	2,000	
Miscellaneous	1,200	
Total		$118,800
Deductions		
Educational and general	67,800	
Auxiliary enterprises	7,000	
Hospital	35,300	
Loan cancellations	700	
Realized investment losses	800	
Total		111,600
Increase in fund balances		7,200
Fund balance, June 30, 1976		$141,100

Table 6–3
Asset and Liabilities Composition, June 30, 1976
(*Thousands*)

Pooled fund

Cash	$ 29	
Commercial paper	775	
Receivables	537	
Government bonds	203	
Corporate bonds	6,639	
Convertibles	170	
Common stock	19,539	
Mortgage notes, other	5,985	
Real estate	2,104	
Liabilities	(2,297)	
		$ 33,685

Other Assets

Plant	135,587
Other (current fund and separate fund)	36,401

Liabilities

Accounts payable, long-term debt	(69,273)
Balance	$141,086

A New Treasurer

George Houston, a Georgetown graduate and professor of accounting who had worked in his own CPA firm, was appointed treasurer of the university in October 1970. With less than 48 hours' notice between his own appointment and the departure of his predecessor from the campus, Houston found himself confronted by limited records and an immediate task of evaluating the position of the university's endowment. At that time most of the school's securities were kept in a custodial account with the Chase Manhattan Bank in New York. Some securities were retained physically at the campus. The cash management of the current fund balances was handled primarily by maintaining a minimum balance of $500,000, based on Georgetown's records, in a local Washington, D.C., bank. A minimum of complaints from the bank indicated that this arrangement was satisfactory. Most purchases and sales of securities were handled through Chase, although some were arranged through local brokers. In mid-1970 the pooled-fund cost and market values were $21,286,000 and $16,231,000, respectively. The pooled-fund portfolio had 239 different issues.

Houston responded to the establishment of an investment committee of the board of trustees that would be responsible for formulating general investment goals but not handling day-to-day portfolio management. Once this committee was formed, it moved to select a portfolio-management firm that would manage the university's securities. After some negotiations, Chase was asked to assume this task in January 1971. Following four months in which the bank put the portfolio in order, recognizing over $2 million of previously unrealized losses and reducing the number of security issues to 95, Chase announced that it would manage the portfolio in accordance with the goals of the investment committee, which had been stated in a resolution passed unanimously in November 1970:

> Resolved that the following recommendations of the Subcommittee on Investments of the Committee on Finance of the Board of Directors be, and they hereby are, adopted as policy for Georgetown University:
>
> 1.   That the Chase contract be modified to provide for actual management on a discretionary basis.
> 2.   That the total portfolio be consolidated at the Chase Bank.
> 3.   That reporting procedures be improved to provide reporting not less frequently than monthly.
> 4.   That appropriate instructions be issued to reduce Georgetown's portfolio to a manageable size as quickly as possible, recognizing that some losses may result particularly among those securities which are not now productive of income.
> 5.   That the basic investment policy adopted in the fall of 1967 be modified to provide that income be the priority objective of this portfolio. The portfolio should be arranged as follows: 50% high quality common stocks with the twin objectives of income and growth; 25% high quality bonds; 25% convertible bonds.
> 6.   That transactions be reported to the University Treasurer as they are made.
> 7.   That all income be sent to the Treasurer monthly.
> 8.   That, in the case of directed business, Chase be given a small list of selected brokers.
> 9.   That the Subcommittee review, at least every six months, the investment policies and practices of the University.

The Unit System

Houston also established the portfolio arbitrarily, as of June 30, 1973, as being composed of 268,355 units each worth $100. For comparison, the Standard and Poor's index of 500 (S&P 500) stocks was also set at 100. Henceforth, the bank and Houston prepared quarterly reports to the investment committee and to the board indicating the course of the pooled fund under Chase management and the S&P 500 (see table 6–4). In this way, two

Table 6-4
Pooled-fund Valuations, 1970-1976 (Fiscal Years Ending June 30)

	1970	1971	1972	1973	1974	1975	1976
Value (millions)	$16,231	$20,814	$26,039	$26,836	$25,655	$29,099	$33,685
Unit value	–	–	–	$ 100	87.04	93.70	99.40
S&P 500				100	82.49	91.31	100.02

goals were met. First, there was an external standard against which the Georgetown pooled fund and its manager, Chase Manhattan Bank, could be measured. This standard was the unmanaged S&P 500 portfolio. Second, the unit system permitted new additions to be made to the portfolio throughout the year without introducing bias in the performance for that quarter or year. For example, if a large gift were credited at the first of the year and the market declined sharply in that period, then actual receipt of the grant at a time other than the first of the year would make the fund appear to have performed better than it actually had. The unit system meant that the valuation of the portfolio was taken as of the date the new funds were credited to the pooled fund. The number of units was determined by the value of the gift divided by the current unit value. From that valuation, so many units (or shares) were added. Deductions from the fund were handled in a similar manner. In this way the pooled fund would operate much as a mutual fund for individual investors operated.

A.G. Becker Evaluations

In addition to viewing how the pooled fund compared with an unmanaged portfolio, Houston was interested in noting how the pooled fund and its managers performed vis-à-vis various other managed funds. After interviewing representatives from several services, he selected A.G. Becker, a firm that did not manage funds but that only offered its performance-evaluation service. The firm evaluated the data quarterly for a large population of funds with similar goals and then indicated where the Georgetown pooled fund stood in relation to the other funds. This evaluation was presented in tabular and graphic form (see table 6-5) for several categories of investment performance.

Houston looked back with some satisfaction on the performance of the pooled fund. Based on Becker ratings, it had consistently been in the top half of all funds reviewed in recent years and had done quite well in relation to the S&P 500. On the other hand, he was concerned about the advisability

Table 6-5
Categories of Investment Performance (All Funds $10 million to
$50 Million Only)

Total fund: Total rates of return	Figure 6-2
Total fund: Percent commitment to equities	Figure 6-3
Equities: Dividend rates of return	Figure 6-4
Equities: Total rates of return	Figure 6-5
Equities: Market sensitivities (beta)	Figure 6-6
Equities: Portfolio market sensitivity	Figure 6-7
Equities: Purchases and sales turnover	Figure 6-8

Source: Excerpted from a larger group of tables and figures available to Georgetown University administrators as part of A.G. Becker's fund evaluation.

of comparing the pooled fund both with the S&P index and with the other funds in the Becker sample. He had been asked by various people about the relevance of this comparison. Clearly, some measure ought to be used, but whether this measure was the correct one was obviously open to question.

Georgetown University: Analysis

Background

In appraising the Georgetown portfolio management prior to the new management, it is useful to note that the endowment is about 25 percent of the total net assets of the university. The school has reduced the number of issues under management to about 95, and has segmented its portfolio by policy into 50 percent common stocks with growth and income qualities, 25 percent corporate bonds and government issues of high quality, and 25 percent convertible bonds. A unit system was established so that performance of the manager over time could be monitored and that the claims of various schools within the university to the pooled fund's income could be evaluated.

Comparative Evaluation

As summarized in table 6-5 of this case, the A.G. Becker tabulations compare the fund with the market and with all funds of comparable size ($10-50 million) having similar goals. There are tabulations along several dimensions for both the total fund and for the equity and marketable-debt portions individually many of which are not shown here. Within each figure are percentile rankings for this fund, the range and interquartile range of all the funds under study, and the average for all funds under study. (The average used in these exhibits is the median, which means half the funds did better than that figure and half did worse.)

Figure 6–2 suggests that the total fund return has had very good and very bad years relative to other funds over the last 10 years. By studying the left axis of the returns, we note that the June 30 fiscal years in which the Georgetown fund did relatively worse than comparable funds (1967, 1969, 1970, 1971, 1972, and 1974) were generally years of market declines, with the exceptions of 1967 and 1971. In 1971 the fund failed to earn the spectacularly high returns of the median fund (36.35 percent), but one notices that it was only marginally lower (31.24 percent). These outcomes may suggest that the fund is less risky than most funds in its class; it rises more than others in good (market) years and falls more in other years. The 1971 outcome suggests that perhaps the fund had become more conservative by 1971 after the bad market years in 1969 and 1970, moving more of the fund to fixed-income securities. If other funds were not quite so conservative in those years, then they would have profited more handsomely than Georgetown from the 1971 rise. Did this happen?

Figure 6–3 provides a clue to this question. The dotted line that declined at the end of 1970 shows that Georgetown did indeed reduce its proportion of equities from about 85 percent to about 70 percent, but that this 70-percent figure was still slightly more than other funds. Notice that there were further reductions in 1972, some additions in 1973, and a sharp reduction in 1974, which was largely offset by the middle of 1975. The market tended to decline in 1972–1974 and rise in 1975 and 1976; Georgetown had fewer funds than the average fund in common equities in the first period (1972–1974) and more in the later period (1975–1976), so one would expect the total fund to out-perform the market. By accident or design, the timing of the Georgetown management was fortuitous for these 5 years to some degree. (If by design, the obvious question is why the movements were not larger. In fact, figure 6–3 suggests that most of Georgetown's relative performance comes from the contrary movement of other funds that on balance reduced the proportions of common equities just as the market rose in 1975 and 1976! Georgetown's equity balance fluctuated in this 5-year period between 60 and 70 percent.)

A look at figure 6–4 shows that the fund has very high relative rankings on the dividend returns of its stock portfolio after 1970. This may suggest that the common stocks in which it invests are higher-yield/lower-return securities (such as utilities) as opposed to the growth or growth-and-income stocks held in some other comparable funds. Again the issue of the volatility of the underlying portfolio is what needs to be studied.

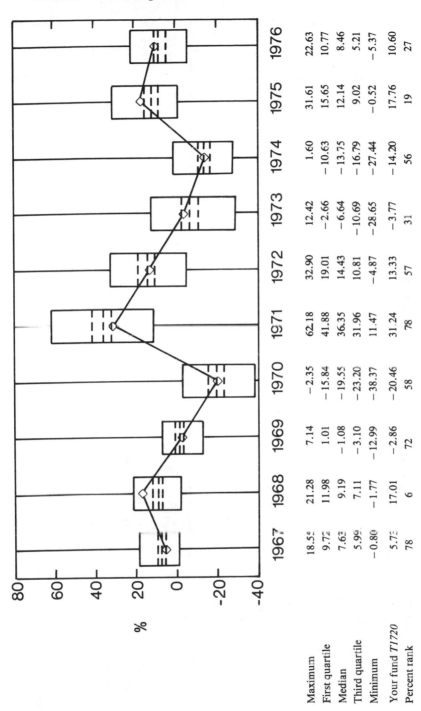

Figure 6–2. Total Fund: Total Rates of Return (Annual Periods Ending June 30)

	1967	1968	1969	1970	1971	1972	1973	1974	1975	1976
Maximum	18.54	21.28	7.14	−2.35	62.18	32.90	12.42	1.60	31.61	22.63
First quartile	9.72	11.98	1.01	−15.84	41.88	19.01	−2.66	−10.63	15.65	10.77
Median	7.63	9.19	−1.08	−19.55	36.35	14.43	−6.64	−13.75	12.14	8.46
Third quartile	5.99	7.11	−3.10	−23.20	31.96	10.81	−10.69	−16.79	9.02	5.21
Minimum	−0.80	−1.77	−12.99	−38.37	11.47	−4.87	−28.65	−27.44	−0.52	−5.37
Your fund *T1720*	5.73	17.01	−2.86	−20.46	31.24	13.33	−3.77	−14.20	17.76	10.60
Percent rank	78	6	72	58	78	57	31	56	19	27

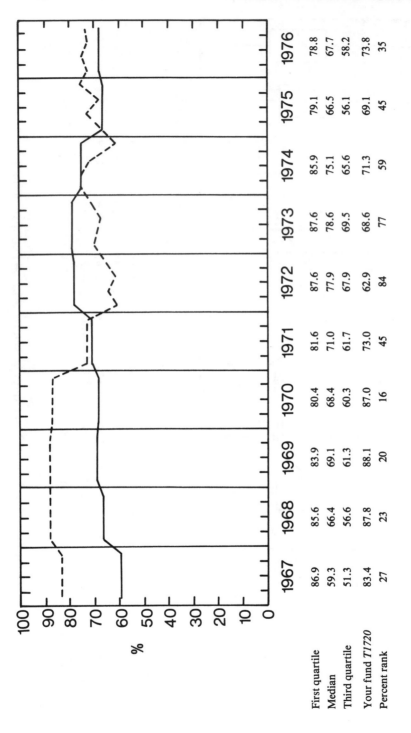

	1967	1968	1969	1970	1971	1972	1973	1974	1975	1976
First quartile	86.9	85.6	83.9	80.4	81.6	87.6	87.6	85.9	79.1	78.8
Median	59.3	66.4	69.1	68.4	71.0	77.9	78.6	75.1	66.5	67.7
Third quartile	51.3	56.6	61.3	60.3	61.7	67.9	69.5	65.6	56.1	58.2
Your fund *T1720*	83.4	87.8	88.1	87.0	73.0	62.9	68.6	71.3	69.1	73.8
Percent rank	27	23	20	16	45	84	77	59	45	35

Key: (———) median; (– – –) your fund.

Figure 6–3. Total Fund: Percent Commitment to Equities (Annual Periods Ending June 30)

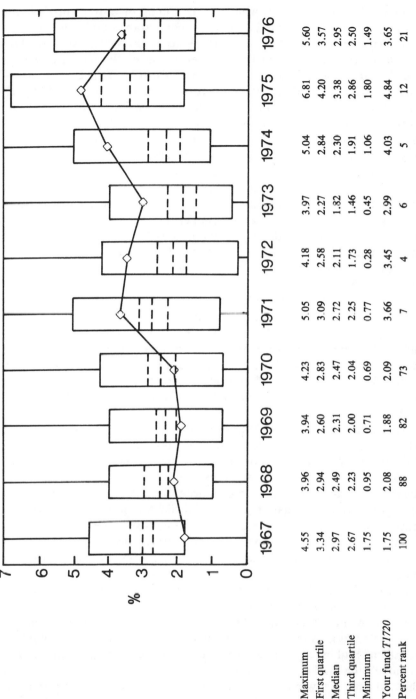

	1967	1968	1969	1970	1971	1972	1973	1974	1975	1976
Maximum	4.55	3.96	3.94	4.23	5.05	4.18	3.97	5.04	6.81	5.60
First quartile	3.34	2.94	2.60	2.83	3.09	2.58	2.27	2.84	4.20	3.57
Median	2.97	2.49	2.31	2.47	2.72	2.11	1.82	2.30	3.38	2.95
Third quartile	2.67	2.23	2.00	2.04	2.25	1.73	1.46	1.91	2.86	2.50
Minimum	1.75	0.95	0.71	0.69	0.77	0.28	0.45	1.06	1.80	1.49
Your fund *T1720*	1.75	2.08	1.88	2.09	3.66	3.45	2.99	4.03	4.84	3.65
Percent rank	100	88	82	73	7	4	6	5	12	21

Figure 6–4. Equities: Dividend Rates of Return (Annual Periods Ending June 30)

Figure 6-5 suggests that, whatever the timing of movements into and out of equities relative to the timing of the comparable funds, the *total* rate of return of the equity portion of the fund has generally been slightly above average in recent years. Notice that this return has not been confined to rising or falling markets. Low-risk stocks will out-perform the general market in market declines (1970) and underperform the market in rises (1971). The high-risk common stocks would provide the opposite performance. Thus this figure suggests that in the recent 5 years (1972–1976), the stocks in the portfolio have done well relative to the market without being dependent on being solely low-risk or high-risk common stocks.

At this point, the question is whether this result is statistically significant and whether the other funds are well managed. The tests of significance are beyond the scope of this book, but generally one looks for consistently superior performance over several periods; for 2 of the recent 5 years the Georgetown fund was slightly below the average, and for one year it was not strikingly high (thirty-fourth percentile). Thus there is evidence of superior portfolio management, but it is hardly conclusive. Moreover, there is the question of market sensitivity for the other funds as a whole.

Figure 6-6 provides the only data on market sensitivity, and unfortunately it is linked to 3-year intervals. The Georgetown equity fund for the recent 5 years has averaged slightly more sensitivity to the market than other funds (1.04). How this measure of beta can be used will be shown in the next chapter. For here, it is sufficient to note that the equity fund has been riskier than the market by a small margin but much less risky than the other funds (percentile ranks below the eightieth for both 1972–1975 and 1973–1976).

If this relatively lower riskiness was true for the individual years 1975 and 1976, then the performance of the equity portion of the fund relative to the equity portion of other funds in a rising market indicates superior stock selection: One would expect in these years of rising markets that the other funds with portfolios having greater market sensitivity would out-perform the Georgetown fund. Again the nature of the data in this figure does not permit a complete answer; the indications are consistent with that outcome.

Figure 6-7 also provides some year-end information on the volatility of the portfolio. The high R^2 indicates that the equity fund is sufficiently large in composition to track broadly the market; a portfolio of all the issues in the S&P 500 in exactly the same proportions as those issues are held in that index would track the market perfectly with an R^2 of 1.0.[6] Notice that most of the comparable funds are relatively well diversified, based on the R^2; undiversified funds would have a much lower coefficient of determination. The median ranking of Georgetown's beta indicates that based on the year-end values, the fund had moved in fiscal 1976 to a lower beta (1.05 versus 1.09) and a much lower beta relative to the other funds. The fact that this

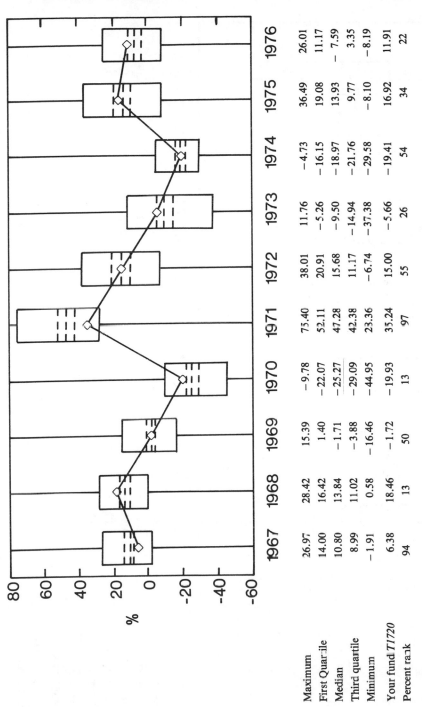

	1967	1968	1969	1970	1971	1972	1973	1974	1975	1976
Maximum	26.97	28.42	15.39	−9.78	75.40	38.01	11.76	−4.73	36.49	26.01
First Quartile	14.00	16.42	1.40	−22.07	52.11	20.91	−5.26	−16.15	19.08	11.17
Median	10.80	13.84	−1.71	−25.27	47.28	15.68	−9.50	−18.97	13.93	− 7.59
Third quartile	8.99	11.02	−3.88	−29.09	42.38	11.17	−14.94	−21.76	9.77	3.35
Minimum	−1.91	0.58	−16.46	−44.95	23.36	−6.74	−37.38	−29.58	−8.10	−8.19
Your fund T1720	6.38	18.46	−1.72	−19.93	35.24	15.00	−5.66	−19.41	16.92	11.91
Percent rank	94	13	50	13	97	55	26	54	34	22

Figure 6–5. Equities: Total Rates of Return (Annual Periods Ending June 30)

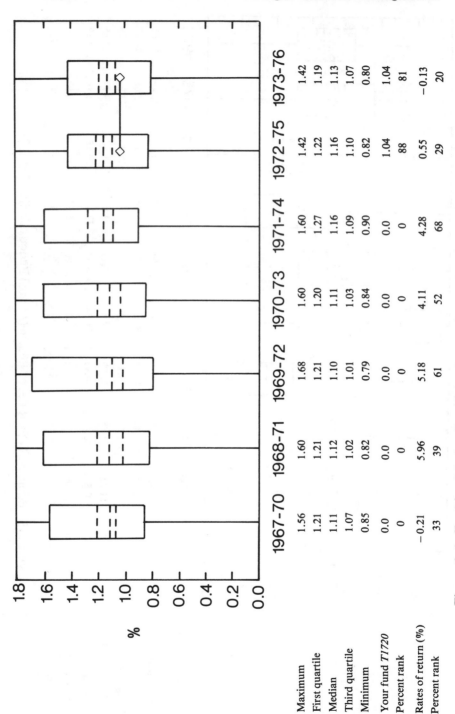

	1967-70	1968-71	1969-72	1970-73	1971-74	1972-75	1973-76
Maximum	1.56	1.60	1.68	1.60	1.60	1.42	1.42
First quartile	1.21	1.21	1.21	1.20	1.27	1.22	1.19
Median	1.11	1.12	1.10	1.11	1.16	1.16	1.13
Third quartile	1.07	1.02	1.01	1.03	1.09	1.10	1.07
Minimum	0.85	0.82	0.79	0.84	0.90	0.82	0.80
Your fund *T1720*	0.0	0.0	0.0	0.0	0.0	1.04	1.04
Percent rank	0	0	0	0	0	88	81
Rates of return (%)	−0.21	5.96	5.18	4.11	4.28	0.55	−0.13
Percent rank	33	39	61	52	68	29	20

Figure 6–6. Equities: Market Sensitivity (Beta) (Cumulative Periods Ending June 30)

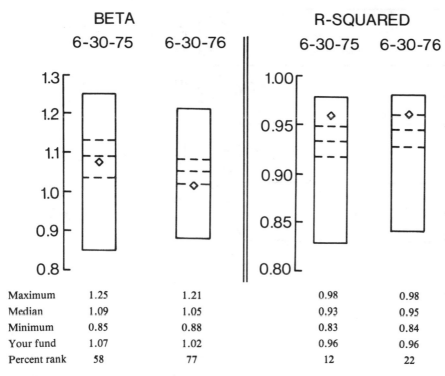

	BETA			R-SQUARED	
	6-30-75	6-30-76		6-30-75	6-30-76
Maximum	1.25	1.21		0.98	0.98
Median	1.09	1.05		0.93	0.95
Minimum	0.85	0.88		0.83	0.84
Your fund	1.07	1.02		0.96	0.96
Percent rank	58	77		12	22

Figure 6–7. Equities: Portfolio Market Sensitivity

movement took place and that the fund out-performed other funds in 1976 when the market declined are consistent; a lower risk portfolio will decline less in a bad market year than other funds. Notice, however, that for 1975 the fund specifically had a beta that was slightly below the average (fifty-eighth percentile) yet still managed to out-perform most of the other funds (thirty-fourth percentile in figure 6–4) in a rising market year. How could this happen? First, the Georgetown fund changed its percentile of equities rather sharply in this year based on figure 6–3. Second, the beta estimate is only for the end of the year. Again one may suspect that the higher volatility in some of the securities in the middle of the year may have helped the performance.

Figure 6–8 provides important information on the cost of movement; excessive turnover may result in high returns but will certainly result in large commissions. Even on large blocks of stocks, the round-trip commission (buying one block after selling another block of stock) will typically be 1 percent or more. For smaller trades, the commission loss can be 4 percent. Thus the new purchase must do at least this well just to break even. Other

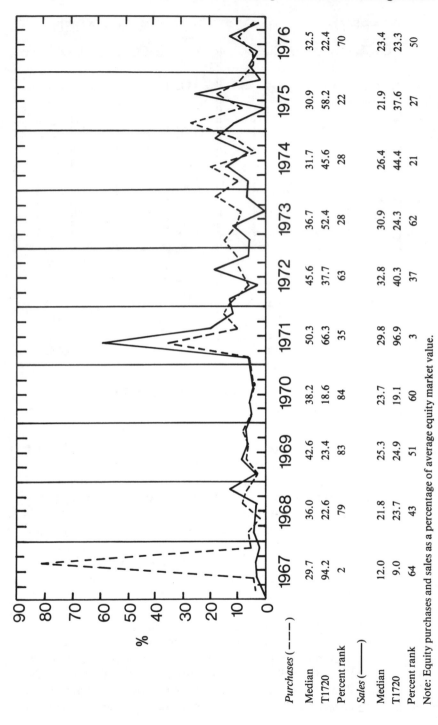

	1967	1968	1969	1970	1971	1972	1973	1974	1975	1976
Purchases (– – –)										
Median	29.7	36.0	42.6	38.2	50.3	45.6	36.7	31.7	30.9	32.5
T1720	94.2	22.6	23.4	18.6	66.3	37.7	52.4	45.6	58.2	22.4
Percent rank	2	79	83	84	35	63	28	28	22	70
Sales (———)										
Median	12.0	21.8	25.3	23.7	29.8	32.8	30.9	26.4	21.9	23.4
T1720	9.0	23.7	24.9	19.1	96.9	40.3	24.3	44.4	37.6	23.3
Percent rank	64	43	51	60	3	37	62	21	27	50

Note: Equity purchases and sales as a percentage of average equity market value.

Figure 6–8. Equities: Purchases and Sales Turnover (Annual Periods Ending June 30)

than the substantial realignment of the portfolio in 1971, total turnover has been around 20 percent, which is not unreasonable; some mutual funds typically have turnovers of from 50 percent to over 100 percent in a few years.

A.G. Becker rates various pension funds, and its most recent tabulation suggested there were few differences in the performances of funds managed by banks, insurance companies, or investment counselors. Using three-, five-, ten-, and fifteen-year periods ending in 1979, the results showed the typical (median) total fund failed to match consistently the inflation rate or the average return on Treasury bills. The median total fund over these periods also lagged the S&P's 500 stock index. For 1979 the median equity fund's return was 21.2 percent, better than the S&P 500's 13.7 percent and more than the Treasury bill return of 10.3 percent and the 13.3 percent inflation rate as measured by the C.P.I. Table 6-6 summarizes the results for these time periods for different funds and the inflation rate as measured by changes in the CPI.

Conclusion

Subsequent to this case, Georgetown continued to use the A.G. Becker evaluation service. The university continued with management by Chase Manhattan and added two additional fund managers through an A.G. Becker manager search service. In early 1980 the university was prepared to embark on a major capital-raising campaign.

Table 6-6
A.G. Becker Pension-fund Performance, 1965–1979

Median Fund	1965–1979 (%)	1970–1979 (%)	1975–1979 (%)	1977–1979 (%)	1979 (%)
Equities	4.3	3.6	13.9	6.4	21.2
Bonds	4.6	6.8	6.7	2.1	1.4
Cash equivalent	a	7.5	7.6	8.2	11.4
Total fund	4.1	4.3	10.6	4.8	13.1
S & P	5.6	5.9	14.8	5.4	18.7
Bond index[b] (b)	3.3	6.2	5.8	−0.9	−4.2
T-Bills	5.9	6.4	6.8	7.6	10.3
CPI	6.2	7.4	8.1	9.7	13.3

Source: A.G. Becker, Incorporated. Reprinted with permission.
[a] Not available.
[b] Salomon Brothers Bond Index

This extended example has served to indicate how some of the policy goals that an investment committee may suggest as prudent may be analyzed with data from an actual investment-fund performance. By studying movements of funds within a category and the movements of funds between categories, and by noting the outcome variability of the given fund relative to the stock market and relative to other investment pools, one has information useful in appraising a manager.

In the next chapter, we move to a discussion of the spending rules. Given the riskiness of an investment fund, how should the college spend from the endowment? As we shall see, the riskiness of the fund should affect the spending rules, and vice versa. We will continue to make use of our beta measure of market sensitivity as we conclude this analysis of endowment management.

Notes

1. See *Managing Educational Endowments: A Report to the Ford Foundation,* Ford Foundation, New York, 1969.

2. The arithmetic mean is found by summing the annual returns and dividing by the number of years. In this example, it is

$$\frac{-0.50 + 1.00}{2} = 0.25$$

or 25 percent. The geometric mean return is 1 minus the Nth root of the product of N years' return relatives, where the return relative is 1 plus the decimal return. In this example it is

$$1 - \sqrt[2]{[1 + (-0.50)] \times (1 + 1.00)}$$

$$= 1 - \sqrt[2]{(0.50)(2.00)} = 1 - \sqrt[2]{(1.00)}$$

$$= 1 - 1 = 0$$

If all income is reinvested in an account, the geometric mean provides the average annual compounded rate of return the investment has earned. It may be easily computed as 1 minus the Nth root of the *ratio* of the ending fund value to the opening value. In this example, it is

$$1 - \sqrt[2]{\frac{\$100}{\$100}}$$

$$= 1 - 1 = 0$$

3. The annual return calculations used to measure performance correctly include income from capital gains and any dividends paid, plus any change in the net asset value per share.

4. For more extensive reading on the literature behind these statements, several collections of articles exist. One such collection is James Lorie and Richard Brealey, ed. *Modern Developments in Investment Management,* 2d ed. (Hinsdale, Ill.: Dryden Press, 1978).

5. The coefficient of determination, R^2, is the square of the coefficient of correlation. It ranges from 0 to 1 and is a statistical measure of the proportion of variance in the Georgetown fund's return that is explained by the movement in the return of the S&P 500.

6. Kim studied the performance of the endowments of a number of small Midwestern colleges for 1962–1972. He found that, on the average, they did worse than the S&P 500 but also held lower risk portfolios. He found some evidence of average performance above the S&P 500 in the 1968–1972 period. However, there are problems with Kim's method of evaluating the risk of his various benchmark portfolios against which he measures the endowments' performances. See Tye Kim, "Investment Performance of College Endowment Funds," *Quarterly Review of Economics and Business,* Autumn 1976, pp. 73–83.

Recall the evidence presented in chapter 2 when options were discussed. These results suggested a covered option writing strategy has *not* been superior to the strategy discussed here of a blend of the market portfolio and borrowing or lending at a (relatively) risk-free rate. See R. Corwin Grube, et al., "Risk and Rewards in Covered Call Positions," *Journal of Portfolio Management,* Winter 1979, pp. 64–68.

7   College Spending Rules

Previous chapters have discussed the different returns from various types of securities and have indicated something about the nature of risk. When risk is defined in terms of the standard deviation of returns, one can see how the returns from a particular investment strategy over the past years have varied and how this variation ex post is related to the returns ex ante. There is also the question of how to spend a given return in an uncertain world. In a certain world, money not spent today is invested to provide more money for the future. In an uncertain world, money not spent today may or may not be available for spending in the future. Finally, it is one thing for an individual investor to elect to spend now or to accept some risk in order to have more money to spend in the future. It is something else to make a decision when the money to spend in the future will benefit someone else. "Future" is a question of time, of course; all of us know that we may leave more or less amounts of money to children, charities, or spouses. In a university environment, however, the future beneficiaries may be as near as five years away or as far away as 100 years. How does one look at these trade-offs?

This chapter will examine these points with the aid of both computer and economic analysis. We begin with the idea of diversification in a category of securities and then move to the idea of portfolio risk across securities. Our discussion ends with an analysis of smoothing rules and risk management for the college.

The Magic of Compounding Values

A point often missed in the analysis of spending is that one can spend smaller amounts in earlier years and enjoy far greater amounts from spending the same percentage of a growing fund value in later years. Assume that one is deciding whether to spend 3 or 5 percent of an endowment, and the assumption is that the endowment will return in dividends and price appreciation an average of 8½ percent per year. The amount that will be withdrawn in the Nth year is then the amount withdrawn in the first year compounded forward at the rate of reinvestment. The rate of reinvestment is simply what is left over after the typical year's return of 8½ percent has been partially spent.

As an example, assume an initial endowment value of $1,000, which would provide first-year spending of either $30 (3 percent) or $50 (5 percent). With the 3-percent rule, second-year spending would be 3 percent of the new portfolio value of $1,055. This figure occurs because $85 (8½ percent of $1,000) was earned and $30 was spent. The second year disbursement would then be 0.03 times $1,055, or $31.65. This amount is 5.5 percent greater than $30. Similarly, the value of the portfolio after spending $50 the first year would be $1,035. The second-year spending would be $51.75, which is 3.5 percent greater than $50.

We can see the relationship between the spending level today, the growth in the portfolio, and the spending level in the future. Stated simply, with the same overall return in the market, money saved today will result in higher spending tomorrow, and the link is algebraically very simple.

To continue the example, it is useful to study the market value of the portfolios under the 3-percent and 5-percent spending rules suggested. Under either rule, the amount spent in the Nth year is the Nth power of the term $(1 + R)$, where R is the reinvestment rate. In the case of 20, 40, 50 years, then the *spending* for the different spending rules given here would be:

	$N =$	*Annual Spending for Different Portfolio Choices*		
		20 years	*40 years*	*50 years*
3%:	$30 (1 + 0.055)^N$	$87	$255	$436
5%:	$50 (1 + 0.035)^N$	99	197	279

The *value* of the $1,000 portfolio in these future years under the assumed 8½-percent total return and different spending rules is also of interest:

	$N =$	*Value of Initial $1,000 Portfolio (Endowment)*		
		20 years	*40 years*	*50 years*
3%:	$1,000 (1 + 0.055)^N$	$2,900	$8,500	$14,542
5%:	$1,000 (1 + 0.035)^N$	1,980	3,960	5,580

Notice that by the twentieth year, the difference in spending between the 3-percent rule and the 5-percent rule has narrowed considerably. It is $12, which is about 15 percent of the amount spent on the 3-percent rule. Second, by the fortieth year, the spending under the 3-percent rule is greater than under the 5-percent rule by about 30 percent. Over time, this spread will widen. It is also instructive that the value of the endowment will escalate rapidly. In only 50 years the value of the portfolio under the more conservative 3-percent spending rule is 2½ times the size of the other portfolio, and 14½ times its own starting value.

There is no magic; it is simply the reinvestment of income and the nature of compounding. There is neither wisdom nor luck, merely algebra. In this context, the large endowments of many old schools are not so surprising, nor so impressive![1]

Common-stock Investment: The Road to Growth

The Returns

For most investors, the most obvious marketable investment for funds that will provide some growth over time is common stocks. There will be periods of loss; however, as the long-term data shown here and confirmed by other studies suggest, the return of common stocks is superior to many other investment areas, although the risk is also greater. One question is how much one would earn from investing in a broadly diversified common-stock portfolio.

The Ibbotson and Sinquefield data shown earlier in table 6-1 suggest that the geometric mean return from 1926-1978 was 8.9 percent, which was superior to the returns for other investment vehicles even after adjustment for inflation. Another way of looking at this issue is to study the value of a $100 portfolio that matched the S&P 500 stock index. The total return in any year from an investment in the S&P 500 would be the dividend yield plus or minus the percentage change in the year-end value of the index. As shown in table 7-1, if one withdrew 5 percent per year beginning in 1960, the final value of the portfolio would have climbed considerably. Had one stopped the calculation in 1973, the value would have been $123.42. However, ending the calculation 1 year later, would have provided a terminal fund value of only $88.76. From table 7-1 one can also compute how the value of the assumed portfolio would grow, and how the spending with a 5-percent withdrawal rule would grow. It is also interesting to compare the figures in table 7-1 with the compounded value of the portfolio in the absence of withdrawals. The values and returns of the portfolio for 1973 to 1979 would have been as in table 7-2.

The Risks

One way to reduce the volatility in the amount withdrawn in table 7-1 is to average the results over several years; the ending portfolio value for the last

X years are averaged together. The larger the X, the less the fluctuation in spending. Recent rises or falls in portfolio value take some time to influence fully the amount withdrawn for spending. This is a common *smoothing* rule that cushions the volatility of annual withdrawals.

One concern is whether the value of the endowment X years in the future will be at least some figure. One way of viewing this problem is to ask: "What is the risk that annual spending beginning in X years will be at least $100 per year, withdrawing the same percentage of endowment as we do now?"

In order for this base to hold, the value of the endowment must be some amount, perhaps $1,000. Yet moving toward that year, for each year that the fund value fails to increase at the assumed rate, there must be a higher reinvestment rate (and lower spending) in order for the horizon value to be met.

At the extreme, take a case in which the school wishes $1,000 in 10 years, and today has $500. If spending is 3 percent of the endowment with no smoothing, then the return will have to average 10.18 percent in order to spend 3 percent and reinvest a sufficient amount to bring the endowment to $1,000 in 10 years. Suppose the actual return the first year is 7 percent. In order for the compounding to be on target, ideally the same $70.18 must be saved; thus, spending should be nonexistent in that year. In fact $.18 should be recovered from past years or from future spending!

This example highlights the fundamental problem: Smoothing of spending for any year by failing to respond to immediate declines in the portfolio return that year either reduces the possibility of reaching the targeted horizon value or implies that the school's administrators think that the average return of the fund will rise in future years. The latter is implausible; each year's return is independent of the previous year's and of future years' returns. A loss in one year does not imply an automatic gain in another year or even in 5 years. All that the historic average return means is what it says: the average figure of the returns in the past.

The Joint Problem

One way of seeing the interrelationships while recognizing several different forms of risk is to view the portfolio in the context of a computer simulation. This simulation involves placing educated guesses about what the returns from the portfolio will be and what the randomness or risk of the portfolio might be. One can then study the effect of alternative smoothing rules on the probability of having various endowment values in the future. In this example, it is assumed that the school administration withdraws the money 1 year in advance; this is not an uncommon period for a budgeting

Table 7-1
Results of 5-Percent Withdrawal Plan with Funds Invested in S&P 500 Index

Year Ending	Total Return	Value before Withdrawal	Withdrawal (5%)	Value after Withdrawal
1959	–	–	–	$100.00
1960	0.3%	$100.30	$5.02	95.28
1961	26.6	120.62	6.03	114.59
1962	–8.8	104.51	5.23	99.28
1963	22.5	121.62	6.08	115.54
1964	16.3	134.37	6.72	127.65
1965	12.3	143.35	7.17	136.18
1966	–10.0	122.56	6.13	116.43
1967	23.7	144.02	7.20	136.82
1968	10.8	151.60	7.58	144.02
1969	–8.3	133.51	6.68	126.83
1970	3.5	131.27	6.56	124.71
1971	14.1	142.29	7.11	135.18
1972	18.7	170.32	8.02	152.30
1973	–14.7	129.92	6.50	123.42
1974	–24.3	93.42	4.67	88.76
1975	35.6	120.36	6.02	114.34
1976	22.9	140.52	7.03	133.49
1977	–6.6	124.68	5.37	119.31
1978	6.4	126.95	6.35	120.60
1979 [a]	17.8	142.08	7.10	134.97

[a]Preliminary

Table 7-2
Values and Returns of the Portfolio for 1973–1979

Ending Year	Value with No Withdrawal	Compounded Return from 1960 (Geometric Mean, %)
1973	$250.38	6.7
1974	189.54	4.7
1975	257.01	6.5
1976	315.87	7.0
1977	295.02	6.2
1978	313.90	6.2
1979	369.77	6.8

lead. Taking into account future inflation, the people who prepared this simulation assumed an average return of 13.3 percent in the stock market in nominal (as opposed to real) terms.[2] This average is higher than the past returns in the market, but it reflects the inflation in the economy that also should inflate the dollar returns. The average amount spent is 5 percent of the endowment value, but this average may be only in the most recent year or may include up to 10 years, depending on which row of table 7–3 one studies. By looking at the value of the endowment for an arbitrary 25-year future, one can determine the range of likely outcomes.

Several explanations are necessary regarding Ennis and Williamson's calculation. First, the adjusted spending fraction in column 2 reflects the fact that the average value of the portfolio will rise and that an average target of 5 percent of the expected market value when many years are averaged implies a greater-than-5-percent spending rule. This is due to the fact that the average value of the endowment will be much smaller than the expected value in the previous year. The purpose of the smoothing rule is not to reduce average spending but to reduce *fluctuations* in spending. Second, the budgeting lead of 1 year and the assumed figures for the average market return mean that the amount spent with even a 1 year "average" is greater than 5 percent. Third, Ennis and Williamson have arbitrarily assumed a spending limit of 10 percent; if the volatility of the market is such that the amount spent is more than 10 percent of the endowment at that time, the amount withdrawn will automatically be reduced to the 10-percent level.

Given these background comments, what conclusions could one draw from these examples? First, greater averaging (more years averaged together) reduces the fluctuations in year-to-year spending by more than 70 percent using these assumed data: Column 3 shows the average fluctuation dropping from 18 percent to 5 percent. Second, uncertainty about the expected value of the endowment rises by more than 25 percent, from .93 to 1.15. Perhaps this second point can be better understood by looking at the final five columns. The initial value is $100. Under 10-year smoothing and a 25-year horizon, there is one chance in four (25th percentile) that the ending value of the endowment will be only $277; with no smoothing, there is one chance in four that the endowment will be less than $364. On the other side (75th, 99th percentiles), there is a probability of an even greater ending value under the longer smoothing period than under a shorter smoothing period. Why? Simply stated, the smoothing rule means that an unusually good period for the stock market in this interval will not let spending rise as rapidly as it would under the shorter averaging rule. More money is invested and, hence, the ending value is higher. Notice that neither the lower ending value nor the higher ending value are certain with the longer averaging period. All these authors are noting that there is greater

Table 7-3
Summary of 25-Year Simulation Results
(Initial Endowment Value = $100)

Case		Average Year-to-Year Fluctuation in Spending	Uncertainty In the Future Value of the Endowment	No. of Times in 5,000 Limit Invoked	Growth in Spending at Median	Value of Endowment at the End of Year 25				
No. of Values Averaged	Adjusted Spending Fraction					1st Percentile	25th Percentile	Median	75th Percentile	99th Percentile
1	0.0570	0.1814	0.9331	0	8.3%	$75	$364	$743	$1,326	$5,581
2	0.0592	0.1236	0.9575	2	8.3	70	355	734	1,324	5,792
3	0.0616	0.0982	0.9825	14	8.3	64	345	733	1,326	5,965
4	0.0640	0.0831	1.0080	29	8.3	58	335	735	1,342	6,132
5	0.0664	0.0730	1.0335	45	8.3	52	324	738	1,352	6,294
10	0.0795	0.0525	1.1513	201	8.3	33	277	688	1,393	6,927

Source: Ennis, Richard M., and Williamson, J. Peter, *Spending Policy for Educational Endowments*, Common Fund, New York January 1976, p. 87. Reprinted by permission.

Note: Spending rule: moving average fund value 1 year apart. Investment portfolio: fully diversified common stock. Spending limit: 10%. Average spending level as a percent of endowment at the time of expenditure: 5%. Budgeting lead: 1 year.

dispersion in the ending values under a longer averaging rule. This dispersion means simply that one can have less confidence about the *minimum ending value* that will be available to the school in 25 years.

The authors suggest that a school make its own judgments about the likely return and volatility of the investment portfolio in the future years and simulate different spending rules and strategies. Then by looking at the values of various outcomes, the school administration can decide if it can live with these outcomes. There is also the chance to revise strategies; if a series of bad outcomes occurs, spending may have to be reduced more sharply than indicated. Ennis and Williamson suggest setting some small fraction for average spending, selecting the variation in spending that can be tolerated (which implies some averaging rule), and then running the simulation. If the ending endowment uncertainty cannot be tolerated, then the example should be resimulated with a shorter averaging period for the spending rule.

Spending Rules and Financial Strategy

Schools tend to strive for leadership in some area. That is useful for attracting student, faculty, and money. One way of reviewing funding in terms of a cost-generated model is to study the cost per student in different types of programs and schools. One set of expenditures per full-time equivalent student in 1975 is given in table 7-4. Even allowing for different types of programs and some extremely high-cost and extremely low-cost programs, one is struck by the wide range between the 25th and 75th percentile.

For any school, one can compute the same table and then ask: Is the cost differential reflected in quality? Even if comparable quality exists for a difference in cost, one must ask if it will continue to exist. Finally, is the quality difference perceived in the market place?

In the context of smoothing, spending rules and educational program funding, the key to the issue is really *flexibility*. Having fixed costs that cannot be adjusted when quality or demand shifts mandate a change in budget emphasis is distressing. It is disastrous when it prohibits budget restrictions suggested by a reduced endowment. In effect, today's fixed costs in particular areas will reduce funding for other areas today and also reduce the funds available for future students. It is in this vein that one sees the importance of keeping costs *variable* and *flexible* in so far as possible. Such flexibility (or mobility, or movement) permits less averaging in the smoothing rules designed to provide an acceptable level of budget variation. Less averaging in turn means that a bad future market experience can be offset more rapidly by reduced spending from the endowment. Such reduced spending in turn permits greater confidence that the pool of funds

Table 7-4
Educational Expenditures per Student (Full-time Equivalent), 1975 (est.)

	Low	First Quartile	Median	Third Quartile	High
Doctoral-granting institutions	$1,500	$2,550	$3,450	$5,700	$13,500
Comprehensive colleges I [a]	675	1,500	1,800	2,250	6,000
Comprehensive colleges II [b]	900	1,650	1,950	2,250	5,250
Selective liberal arts colleges	1,350	2,700	3,600	4,200	8,850
Other liberal arts colleges	525	1,800	2,250	2,775	5,850
Public two-year institutions	375	1,200	1,500	1,725	3,225
Private two-year institutions	825	1,425	1,950	2,475	3,750

Source: *Colleges and Money: A Faculty Guide to Academic Economics* (New York: Change Magazine, 1976), p. 35. Reprinted by permission. Information is from Carnegie Commission on Higher Education, *New Students and New Places,* McGraw-Hill, New York, 1971, pp. 70–80. The data are estimates and updated.

[a] Institutions with a liberal arts program, at least two professional or occupational programs, and at least 2,000 students.

[b] Private institutions with at least 1,500 students and public institutions with at least 1,000 students offering liberal arts and at least one professional or occupational program.

from which future expenses will be paid will be at least at some minimum level.

It is this concern for future income that induces a worry about budget flexibility today. And budget flexibility today is reflected in a concern for fixed and variable costs. Those issues are discussed in chapter 8, where we indicate the influence of tenure decisions and long-run program enrollments on the operating budget of a college.

Notes

1. Reducing spending is often one goal of trustees, whose emphasis on fiscal conservatism and reinvestment of "income" is often dominant. In addition, when the investment adviser is compensated by a fee based on the portfolio value, a large reinvestment of the annual income leads to a larger fund value (with larger management fees) in future years compared to a higher spending policy.

2. Based on historical data discussed earlier and summarized in table 6-1, Ibbotson and Sinquefield completed simulations of common-stock returns through the year 2000. They suggest mean common-stock nominal and real returns of 13.0 and 6.3 percent, respectively, implying an average inflation rate of slightly less than 7 percent from 1976 to 2000. Twenty-year

government- and corporate-bond nominal returns had an expected value of 8.0 percent and 8.2 percent, respectively. See Roger G. Ibbotson and Rex A. Sinquefield, ''Stocks, Bonds, Bills and Inflation: Simulations of the Future (1976–2000).'' *Journal of Business,* July, 1976, pp. 313–338.

8 Long-run Financial Planning

The previous chapters have presented certain concepts that colleges can apply to various economic and financial decisions they must make. This chapter surveys the general programs of a major state university, considering how concepts such as state-funding formulas and the granting of tenure to faculty members, as well as other features of college administration and governance, have an impact on the financial situation of the college.

Wichita State University

In May, 1976, Dr. Clark Ahlberg, president of Wichita State University, Dr. John B. Breazeale, vice-president for academic affairs of the university, and others of the administration and faculty were considering what policies should be developed regarding the changing conditions under which the university would operate in the future (see figure 8–1). As part of this evaluation, the financial consequences of various policies were certainly an issue. The university was part of a major state system and not directly dependent on endowment income, but there was a question about whether state legislators would continue to vote the budget increases to which the system administrators and faculties had been accustomed. Although the general economy of the Kansas area had been relatively stable during the recession of the early 1970s, inflation had caught the Kansas taxpayer as it had everyone. Possible declining enrollments stemming from such factors as the end of the military draft, lessened job opportunities for college graduates, the increased cost of college at both public and private institutions, and declining college-age population pools for the future decades meant that many universities could no longer assume that increasing numbers of students and increasing appropriations per student would be forthcoming. On the other hand, there was some evidence that many students from upper-middle-class families were being "priced out" of the market for private universities, whose tuition levels had increased more rapidly than the general cost of living. These private universities, usually unable to increase scholarship funds to offset fully the cost of tuition increases for families from middle- and upper-middle-income ranges, thought they might lose students to public universities. All these issues had been raised (but hardly resolved) in various university journals in recent years. It was with a view to these factors in

---

Colleges Healthy Despite Inflation

American colleges and universities have "a way to go before financial tautness" hurts them, a noted educator said Sunday.

Dr. Howard Swearer, president of Carleton College in Northfield, Minn., said it would be some time before inflation, which has risen more sharply in education than in the general economy, would force institutions of higher learning to cut expenses.

"We should try to plan ahead," Swearer said, "and make sure those cutbacks will not jeopardize any academic programs."

Swearer said the recent trend of high school graduates to consider alternatives to a college education would both help and hurt colleges.

"It means fewer students in college, but we weren't going to have as many students in 1980, anyway, because of demographics," he said.

"But, I don't think everyone should go to college. The only people who should attend college are those who think they will benefit by it."

Swearer, a former Wichitan who graduated from East High School, said the lessening of college graduation requirements—begun in the late '60s—is being reversed.

"What it made us do, though, is rethink our requirements," he said. "Many of them had been carried along simply by tradition."

However, Swearer said many of the requirements, particularly the traditional foreign language requirement, are necessary.

He said American colleges and universities should define their missions and what they want to be.

Source: *The Wichita Eagle,* March 15, 1976. Reprinted by permission.

Figure 8-1. Statement by College President

general and the possible action of the Kansas state legislature in particular that WSU administrators and faculty had to consider how vulnerable the university might be.

Background

Six institutions comprise the university system of the state of Kansas: Wichita State University (WSU), Kansas State University (KSU) and the University of Kansas (KU) (both 100 miles from Wichita in the northeastern part of the state), Kansas State College of Pittsburg (KSC Pittsburg) (80 miles from Wichita in the southeastern part of the state), Kansas State Teachers College of Emporia (KSTC Emporia) (located 70 miles from WSU), and Fort Hayes State College (FHSC Fort Hays) (located 130 miles from WSU). Enrollments in the fall of 1975 at these schools were as shown in table 8-1.

All these schools operate under the Kansas Board of Regents, and

Table 8–1
Fall 1975 Enrollments, Kansas State University System

	WSU	KSU	KU	KSC Pittsburg	KSTC Emporia	FHSC Fort Hays
Undergraduate	10,100	14,225	15,051	3,623	4,438	3,623
Graduate	5,614	3,676	6,687	2,065	2,073	2,065
Total	15,714	17,901	21,738	5,688	6,511	5,688

cross-school raiding or lobbying is minimal compared with many public university systems. The board of regents, the budget director (responsible to and appointed by the governor), and the state legislature are the three parties involved in the budgeting process. In addition, each campus president has the right to request extra funding for new programs at his or her campus. Typically, WSU and the others had requested $500,000 to $700,000 and received 50 to 70 percent of their requests. These projects were outside the normal budgeting procedures, and funding tended to be obtained face to face with the budget director or legislative committee chairperson.

State Appropriations

Funding from the state of Kansas was on the basis of equivalent full-time students (EFT). Increasing or decreasing enrollments were the key to this appropriation, and the budget allocation at WSU was 18 EFTs for each faculty, administrative, or library person funded. These positions were unclassified. One classified custodial and maintenance position was added for every three new unclassified positions. Additional budgeting for operating expenses per student currently were at the level of $258 per EFT. In recent years special salary increments for the faculty positions had been obtained through the efforts of Dr. Ahlberg and others to bring faculty salary scales into parity with 18 peer institutions, including urban universities, AAUP Class IIA institutions, and other regional neighbors.

As shown in table 8–2, the state appropriations were central to the university's budget, and one issue was how the state legislature would react to continuing budget requests if enrollments declined and the tenured faculty were reduced. Kansas tended to be in the lower half of the fifty states on expenditures per student, an argument for increased funding. On the other hand, on the basis of per-capita income, age profiles, working population, and student-attendance figures, it was in the top half of the states in outlays per dollar of state income, both total and per capita.

Table 8–2
**Percent Comparison of Revenues and Expenditures for the Fiscal Year
Ended June 30, 1975**

Revenues by Source ($18M)	
Sales and services of auxiliary enterprises	2.03%
Sales and services of educational activities and other sources	4.89
Grants, contracts, and gifts	15.92
Tuition and fees	23.76
State appropriations	53.40
	100.00%
Expenditures by Object ($18M)	
Transfer and other	6.10%
Capital outlay	3.45
Other operating expenses	21.68
Salaries and wages	68.77
	100.00%
Expenditures by Activity ($18M)	
Auxiliary enterprises	4.05%
Scholarships and mandatory transfers	4.01
Institutional support, and operation and maintenance of plant	15.66
Student services	8.63
Academic support	11.82
Instruction	52.84
Research and public service	2.99
	100.0%

Student Enrollments

The students currently enrolled at WSU were about half in the 18–22 age
group and about half older; the average age of the students was 26.4 years.
Of the enrolled students, 75 percent were from Sedgwick County, in which
the university was located. Some of the programs such as the special health
and judicial administration professional programs were promoted region-
ally, and enrollments came from a broader geographic area.

Nationally, about 50 percent of high school graduates attend some
form of post-high school education. In Kansas 65 percent of this group
seeks higher education. Members of minority groups and women are under-
represented in this group in Kansas compared to national patterns. However, WSU did attract a higher proportion of these students than other state
schools, though not 65 percent of the local high school pool.

Enrollments in general are the source of concern. High school senior enrollments in the state of Kansas are expected to decline 30 percent in the next decade, as shown in table 8–3.

Projected enrollments through 1980 for four different categories of Kansas institutions are shown in table 8–4. Of these four categories of institutions, only Type II institutions, the 19 community junior colleges, were expected to have an aggregate increase in enrollments. The 7 state and municipal colleges and universities, the 16 independent four-year colleges and universities, and the 4 independent two-year colleges were expected to have absolute decrease.

Increasing Future Enrollments

There were several major programs currently under consideration for attracting more students in the future. First, a community outreach study had evaluated the desires of potential students in specific areas of the city and the area. These included Derby, a small town located 30 miles south of the WSU campus; the western part of the city, located about 10 miles away from the WSU campus in the northeastern section of Wichita; a low-income model neighborhood near the campus; and the downtown area of the city, with workers in various types of jobs. More than three fourths of the individuals surveyed felt that nothing WSU could do would change their decision that course requirements, various personal time conflicts, and the lack

Table 8–3
Predicted Decline of High School Senior Enrollments for the Next Decade

Year	Number	Percentage of Base (1969–1972)
1976	34,399	101.0%
1977	34,146	100.2
1978	32,831	96.4
1979	32,000	93.9
1980	30,187	88.6
1981	28,729	84.3
1982	28,215	82.8
1983	26,223	77.0
1984	23,770	69.7
1985	24,175	71.0

Table 8–4
Type I–IV Institutions: Actual and Projected Fall Headcount Enrollments

	Type I	Type II	Type III	Type IV	Total
Actual					
1970	67,076	17,140	12,119	1,798	98,133
1971	69,600	18,856	11,463	1,664	101,583
1972	68,675	19,651	10,957	1,497	100,780
1973	69,685	21,134	10,715	1,413	102,947
1974	73,569	22,740	10,561	1,419	108,289
1975	78,262	25,806	11,006	1,735	116,809
Projected					
1976	77,660	27,010	10,345	1,609	116,624
1977	76,983	28,185	9,666	1,489	116,323
1978	76,141	29,301	8,984	1,354	115,780
1979	75,004	30,272	8,262	1,216	114,754
1980	73,446	31,049	7,522	1,086	113,103

Type I: 6 state colleges and universities and 1 municipal university.
Type II: 19 community junior colleges.
Type III: 16 independent four-year colleges and universities.
Type IV: 4 independent two-year colleges.

of any perceived benefit prevented any further education. However, a third of the total respondents indicated interest in a local neighborhood "mini-campus" for evening courses, as opposed to their commuting to the WSU campus for an evening program once a week. This statistic was balanced by the fact that of the 25 percent of respondents who indicated they might take courses if some changes were made, less than 10 percent mentioned reloca-tion of the class offering as a factor that might influence them to enroll. Of those with an interest in courses, most seemed attracted by business and liberal arts programs even though they were generally unaware of the uni-versity's current offerings in these areas. Based on the existing students' responses shown in table 8–5, the authors of the study did not believe that new programs would pull substantial numbers of students away from the present campus.

A related issue was the educational profile of the respondents. From the sample data gathered, the breakdown by educational achievement was as shown in table 8–6.

One unresolved question was what the market for students would be. Clearly, a decision on that issue would affect course offerings, degree versus

Table 8-5
Preferred Location for Courses by Current Students

	Derby Students	West Wichita Students	Model Neighborhood Students	Students Who Work Downtown	Total
At WSU	28%	37%	54%	25%	41%
Central location	52	42	25	33	38
Location near work	6	6	3	8	5
Other	2	4	3	17	4
No preference	11	11	15	17	12
Totals	100%	100%	100%	100%	100%
Number of respondents	82	216	158	24	480

Table 8-6
Educational Attainment of Respondents by Area

Furthest Educational Attainment	Derby	West Wichita	Model Neighborhood	Downtown	Total
Grades 1-11	10%	24%	30%	4%	15%
Grade 12	45	37	35	35	38
Some college	28	27	23	27	28
College graduate	7	6	4	16	8
Graduate work	10	6	8	17	10

Note: May not add to 100 percent because of rounding.

nondegree offerings, and marketing efforts. The current occupation of respondents is shown in table 8-7.

As part of this study, special questions were asked of residents of a relatively high-income neighborhood near the campus. Eastborough and Vickeridge residents expressed interest in nontraditional, noncredit courses offered in the homes of the students on a rotating basis. In this survey 75 percent of those interviewed indicated a high probability of taking an existing course. Forty-five percent indicated an interest in the home seminar courses. When the entire group was offered the choice between courses at home or on campus, the responses were equally divided between home location, campus location, and indifference. This neighborhood also had a

Table 8–7
Occupation of Respondents by City Area

Occupation	Derby	West Wichita	Model Neighborhood	Downtown	Percent
Professional	25	13	4	23	11.2%
Proprietors, managers, officials	13	14	8	27	10.7
Wholesalers, retailers	0	1	3	13	2.9
Secretaries, clerks	27	22	13	24	14.9
Skilled workers	5	7	11	13	6.2
Semiskilled workers, military	9	11	11	6	6.4
Manufacturing workers	4	5	7	2	3.1
Unskilled laborers	8	13	10	4	6.0
Domestics	0	2	13	0	2.6
Retired	3	2	17	2	4.2
Housewives	62	62	41	1	28.7
Unemployed/ handicapped	1	0	2	1	0.7
Other	–	7	2	7	2.4
Total	157	149	142	113	100.0%

higher level of college graduates than the other areas. Course interests were similar, however, to those in the other areas studied.

Beyond an array of evening and continuing-education programs, a second possibility for attracting students was expansion of a special nondegree student category. As opposed to normal admissions procedures that required submission of transcripts, adults could be admitted to the university's Division of Continuing Education for a cumulative total of 15 hours if they had not attended high school or college in the previous 3 years and had earned a high school diploma or equivalent, or if they were at least 25 years of age. In the event these students desired to continue in degree programs or in nondegree activities at the university beyond the 15 hours, then regular application procedures were to be followed after completion of the 15 hours. This process might attract students who felt inadequate high school work or previous poor academic performance in a university would make them unqualified for admission to a regular degree program. The main purpose of the program, however, was to attract students as a result of the convenience associated with the enrollment procedure. By succeeding in the continuing-education courses, these students were given another chance to perform at the college level. Upon completion of these courses with a satisfactory grade, many students were then welcomed to regular degree programs of the university that might otherwise have rejected their applications. Currently about 537 students from the total of 1,730 students in the continuing-education program were admitted under this special procedure.

Special-student Programs

For several years the university had been involved in developing a variety of special programs for particular groups. These groups were seen as possessing particular qualities or time constraints that made the traditional weekday semester credit-course offerings inappropriate. Among the programs offered were the following:

Special-group Programs. The university designed special programs for particular groups such as senior citizens. Another special program was for women living in proximity to the school. As the university's statement of objectives and procedures for the women's program noted:

> Women form a vast reservoir of talent. While most of them are fully occupied with their homemaking duties when their children are quite young, they now realize that many productive years lie ahead of them following that period. They seek ways in which they can perform functions that require commitment, expertise and judgment—characteristics which accrue with maturity.

> The program strives to respond effectively to, not incite, the restlessness of modern women. Emphasis is on helping them examine their present status and their aspirations for the future in order to focus the resources of the university and the community on meeting their educational and/or occupational objectives.

> During the early years, 1967–1970, one full-time professional and one full-time secretary were committed to the program. Women applied for admission to the program and were afforded special services in pursuing their interests and objectives. In addition to an on-going effort in the credit area, special noncredit conferences and spaced learning courses were developed around general interest and career topics. Special attention was given to remedial courses for the disadvantaged.

> Subsequent to the termination of federal funding in 1970, the reduced staff and budget permitted the continuation of major components of the program as follows:

> *Credit Area*

> 1. Each fall, women in the area are invited to attend an information/orientation session to learn about WSU's programs and services and their relevance to them.

2. A streamlined advising/registration period the following day permits the enrollment of those wishing to enroll in the fall courses.
3. The women are invited to attend a group-counseling session about mid-term to discuss their problems or triumphs or both. Special "Help!" sessions are organized to meet their particular needs in writing examinations, using the library, and so on. Appointments are set up for individual counseling sessions.
4. Special instructions for preregistration are provided to encourage the women to fit into the regular calendar activities of registration.

Noncredit Area

General-interest, noncredit courses of primary interest are scheduled during day-time hours; occasionally a second session is offered also on Saturday for working women. Special one-day conferences devoted to employment opportunities and analysis of women's interests and skills are provided as staff and budget will permit.

"Free-form" Options: Alternative Adult Studies. A more flexible program for those who wished to continue liberal arts studies without the confines of a traditional curriculum or credit program was offered in these courses. Enrollment was open, and course offerings and costs were negotiated with a group of prospective students by administrative personnel of the university. Faculty were contacted to learn of individual faculty members' interests and availabilities, after which the administrators again met with the group of prospective students. Meeting times and total course hours then were established by additional dialogue between university personnel and students. The nucleus of the original members of this program was women community leaders. The program involved 3–10 members of the professional staff of the university on a part-time basis.

Project Together. This program was initiated in July, 1970, and was designed to help minority and low-income students adjust to college life by providing individual tutoring, instructional counseling, and student-development programs. For example, students needing additional help in their courses used the tutorial program developed by Project Together. A formal reporting process is conducted so that the performance of the tutors and the students tutored can be evaluated. In 1975 Project Together completed a survey to determine the accessibility of campus facilities to *handicapped* persons. As a result of this survey, additional alterations of campus facilities were made or planned.

Outreach Programs and Weekend University. The administration of justice department provided special 8-week and 12-week courses at Fort Riley as a service to military personnel. Off-campus courses in sociology, psychology, and history began in order to telescope classroom contact hours and to develop a more flexible approach to research and independent study. During the past 7 years, the instructional-services department offered short-term courses (generally for less than four weeks) that appealed to the special interests of non-degree-bound professional educators. Approximately 100 short-term courses were available to these students in the 1975–1976 academic year.

The university was increasing its efforts to provide courses for those who, for various reasons, could not come to the campus. Off-campus offerings as a result steadily expanded to meet the needs of those students. The recent growth of the Division of Continuing Education, which coordinated these courses and dealt primarily with adult, part-time students, was an indication of this expansion. It coordinated more than 100 off-campus courses, three times the number of off-campus courses offered 3 years previously. A variety of credit and noncredit institutes and workshops were also coordinated by the Division of Continuing Education.

More recently Wichita State began a program to provide Saturday college courses for students who are not able to take advantage of the regular day and evening programs. This new program, called Weekend University, offered 23 courses from 18 departments in the fall of 1976.

In sum the university was concerned with meeting the needs of part-time students as well as full-time students; it sought to serve its regional as well as local clientele; and increasingly it was adapting its systems to serve short-term, ad hoc instructional needs and interests in addition to long-term, degree-oriented interests.

Tenure and Promotion Decisions

In the early 1970s many schools realized that making promotion decisions would become increasingly difficult. Assume a growth of 10 percent per annum in the faculty, a target tenure/nontenure ratio of 50 percent, which was also the current ratio, and that 5 percent of existing tenure positions would become available through death, retirement, or resignation. Then the possibility of tenure for the average nontenured faculty member in the sixth year was 87 percent. This is the maximum case which assumes that all the growth and replacement slots in the tenured faculty are filled by promotion from within. On the other hand, if growth stopped, then only 30 percent of the nontenured faculty could be promoted under the remaining assumptions.

Beginning from any level of tenured/nontenured faculty and with various assumptions about promotion rates, internal/external appointments, attrition rates, and the total number of faculty members, then it is possible to determine both promotion possibilities and the pattern of promotion decisions. Examples of the calculations and application to WSU are presented in appendix 8A.

In late 1973 various university officials reviewed this model and other information. As a result, a policy statement regarding promotion decisions at the university was prepared. Based on an equilibrium percentage of tenure positions of 70 percent of the faculty, a 3.9-percent attrition rate for tenured faculty, and the assumption that 95 percent of the positions would be filled by internal promotions, the calculations shown in appendix 8A suggested 8.66 percent of the nontenured faculty could move to a tenured slot each year. Based on the average number of candidates under consideration, then 52 percent of those reviewed each year could receive tenure. This figure was used as the basis for the 1973 statement on promotions at the university.

Tenure and Promotion Decisions: 1976 and Later

By 1976, updated information was available on several of the assumptions inherent in WSU's 1973 application of the faculty model. Although the faculty had increased slightly, the constant faculty-size assumption remained plausible. The attrition rate in the 5 years preceding the 1973 study ranged from 6.9 to 2.9 percent and the average of the recent years of 3.9 percent was used in the projections. However, the actual attribution in the subsequent 2 years was only 1.2 and 1.9 percent. For future projections an attrition rate of 2.0 percent seemed more reasonable. In addition, increasing outside appointments meant that 90 instead of 95 percent of tenured positions probably would be filled internally.

Using these revised calculations, the overall average tenure award would be 4.2 percent instead of the 8.7 percent assumed in the earlier studies. Although this rate could be phased in over several years, it was possible for such a change to create difficulties in implementing the policy. Table 8-8 indicates the distribution of faculty by rank and tenure within various colleges and departments.

At this point it was appropriate for university officials to wonder whether any major changes in the guidelines for awarding of tenure were required. These guidelines presumed that "all nontenured members of the faculty are afforded essentially the same opportunity to achieve tenure now, 5 years from now, or at any point in time." The guidelines suggested that tenure would be awarded in about 50 percent of the cases across all colleges and all years in the coming years. The report did note that the guidelines were not rigid rules since institutional flexibility had to allow "for occasional decisions that are exceptions to them."

A document prepared by an ad hoc committee of the University Senate and approved by the university faculty in the spring of 1976 provided an

Table 8–8
Status of Full-Time Faculty, Fall 1975 (Fiscal Year 1976)

College and Department	Prof. No.	Prof. Ten.	Prof. Prob.[a]	Assoc. Prof. No.	Assoc. Prof. Ten.	Assoc. Prof. Prob.[a]	Asst. Prof. & Instr. No.	Asst. Ten.	Asst. Prob.	Asst. Tmp.	All Ranks No.	All Ten.	All Prob.	All Tmp.	% Ten.
Business Administration															
Accounting	4	4	0	2	2	0	4	1	2	1	10	7	2	1	70
Administration	8	8	0	3	3	0	9	1	3	5	20	12	3	5	60
Economics	4	4	0	6	6	0	5	0	2	3	15	10	2	3	66
Business education	0	0	0	1	1	0	3	2	0	1	4	3	0	1	75
Total	16	16	0	12	12	0	21	4	7	10	49	32	7	10	65
Education															
Personnel services	4	4	0	2	2	0	1	0	1	0	7	6	1	0	85
Instructional services	2	2	0	11	10	1	17	2	11	4	30	14	11	5	46
Logopedics	3	3	0	3	3	0	2	1	1	0	8	7	1	0	87
Physical education	1	1	0	1	1	0	11	5	4	2	13	7	4	2	53
Industrial education	0	0	0	1	1	0	3	1	0	2	4	2	0	2	50
Total	10	10	0	18	17	1	34	9	17	8	62	36	17	9	58
Engineering															
Aeronautical	6	6	0	2	2	0	1	1	0	0	9	9	0	0	100
Electrical	4	3	1	4	4	0	2	0	1	1	10	7	2	1	70
Industrial	0	0	0	1	1	0	4	1	3	0	5	2	3	0	40
Mechanical	2	2	0	2	2	0	2	2	0	0	6	6	0	0	100
Total	12	11	1	9	9	0	9	4	4	1	30	24	5	1	80

Table 8-8 continued

College and Department	Prof. No.	Prof. Ten.	Prof. Prob.a	Assoc. Prof. No.	Assoc. Prof. Ten.	Assoc. Prof. Prob.a	Asst. Prof. & Instructors No.	Asst. Ten.	Asst. Prob.	Asst. Tmp.	All Ranks No.	All Ten.	All Prob.	All Tmp.	% Ten.
Fine Arts															
Art education	0	0	0	0	0	0	3	1	0	2	3	1	0	2	33
Art history	0	0	0	1	1	0	2	0	2	0	3	1	2	0	33
Graphic design	2	2	0	0	0	0	2	0	1	1	4	2	1	1	50
Studio arts	1	1	0	3	3	0	3	0	3	0	7	4	3	0	58
Music education	1	1	0	0	0	0	4	2	2	0	5	3	2	0	60
Performance	1	1	0	12	10	2	14	3	8	3	27	14	10	3	52
Music composition	1	1	0	1	1	0	4	0	2	2	6	2	2	2	33
Total	6	6	0	17	15	2	32	6	18	8	55	27	20	8	50
Health-related Professions															
Health sciences	0	0	0	1	0	1	1	0	1	0	2	0	2	0	0
Community health education	0	0	0	0	0	0	1	0	0	1	1	0	0	1	0
Health-care administration	0	0	0	1	0	1	0	0	0	0	1	0	1	0	0
Nursing	0	0	0	3	0	3	12	0	12	0	15	0	15	0	0
Nurse clinician program	0	0	0	0	0	0	2	0	1	1	2	0	1	1	0
Dental Hygiene	0	0	0	0	0	0	4	0	1	3	4	0	1	3	0
Respiratory therapy	0	0	0	0	0	0	2	0	1	1	2	0	1	1	0
Medical technology	0	0	0	0	0	0	1	0	1	0	1	0	1	0	0
Physical therapy	0	0	0	0	0	0	3	0	3	0	3	0	3	0	0
Physician's assistant program	0	0	0	0	0	0	1	0	1	0	1	0	1	0	0
Total	0	0	0	5	0	5	27	0	21	6	32	0	26	6	0

Liberal arts

	C1	C2	C3	C4	C5	C6	C7	C8	C9	C10	C11	C12	C13	C14	%
Administration of justice	2	2	0	0	0	0	9	2	4	3	11	4	4	3	36
American studies	1	1	0	1	0	1	0	0	0	0	2	1	1	0	50
Anthropology	3	3	0	1	1	0	3	2	1	0	7	6	1	0	86
Biology	4	4	0	2	2	0	11	4	6	1	17	10	6	1	59
Chemistry	5	5	0	3	3	0	5	1	3	1	13	9	3	1	69
English	7	6	1	4	4	0	11	5	4	3	22	15	5	2	68
Geology	4	4	0	0	0	0	3	1	2	0	7	5	2	0	71
German	1	1	0	1	1	0	3	2	0	1	5	4	0	1	80
History	6	6	2	9	9	0	0	0	0	0	15	15	0	0	100
Journalism	2	0	0	1	0	1	1	0	0	1	4	0	2	2	0
Mathematics	3	3	0	9	9	0	12	5	4	3	24	17	4	3	71
Minority studies	0	0	0	1	1	0	2	0	1	1	3	1	1	1	33
Philosophy	0	0	0	4	4	0	2	0	1	0	6	5	1	0	83
Physics	1	1	0	3	3	0	3	1	1	0	7	6	1	0	86
Political science	5	5	0	3	3	0	3	2	3	0	11	8	3	0	73
Psychology	4	4	0	3	3	0	7	0	3	1	14	10	3	1	71
Religion	0	0	0	1	1	0	3	3	1	0	4	3	1	0	75
Romance languages	3	3	0	2	2	0	10	4	5	1	15	9	5	1	60
Sociology	1	1	0	1	1	0	9	2	7	0	11	4	7	0	36
Speech	2	2	0	2	2	0	8	3	5	0	12	7	5	0	58
Composition	0	0	0	1	0	1	13	1	4	8	14	1	5	8	7
Total	54	51	3	52	49	3	118	40	55	23	224	140	60	24	63
Unassigned Total	1	1	0	0	0	0	8	2	5	1	9	3	5	1	33
Total University	99	95	4	113	102	11	249	65	127	57	461	262	140	59	57

a Only one temporary faculty member.
Ten. = Tenured.
Prob. = Probationary (nontenured).
Tmp. = Temporary.

orderly process for dealing with retrenchment owing to financial exigency. Briefly, the document called for the termination of nontenured faculty before tenured faculty (except in cases where serious distortion of the academic programs might result) and for termination of tenured persons at the lower ranks first according to the number of years in rank. The document also required thorough participation by the faculty in termination decisions and provided an elaborate appeals procedure. A companion document detailing procedures for termination of tenured faculty for inadequate performance was prepared by the same committee and was under consideration by the faculty.

In addition to consideration of whether the tenure award ratio and perhaps some departments chairpersons' expectations should be revised, the university faced a problem of deciding on tenure for administrators. A recent draft report prepared by an ad hoc committee of faculty and administration had suggested that many members of the university involved in nonacademic roles such as the library, computer services, and media facilities also should receive a tenure decision at the end of 6 years. The implications of this report, if enacted, were unclear. In addition, there was a question as to the appropriate response of the university administration and faculty to this report, which had grown from confusion about the role of these nonfaculty people in the university's tenure system.

Collective Bargaining

Neither faculty nor staff at WSU were unionized. Apart from ideological considerations, most administrators at American universities probably preferred to avoid unionization of faculty and/or staff for the same reasons corporate executives wished to avoid it: organization was presumed to reduce the flexibility of the manager in running the organization. With the possibility of tenure quotas in the air, collective bargaining was an additional constraint that would severely restrict the operating freedom of the university administrators. WSU operated under the Kansas "meet-and-confer" law, which provided that any five employees could request a collective-bargaining election.

During 1974 a University Senate ad hoc committee on collective bargaining, formed at the request of the university's president, distributed extensive information to all faculty and held several campus-wide discussions and conferences so that the faculty could be well informed on the subject of collective bargaining in higher education. The returns of the Faculty Perceptions Survey indicated that 60 percent of the faculty opposed formal organization for collective bargaining at Wichita State, with 43 percent of the faculty strongly opposed. The overall distribution of responses indicated little interest in collective bargaining at that time.

Faculty Development

In conjunction with a review of promotion procedures and an early process for staff reduction if financial cutbacks were required, the university administration and faculty also were concerned about retraining of faculty as well as general faculty development. A request for funding from the Kellogg Foundation outlined the thoughts behind a proposal for retraining:

> The university's greatest resource is its faculty. To maintain the viability of this resource, and ultimately of the institution in the steady state, more significant investments in faculty development are essential. While the university has an effective process for the review of tenure and promotion and engages in faculty-development activities of a traditional nature, there are needs for a profile of the faculty, systematic evaluations of tenured faculty and administrators, and a comprehensive program of faculty professional development.

> A comprehensive program of faculty professional development will be planned on a pilot basis to provide for the continued development of effective faculty and the redevelopment and redeployment of other faculty members.

> Development activities will be conducted in the following areas:
> New instructional methodologies
> New curricular and delivery system developments
> Emerging professional service and research opportunities,
> Student-relations skills, including advising and counseling.

> Methods such as the following will be utilized:
> Seminars and workshops,
> Faculty-exchange programs,
> Internships in other universities and organizations,
> Formal instructional improvement programs

> An office to provide professional counseling services to faculty will be initiated, particularly in relation to the evaluation process and the planning of alternative futures for those interested in redevelopment and redeployment.

Conclusion

In late 1976 the issues confronting the university included the possibilities for additional programs for students to improve the revenues of the school. In addition, there was the issue of relative balance among the various programs for dealing with the faculty under a situation of financial hardship. What were the alternative costs of dealing with hard times? Should a plurality of programs be attempted, or should the university seek leadership? Should departments be constrained in their granting of tenure and hiring of faculty?

Thus as a university administrator could remark to an outside observer, "What would *you* do with it?"

Wichita State University: Analysis

In the context of a discussion about long-run financial planning and strategy, the situation faced by the administration of Wichita State University is not unusual.[1] What is unusual, at least at the time of the case, is the commitment to assembling data and confronting the faculty with the implications of the data as perceived by the administration if certain events should take place. For thinking about this case, probably the most relevant question is: As the financial vice-president of Wichita State University, what issues would concern you?

Returning to the analysis of earlier chapters, it seems that the issues might be grouped around:

Long-run versus short-run costs and revenues

Fixed versus variable costs and revenues

Controllable versus noncontrollable costs and revenues

These three areas interrelate: Fixed costs in the short run are often costs that become variable over a longer period (for example, the costs of a particular department or the maintenance charges of particular buildings that may ultimately be demolished). The legislature might be persuaded that the levels of certain areas of revenue and expense could be left to the judgment of the administration, at least within ± 10 percent of some state-mandated figure; thus noncontrollable amounts become (semi) controllable in the long run. Active versus passive management should not be ignored, for the university administrator who finds certain areas creating significantly more costs of an uncontrollable nature may wish to emphasize moving these costs into a controllable category in the long run.

Revenues

Within the last few years many schools have moved to a variety of special programs designed to appeal to nonstandard potential students. WSU is moving rapidly in this direction: The brief description of programs involving senior citizens, women, free-form enrollment, the Weekend University, Outreach, and Project Together exemplify this pattern. This interest nationally and at WSU results in part from the well-known decline in high school enrollments over 10 years as shown in the case. The pool from which most schools draw their entering classes will decline 30 percent over this decade. On the other side of the coin, three fourths of the respondents to the WSU survey indicated that nothing the university could do would attract them. Consistent with the economic concepts mentioned in the first chapter of this book, one must also ask what the *draw effect* would be: How many students are shifted from regular programs to these special programs, creating no additional funding at all?

In the short run and long run, student tuition is a variable-revenue item. First, these students pay tuition of some low amount. Second, the state of Kansas provides $258 per equivalent full-time student (the important EFT that WSU and many universities study with good reason). EFT students do *not* directly relate to faculty salaries, and other operating expenses according to figure 8-1 are 21.68 percent of the total object allocation.[2] In the short run then, additional students contribute variable revenue that more than offsets their variable costs *if* one assumes that no additional faculty are hired or that those faculty hired cost less than this contribution.

There are two major problems with these assumptions. First, can the students be recruited in areas where existing faculty can teach? If the students go into existing classes, well and good. If they have classes at special times, as implied by most of the special-program themes, then one must assume that existing faculty can be reallocated from normal classes. Any retraining or special-preparation funding for this reallocation ought to be considered. In addition, even if part-time faculty were hired for these special classes, there is the problem of whether additional funds from the state and/or tuition income can be sufficiently reallocated to pay the salaries. Often income is *franked* by budget category, limiting the ability of an administrator to transfer funds from one budget category to another. A related issue is whether the special students recruited under these innovative programs will refuse to continue in sufficient numbers because they feel they are not taught by "regular" faculty; this too represents a cost.

These amounts then represent variable-revenue items but only semicontrollable. They are "controlled" in the sense that the school can seek new applicants for the special programs. Several other areas of revenue generation seem relevant in this context, and these areas may be much more susceptible to control.

First, allocation of funding for faculty salaries may be based heavily on cost of living, peer institutions, or aspirant-peer institution salary arguments.[3]

Second, differential tuition levels and funding/support levels from the state may be sought. What is the ultimate economic impact of in-state/out-of-state tuition differentials? What of undergraduate/graduate tuition or funding differentials? What of engineering and science differentials versus funding for liberal arts and business? Within this tuition-level argument, note that there are sharp short-run/long-run differentials. In the short run, the marginal cost of funding an engineering student may be only slightly above a history major. In the long run, when one considers probable trends in engineering faculty salaries versus history faculty salaries, the increasing costs for specialized equipment in instruction and laboratory facilities, and the like, the marginal cost of an engineering student is probably considerably higher than that of the history student. In this same vein, notice that there are difficult evaluations for graduate versus undergraduate education. The graduate student may require more individual attention and greater financial aid. Offsetting this variable cost is the substitution of graduate assistants for outside research or teaching personnel. Here again the administrator would consider marginal cost and marginal revenue of such a policy of additional support for graduate education. (In the WSU case, the out-of-state tuition differential may not be much of an argument, for students tend to come from Kansas anyway. With other public universities, there is also the problem of continuing legislative and judicial easing of requirements that a student must meet in order to be considered a resident.)

Third, cooperation with other public and possibly private universities may be appropriate as a revenue-generating tactic. In the public sector, assuming continuing inflation and limited lack of enthusiasm for higher education per se among high school pools, effective lobbying at the state and national level to limit grants to students in private schools (directly to all students or indirectly through grants to the private schools) helps stimulate demand for the public sector. If grants are inevitable to students in private schools, then the two principles of marginal cost and revenue and substitution would suggest that public-school administrators using this avenue of revenue generation would seek to spread the grants to public-school enrollees as well. Thus with inflation raising the effective cost of other goods, if the real income of the student does not rise, then education as a service industry is likely to have cost increases even greater than the national average. Not only do students have less money to spend on all goods if their real income fails to maintain its level (the income effect), but as some goods such as education are perceived as becoming even more expensive relatively, students will substitute other goods such as technical schools or recreation (the substitution effect).

As part of this substitution effect, however, the public universities that lose students who opt for other goods will also *add* some students who substitute the public university for the private university. Grants solely to the private student remove some of this private-student-substitution inflow to the public university by making these students less inclined to make the substitution. However, grants to *all* students would presumably offset some of this reduced public inflow by reducing the outflow of public students to other markets as the real cost of higher education increases relative to their incomes. Private schools, of course, would look at these arguments in reverse, and their policy arguments to legislators and the public would no doubt be opposite to what is suggested here.[4]

These are nonexhaustive approaches to the area of revenue generation, using some of the concepts of economics that were outlined earlier. Any administrator would be forced to apply guesses to the levels of various changes, seeing what the benefit or cost is likely to be. Even when these guesses are not easy to come by, some estimate must be made. In many cases, a breakeven estimate can be calculated: If a university will lose this many students because of policy x, how many additional students at various tuition/expense funding levels have to be added to offset this loss? Again some basic economic arguments can be used to advantage, as discussed in chapter 1.[5]

Expenses

Not atypically, WSU has two-thirds of its costs in salaries and wages and one-half of its costs in instruction when one studies the object and activity tables.[6] In controlling expenses then, one obvious idea is to focus on the large items. It may well be that other areas are more controllable and more variable in the short and long run; the analysis here will emphasize these two categories of analysis.

The interrelationship of revenue and expense items in one area has already been mentioned: Ph.D. programs take faculty time and usually more financial aid, creating high student cost, yet the Ph.D. students can aid the faculty in teaching and research, permitting lower effective salaries to faculty in some cases. To some degree this argument applies to master's candidates as well. Moreover, the administrator needs to be aware of a short-run/long-run and a fixed-cost/variable-cost comparison that is often not obvious in this analysis. Many faculty emphasize the importance of research and stress that they would like to do more research if teaching loads (class hours or class size or whatever) were not so heavy. One would presume that such improved conditions would permit slightly lower salaries (which is the pattern in the more prestigious research universities, certainly among junior faculty). Even if no salary adjustment were in the back of the administrator's mind, he or she may well assume that greater publication leads to more visibility and status for the university, improving the quality of students, perhaps leading to more grants, and possibly permitting more generous state funding to a "flagship" institution.[7] The difficulty in this logic is something that became apparent to Mayor John Lindsay in the public sector: Improving conditions may permit attracting better people (where "better" is defined along the norms suggested), but it also results in a windfall gain to the existing faculty, many of whom will not leave under current conditions and will not do much research under any conditions. Hence if this strategy is adopted, it would seem wise to make sure that deans and department chairpersons are prepared to make differential adjustments in teaching loads, compensation, assistant support, and the like; given the environment of many departments (where the chairperson will return to the club), this is often not likely.

Much of industry can accommodate some inflation in salaries in productivity increases. But using the forum of a legislature or a board of trustees, what is the productivity measure in universities? There may be some adjustment for quality variables (better instruction, smaller classes, academic field differentials, or the like), but these are often lost amid argument and dispute. On the other hand, course hours taught, students taught, departmental majors, and graduates are tangible measures. How does one increase this variable? Larger classes? Heavier teaching loads? These solutions are not what most faculty members have in mind. On the other hand, faculty and staff want cost-of-living and other salary increases, arguing that the fact they are in an industry that has difficulties generating productivity increases does not mean that it costs them any less to feed, house, clothe, and educate their own children.

If one recalls the economic issue of risk discussed in earlier chapters, then the whole issue of *tenure* become overwhelming.

1.   The major costs are in instruction (by activity) and salaries and wages (by object).
2.   Inflation forces higher salaries and wages, yet offsetting productivity increases are hard to achieve in this service industry.
3.   An administrator prefers variable and controllable costs to fixed and noncontrollable costs.
4.   With enrollment shifts and a declining addition of new standard students, there is a need for *flexibility* in staffing that has never been as critical as it will be in the next two decades.[8]

With growth one can add funding where departments are growing; slow (relative) growth departments can be handled easily by nonaddition and perhaps by some reduction of faculty as retirement takes place or by reappointment of part-time and temporary people at the lower ranks. In a no-growth environment, the difficulties are compounded, as many administrators have realized in recent years. The appendix to the Wichita State University case, using the AAUP tenure model, is noteworthy. One can elaborate on this model by allowing growth in N, the number of faculty members, and it is this growth that allowed most schools to have very high promotion ratios in the 1960s. Table 8–9 shows the world of a university under several different assumptions. Rather than the sterile case *A, B,* and *C,* I have chosen to call these cases 60, 70, and 80. Notice that starting with an assumed faculty of 100, a target faculty tenure ratio of 50 percent, and a 6-year probationary period in all cases, the probabilities of tenure for a junior faculty member differ sharply in the three cases. In case 60, relatively large mobility of faculty and a 6-percent growth in total faculty size permit the person to have a .72 chance of promotion. In case 70, there is decreased roll-over of existing tenure slots and no growth, and the movement of non-tenured faculty to tenure is now a .24 probability. Finally, in case 80, there is a reduction of faculty size mandated (perhaps) by declining enrollments, and the probability of promotion for a junior person is 0.

Crudely these figures refer to the 1960s, 1970s, and 1980s. The attrition

Table 8–9
Promotion Ratios under Alternative Conditions

	Case		
	60	*70*	*80*
Faculty size	100	100	100
Tenure ratio	.50	.50	.50
Target tenure ratio	.50	.50	.50
Attrition of tenured faculty	6%	4%	4%
Growth in faculty size	6%	0	– 4%
Probationary period	6 yr	6yr	6yr
Tenure slots available from:			
Growth	3	0	– 2
Attrition	3	2	2
Total	6	2	0
Candidates for tenure (50/6)	8.3	8.3	8.3
Tenure slots/candidates	6/8.3	2/8.3	0/8.3
Probability of promotion	.72	.24	0
With seven-year probationary period, candidates for tenure per year are 50/7 = 7.1, and the probability of promotion for any candidate becomes:	.85	.28	0
A higher attrition percentage also would arise under this condition because the age at which tenure is granted is later, meaning fewer years per person in a tenure slot. This increase in attrition would make more slots available, further increasing the probabilities of promotion.			

figures may be suspect: After all, moving people from one university to another should not in the aggregate affect the promotion ratio, nor should it affect any given university that imports as many faculty as it exports. Yet in the 1960s the universities on balance could be net exporters in the typical case because of the aggregate expansion created by totally new campuses. In the 1980s universities may again be net exporters as faculty move to the private or government sector of the economy.

Another way of viewing the problem that is even more pessimistic is to study discretionary dollars available to administrators, the fixed/variable discussion we have used before. In this case, a tenure ratio of 50 percent probably means that far more than 50 percent of the budget is fixed because tenured faculty are typically in higher salary categories than the non-tenured, and their mandated support is higher (teaching loads lower, secretarial staffing greater).

It may also be useful to view the tenure decision in the context of the present-value analysis used in some project and portfolio discussions earlier in this book. We introduced the idea of the cost of a tenured faculty member as an example of present-value analysis. Table 8–10 elaborates on those concepts and that example.

Case A uses an assumed $20,000 salary for a newly tenured faculty member, and 15 percent fringes. Net real growth in salary and fringes is assumed to be 2 percent, implying a peak full-professor salary in 30 years of ($20,000 $\times$ $(1 + .02)^{20}$ =) $36,227 in *real* terms. An arbitrary staff charge of $10,000 is included with no growth. Using the present-value formulas from earlier in this book, one can compute the present value today of a 30-year commitment to pay a professor's salary of $20,000, plus 15 percent fringes, with growth in the salary and fringes of 2 percent in real purchasing power. Using a 5-percent discount rate, the calculations are completed using a net discount rate of the 5-percent rate minus the 2-percent growth in the cash flow, or 3 percent in case A. The present value of these flows is then $450,810 as shown in column 10. A similar analysis can be completed for the staff-support costs associated with a faculty member. Case D is the alternative of a junior faculty member, with less fringe and staff costs and no growth assumed. The differential of $358,575 in this present value over the base case A is noteworthy. Case E is a part-time instructor. Several of these instructors would be equivalent to one junior faculty member in institutional cost, perhaps two as in this case. Note the lower fringe and staff costs. Cases F and G show the same comparison for cases A and D where inflation occurs in the form of increasing the *percentage* changes for salaries and fringes. This change widens the dollar salary scale between senior and junior faculty and increases the present-value differential. Notice that any identical dollar increase for both (that is, larger percentages for junior faculty but keeping the same base $10,000 salary differential) would not change the present-value spreads between them. What are the differentials?

Table 8-10
Tenure Present-Value Calculations

Case	1 Salary	2 Fringe	3 Growth S & F	4 Discount Rate	5 4 – 3 (Approx.)	6 Staff	7 Growth Staff	8 4 – 7 (Approx.)	9 PV Staff	10 PV Salary & Fringe	11 9 & 10 Total PV	12 Differential over Case
A	$20,000	15%	2%	5%	3%	$10,000	0%	5%	$153,724	$450,810	$604,534	–
B	20,000	15	3	5	2	10,000	0	5	153,724	515,119	668,842	
C	20,000	15	2	8	6	10,000	0	8	112,578	316,591	429,169	
D	10,000	10	0	5	5	5,000	0	5	76,862	169,097	245,959	$358,575 A
E	5,000	5	0	5	5	1,000	0	5	19,216	76,862	96,078	508,456 A
F	20,000	15	5	5	0	10,000	3	2	223,965	690,000	913,965	309,431 A
G	10,000	10	3	5	2	5,000	3	2	111,932	246,361	358,343	555,622 F

a. Would *staff* costs be spent anyway? Should they be charged to a tenured slot?

b. *Sabbaticals:* If these are more likely to be taken at higher levels with higher costs, they should be charged to the fringe benefit. This adjustment (and other salary changes) are easy to make by increasing the $S + F$ total. Notice the cost of a sabbatical is not just salary and fringes but the cost of a replacement as well.

c. What of *visitors?* They might cost more, but the key element is locked-in cash flows (department) with a tenured senior faculty member versus flexibility with the junior one. (Thus these present values are more unnerving than at first appears!)

All these figures can be proportionately adjusted for different initial salary spreads and different staff assumptions.[9] As an example, case B uses a 3 percent real growth in salary and fringes compared to case A's 2 percent. Case C uses an 8 percent discount rate instead of case A's 5 percent.

These arguments show the compelling need to consider tenure. Tenure represents a commitment to a large fixed, noncontrollable cost that will continue for perhaps 30 years; a tenure decision represents a major commitment of the university's future income valued in present-worth terms. What are the options to move this fixed cost to variable, from a noncontrollable to a controllable cost?[10]

First, at the societal level the elimination of tenure could be valuable. Yet faculty consider it a major aspect of the academic life, protecting them not so much from a trustee or a hostile legislator as from each other: Tenure permits the scholar-teacher to pursue truth as he or she perceives it. Although tenure is a relatively recent addition to academics, being introduced nationally in the United States only in the latter part of the nineteenth century, it is a part of the academic scene. Even if one considers that tenure de facto is a large part of the American *corporate* scene (except perhaps at the top executive officer level), and de jure in many governmental positions through civil service, it may still be argued that its formal entrenchment is a unique part of academic life versus other career opportunities.[11] From an economist's perspective, paying, for instance, 20-percent higher salaries to induce more people to take nontenured positions would be an option.

However, both the option of eliminating tenure and paying the new or old faculty member to surrender tenure will fail unless all universities follow suit: One university, like one firm in a competitive industry, cannot unilaterally eliminate tenure or raise prices and survive. Over time our society may eliminate tenure by the flood of Ph.D.'s willing to work without tenure. However, the trade associations are likely to resist the removal of tenure, especially given their concern for existing faculty members (who are the dominant proportion of the associations' membership).

What then can the administrator do? One option is tenure by *system:* A large public university grants tenure in the system, permitting the movement of faculty members to other campuses under stringent conditions.

A second option is tenure by *school* but not by department. Here enforced reallocation of the faculty member to another field with suitable retraining support is possible.

These are fall-back options: They are unpleasant for the administrator, the members of the department, and most of all for the affected faculty member. Intellectual growth is possible, yet the emotional and physical upheaval of a faculty member who did nothing more than, with hindsight, choose the wrong discipline and perhaps the wrong academic institution is tragic. Accordingly, to gain flexibility short of these measures, several other choices are possible.

One may limit department size. Until someone retires, no additional hiring may occur without the specific approval of the central administration. Attrition of young people and retirement of old people will not automatically free a position for a new person. The positions may be eliminated or at least recaptured at the school, if not at the university level.

One may limit tenure by department, a quota system. Within the context of the WSU system, one may ask how the faculty might approve such an arrangement. In the short run, faculty may oppose tenure quotas: Senior faculty recognize that new young people are needed to rejuvenate the system (if not to do the more onerous teaching); junior people recognize that quotas will reduce their chances for promotion in many cases. Furthermore, this short-run departmental bias may carry over in a voting pattern on policy for the university. Thus one may look at WSU in terms of the percentage of liberal arts and total faculty who are in departments that are more than X percent tenured. These figures are as follows:

Departmental Tenure Ratio	Liberal Arts		Total	
Greater than 80%	36/140	25%	64/262	25%
Greater than 66%	102/140	73%	157/262	60%

If one has a vote by individual department, a vote by school, a vote by the entire faculty, or a vote by tenured faculty only, one may have sharply different percentages of the electorate with a prior disposition sharply against a tenure quota. Thus 55 percent of the total tenured faculty are in liberal arts at WSU. Of these, 73 percent are in departments that already have a tenure ratio greater than 66 percent. If only the tenured faculty vote on this issue, then the fact that only 60 percent of the total faculty are in departments with more than a 66-percent tenure ratio suggests that one would prefer a vote with each school having one vote as opposed to the whole faculty counted equally. (Most of the other departments are unlikely to have such a high tenure ratio, given the preponderance of liberal arts department members in these totals, a judgment confirmed by table 8–4). Since such a vote is probably precluded by faculty by-laws, one might assume that at least the committee of the faculty that studies this issue for a recommendation to a faculty senate should have a preponderance of members from outside the liberal arts departments.

On the margin, tenure decisions often seem to present positive present-value changes for a college: a newly tenured researcher who will obtain grants with large overhead reimbursement to the college can more than pay his or her own way. There are several difficulties with such a judgment. First, grant money is increasingly hard to obtain and will shift over time. What happens when the person tenured is in a field for which grant money ebbs, yet the tenure decision is relatively permanent? Second, does the overhead cost recovery really cover the cost of grants in total? As one dean remarked to the author, "We encourage faculty to earn outside a replacement for half their salary on an annual basis with 70–80 percent indirect cost recovery. Yet we add additional support for them, which is used up in seeking many grants that never materialized. Thus we probably lose money on this whole operation. But that is the university's style." Third, by expanding faculties and by tenuring grant-dependent faculty, massive disruption can occur for the entire college if a large portion of the college's budget is dependent on grants and the grants disappear. The Harvard School of Education faced exactly this situation some years ago and had a rather wholesale early retirement/forced retirement of many seemingly permanent faculty. Finally, the administrator may create a two-class faculty: a few stars paid high salaries who have effectively bought their position and many satellites who carry out the large teaching requirements.[12]

This section of the chapter has dwelt on tenure and the need to bring tenure under some control so that administrators (and ultimately faculty themselves) will have flexibility in a period of declining growth in the student population. Coupled with shifting enrollments, the decline can create a feast/famine situation among departments. That is not to say that economics should rule the university, as has been emphasized before. Rather it is merely to emphasize that the cost of no tenure ceiling, the cost of letting the university "unfold" as nature buffets it, will mean chaos. The cost of avoiding a tenure ceiling may mean that growth departments cannot attract faculty in the future and will fail to enroll the students needed to serve the public and/or keep the trustees and legislators happy. This situation of course is well known among engineering and business faculties in the late 1970s!

What Happened

As noted, the purpose of this case is to outline a variety of approaches that one major state university took to the possibilities of budget cutbacks coupled with the certainty in the decline of high school graduates that produce the typical input for the undergraduate enrollment base.

Subsequent to the case, an enrollment decline forced a reduction of 24 slots at the university. Several options were available. First, whenever a vacancy occurred in any department, it reverted to the college as a whole rather than just the department. Second, it became a slot available at the assistant-professorship level, with corresponding salary. At the time of this case, the university administration was waiting to see if the decline in enrollments would continue.

As part of that wait, some preliminary evidence gathered by Drs. Breazeale and Ahlberg indicated that the university really had about 40,000 students, of which the full-time equivalent was 15,000. From the fall enrollment of 15,700, only 10,000 carried over to the next semester. The task for the administration then was to understand why there was turnover of this magnitude. Economic booms tended to hurt enrollments on balance; opportunities for good jobs apparently drew students away from both full-time and part-time programs.

1980 Events

By 1980 the six regents' universities in the Kansas system were each related to five comparable universities in the Midwest. Data were prepared comparing the funding per credit hours in various disciplines at these peer institutions. Because the Kansas universities showed a deficit compared to the average for these other institutions, there was hope that the legislature would close this gap in funding over several years.

Until the recent year the legislature had provided funding for the university on an average basis, without concern over the detailed mix of engineering versus history nor with particular attention to the allocation of funding to administrative and other support costs versus teaching. There was evidence that this attitude was changing; the legislature indicated it would pay attention to factors such as these in decisions on future funding.

The board of regents moved to a program of 5-year budget forecasts for the schools in this system. Although the average was a forecast of 10-percent declines in enrollments over this period, the regents' forecast for WSU was a 4-percent decline.

By 1980 WSU was in a better position than forecast at the time of the case in terms of the tenure levels overall, in part because of some growth in faculty that is not considered in the AAUP model. With only 58 percent of the faculty tenured versus the 65 percent forecast in the case, the administration had some latitude. Using an expanded model that allowed for changing the size of the faculty, Dr. John Breazeale and others at WSU felt the university would be in relatively good condition for the foreseeable future.

However, the regents had also become aware of the decreasing flexibility available to administrators with tenured faculty as a result in part of an incident involving nonrenewal of contracts and reductions in positions at another regents' university. The regents adopted a rule relating to financial exigency. In general, the definition adopted said that when declining enrollments and/or declining appropriations required a reduction in nontenured faculty and expenditures where further reduction would produce programmatic distortions, the president of the institution could declare that financial exigency existed and report to the board of regents. Then tenured faculty could be dismissed even though there were still nontenured faculty in the institution as a whole. (This definition is in contrast with the AAUP guideline, which in essence relates to the "eminent collapse of the entire system.")

With these concerns in the background, a series of one-day faculty workshops were organized in the summer of 1979. Faculty members were given background papers and simple case exercises of a hypothetical college that faced declining or shifting enrollments. As became apparent to the faculty participants, the Kansas funding system meant that a decline in a relatively "high-productivity" area with large lectures reduced funding overall, perhaps hurting many other areas as well, even though some of those other areas would have growth in enrollments. In some of the hypothetical situations, one out of four faculty members called for the president to declare financial exigency, terminating some tenured faculty in an old-line department with no growth in order to preserve a newer department that had the only prospect to enroll additional students in future years, preserving some state funding. (Obviously it is not clear whether any faculty member would call for such a declaration at his or her own university!)

In addition, at the workshops it became clear that there could be additional considerations of the balance among and across areas in relation to the mix of credit hours per equivalent full-time faculty. A common assumption had been that clinical instruction would relate to 100 credit hours, laboratory work would relate to 200 credit hours, and general studies would relate to 300 credit hours. No discipline was 100 percent in one type of instruction versus another, but the mixture could be changed. However, given the state funding system and enrollments by area, deciding on two of the three types of instruction implied the third for a unique number of credit hours. Clearly, having more of the individual instruction by clinical study would typically require far less instruction in smaller groups (laboratory) and more instruction in larger lectures (general studies).

As noted in the case, there was legislation relating to collective bargaining. Under the Kansas meet-and-confer law, 5 people can petition for the determination of a bargaining unit. In the fall of 1979, 16 people signed such a petition, although it was not clear that they ultimately wished to have collective bargaining. The issue related more to whether chairpersons, part-time faculty, and temporary faculty would be included in the unit. One of the regents' universities had a union, and two others had bargaining units defined; thus this step was simply seen as moving WSU in the direction of some of the other universities.[13]

WSU had not moved to tenure quotas, although the administration had indicated that a hard look would be taken at departments where the tenure level was high. In those departments where there were high levels, the decision was made not to change the rules for awarding tenure to the people currently in the nontenure ranks, simply indicating that it was expected that one half of them would move to tenure positions. The decision was made to halt recruiting in these four departments so that the positions would not be replaced as they became vacant.

Howard Swearer, the local high school graduate whose comments as president of Carleton introduce the case, went on to become president of Brown University. One wonders if the budget cutbacks facing other schools will eventually cause him to temper some of his thinking. One hundred thirteen private schools ceased operations between 1970 and 1976; for the future, Boston University's president predicted 500 of the 1,500 private universities and colleges closing, merging, or consolidating.[14]

Conclusion

I have concluded the book with this analysis in cursory form of Wichita State University because the administrators there, well before any "crisis" descended upon the plains of Kansas, had developed a set of data and a concern for contingencies that was rare among universities at this time. Many of the simple issues I have raised here are at the expense of equally compelling topics that could have been used in their place. However, the basic idea of using management concepts from economics such as risk evaluation, contingency planning, marginal cost and revenue determination, long-run/short-run differentiation, fixed- versus variable-cost analysis, and controllable versus noncontrollable segmentation seem useful. Present value, a concept long a part of corporate planning and of analysis in the governmental sector, also offers an insight to the university administrator concerned about where the institution will move in the future.

Ultimately, the standards used for evaluating a university in the public or private sector are beyond economics and probably beyond measure. Quality is always the key point, yet at what cost? Even then how does one trade off a marginal quality improvement in one area (perhaps percentage of students earning X dollars in 10 years) versus quality in another area (percentage of faculty receiving at least Y dollars in research grants in a given year)? Even if one argues faculty quality is important in the long run, how one measures it is superseded by whether anyone really cares on the consuming side about "quality." As has been pointed out, in contrast to industry, education is an odd "firm." The people who produce the services do not sell them; the people who consume the services do not pay for them; and the people who pay for the services do not consume them. Since most of the cost of education is borne by parents, the public at large as taxpayers, or previous donors to the public or private university, the statement seems apt. In the long run, though, accountability is a major emerging issue. Concern is rising among Americans about the high levels of property taxes (most of which go for local schools), state income taxes (some of which go for medical and educational facilities), and federal taxes (some of which go for student grants and federal research funding in defense and nondefense areas to the universities). There is also the paradox of a bad economy: Many universities find that students tend to return to school since the opportunity cost is low; there are few jobs for them at the entry level anyway. Yet this same period is when state and local tax receipts decline, meaning legislators are likely to scrutinize public-school budgets with even greater intensity.

Ultimately then management analysis does not say what should be done; it merely suggests that some ways of doing things are more costly along one or more dimensions of cost than other ways. The cost is not always dollars. Furthermore, management analysis suggests that elbow room or flexibility may be the most important quality of any program for university administrators planning for a volatile and economically hazardous future. Growth is always more fun than contraction, but unless administrators manage the house of academe effectively as stewards for the public trust, one may be sure that the public will impose its own managers with a vengeance. Private enterprise in many nations has learned this the hard way; let us hope those of us committed to education can benefit from their experience.

Notes

1. Part of the problem in enrollment declines now is that there were massive increases concentrated in the latter part of the 1950–1970 era. As Freeman notes, 60 percent of the 5 million plus growth in the traditional college-age population between 1950 and 1970 came in the years 1965–1968.

The anticipated decline of the 1980s was noted in this 1965 publication, as was the fact that the *growth* in the enrollment ratio (percentage of high school graduates enrolling in institutions of higher learning) was leveling off in the early 1960s. See Roger A. Freeman, *Crisis in College Finance? Time for New Solutions* (Washington, D.C.: Institute for Social Science Research, 1965), p. 21.

The Ford Foundation bestowed $218.5 million on American colleges and universities from 1960 to 1963, usually requiring matching grants to be raised within 3 years of the initial grant. These matching grants totaled $556.5 million. Thus an extra $775 million went into (mostly) private colleges and universities in the mid-60s. How much this infusion helped the short-run situation by creating overcapacity is debatable. For one tabulation of the specific allocation by college and university, see *Toward Greatness in Higher Education: A First Report on the Ford Foundation Special Program in Education* (New York: Ford Foundation, 1964), pp. 30–33.

2. Notice that 21.68 percent of $18 million in funding is $3.902 million, about the level of $258 per EFT times 15,714 EFT students equals $4.054 million.

3. Increasing hostility of legislators to salary needs of public university faculty versus all state employees are well reported in the account of the University of California at Berkeley. See "University Challenge," *The Economist* (London), January 27, 1979, pp. 34–35.

4. There is a familiar slogan from the officers of private colleges along the lines that it is hard to sell education for a fair price when someone else is giving it away down the street. Chambers aptly points out the problem with this statement: "The statement is inept and pointless for two very important reasons: (1) Education is primarily a service to the society, not merely a consumers' good to be bought and sold for what the market will bear. (2) The facilities and opportunities offered by private institutions are not and ought not to be the same as those offered by public institutions. Their differences and their individual character constitute one of the principal reasons for their continued existence." See M.M. Chambers, *Higher Education, Who Pays? Who Gains?* (Danville, Ill.: Interstate Printers and Publishers, 1968), p. 265.

The public sector as a whole is far more involved in education than most people realize. Using 1974 data, of $30.5 billion of income reported by all institutions of higher learning, 21 percent was from student fees, 37 percent from state government, 5 percent from local government, 12 percent from the federal government, 2 percent from endowments, 3 percent from gifts, 12 percent from auxiliary charges, and 8 percent from miscellaneous sources. Thus 54 percent of the income was from government in some form. See "Colleges and Money: A Faculty Guide to Academic Economics," *Change* 1976. Total enrollments by students have also indicated a marked shift to the public sector, as I have calculated below from data in the *Chronicle of Higher Education,* September 19, 1977, p. 8.

	Public Percentage of Total			
	1965	*1971*	*1977*	*1985 (est.)*
Four-year institutions	62%	69%	70%	72%
Total number (000s)	4,748	6,463	7,682	7,623
All institutions	67%	76%	80%	83%
Total number (000s)	5,921	8,949	12,146	13,360

The expansion in the public sector began many years ago. Freeman notes that enrollment was about evenly divided between public and private colleges as late as 1950. However, in the next 12 years, four out of five students added chose a public institution. See Roger A. Freeman, *Crisis in College Finance? Time for New Solutions* (Washington, D.C.: Institute for Social Science Research, 1965, p. 36

5. One study completed in 1976 suggested that generalizations can be made about the financial state of higher education by categories of institutions: Larger universities were healthier than smaller one, public institutions were healthier than private ones, and two-year institutions were healthier than four-year institutions. The study, however, stressed the variance within each of these categories, as would be expected. The same study also emphasized the importance of general demographics and regional location of the colleges in determining their financial health: Growing populations (as in the "Sunbelt") substantially helped in the aggregate higher educational institutions which were fortunate enough to be in that area. Colleges offering the doctoral degree tended to be very healthy or very sick. See "Financial State of Higher Education: A Special Report," *Change,* September, 1976.

6. How one computes cost is always arguable, and the general index for all colleges (weighted averages of salaries, wages, supply costs, and so on) may not apply to the typical college. However, several recent tabulations of higher education price indices by D. Kent Halstead of the National Institute for Education are probably representative. Thus for fiscal 1978, the average of prices for all goods and services rose by 6.7 percent, compared to increases of 8.6 percent, 6.6 percent, and 6.5 percent for fiscal 1975 through fiscal 1977. Faculty salaries rose by 5.3 percent versus 7.8-percent increases in salaries and wages for nonprofessional employees. Average fringe benefits for all personnel rose by 9.9 percent. The sharpest single-component increase appeared in utility costs, which rose by 13.3 percent. See "Inflation Hit Colleges Harder in Fiscal 1978," *Chronicle of Higher Education,* September 22, 1978, p. 8. Also see the annual publication of the U.S. Office of Education, *Higher Education Prices and Price Indexes.*

7. Budgeting in the past has been found to be related to "maximizing prestige subject to an over-all budget limitation." A recent study found some movement toward long-range planning and management-information systems, at least in larger colleges and universities. Among the major defects in most college planning systems was the lack of any comprehensive attempt to project future total costs of a new program. In addition, there was lack of recognition of the joint cost and revenue effects of new program proposals and existing programs. See R. Charles Moyer and William J. Kretlow, "The Resource Allocation Decision in U.S. Colleges and Universities: Practice, Problems and Recommendations," *Higher Education,* February, 1978, pp. 35–46.

Problems of the trade-offs in educational program goals and in the difficulty of measuring program quality are addressed in Seymour E. Harris, *Higher Education: Resources and Finance* (New York: McGraw Hill, 1962), chap. 46, pp. 557–567. A spendid comprehensive analytical approach to college planning is found in Frederick E. Balderston, *Managing Today's University* (San Francisco, Calif.: Jossey-Bass, 1975).

8. Some ideas for achieving flexibility in costs are presented later in this chapter.

9. Columns 5 and 8 make use of a mathematical approximation where growth is constant and the present-value analysis is useful. Essentially growth at one rate per annum commencing at the same time as discounting at a higher rate per annum permits a reduced series equation that can be quickly solved with the present-value table. These figures are for reference only, for they involve some rounding.

10. West, in a lucid article, cautions administrators that traditional measures of tenure proportions are often misleading. First, what is the faculty base: all faculty or all full-time equivalent faculty? Then how much of the funding of the school is linked to tenured faculty salaries? And finally, what is the hard-money budget of the school? West argues that the percentage of hard-money (permanent) funding committed to tenured faculty salaries is the key variable. This link between dollars committed to faculty who are tenured and the total budget is consistent with the theme of this book. West alludes to the idea of present-value analysis of tenured faculty in a footnote. See Richard R. West, "Tenure Quotas and Financial Flexibility in Colleges and Universities," *Educational Record,* Spring, 1974, pp. 96–100.

11. Law partnerships and accounting firms are notorious for their "tenure" situations. For a flip but candid survey of academic life, see Oliver P. Kolstoe, *College Professoring, or Through Academia with Gun and Camera* (Carbondale and Edwardsville: Southern Illinois University Press, 1975).

12. Analogies are always dangerous, and an especially dangerous and misleading one is the use of the term borrowed from athletics, "superstar,"

to describe a particular luminary in academics. As one writer has pointed out, in sports these people are supposed to make money. In contrast, in academics they usually turn out to add to insolvency rather than providing extra income to the institution: heavy compensation, light teaching loads, and the requirements to provide extensive staff support contribute to their being a drain on the usual college budget. See Bruce C. Vladeck, "Why Non-profits Go Broke," *The Public Interest,* Winter, 1976, pp. 86–101.

The issue of *differential salaries across fields* versus a compact system (as tends to be the pattern in the United Kingdom) is discussed in William G. Bowen, *Economic Aspects of Education* (Princeton, N.J.: Princeton University, 1964), p. 70. Within the U.K. experience cited by Bowen, there seems to be little emphasis on merit increases once a person becomes a tenured faculty member; step increases for all faculty in all disciplines other than medicine are the pattern.

Bowen and Douglass discuss the concepts of efficiency and cost effectiveness in universities using alternative methods of teaching. Their suggestions for various types of colleges and programs are presented in Howard R. Bowen and Gordon K. Douglass, *Efficiency in Liberal Education* (New York: McGraw-Hill, 1971).

13. In early 1980, the U.S. Supreme Court held by a narrow 5–4 vote in *National Labor Relations Board v. Yeshiva University* that professors were managerial personnel and thus did not have guaranteed bargaining rights under federal law because they participated in decisions related to hiring and promotion, teaching schedules, salary rates, and so forth. The impact of this case on WSU's union activities and universities in general is not clear.

14. See "U.S. Colleges: Life and Death Struggle," *U.S. News and World Report* 84 (No. 21) (1978): 64–66.

Appendix 8A: The AAUP Faculty Model

The summer 1973 issue of the AAUP *Bulletin* describes a faculty model for an institution with a faculty of fixed size that can be used as a basis for considering policy alternatives and discussing those alternatives with faculty groups.

Definitions:
N = total number of faculty members
N_t = number of faculty members holding tenure
N_n = number of nontenured faculty members
T = ratio of tenured to total faculty (N_t /N)
r = annual attrition rate of tenured faculty
p = annual tenure award rate for nontenured faculty
λ = fraction of tenured vacancies filled by nontenured appointments

Consider the equilibrium case where T is constant. Then the attrition of tenured faculty will be balanced by new awards of tenure.

Loss of tenured faculty equals new awards of tenure plus new appointments with tenure

$$N_t r = N_n p + N_t r(1 - \lambda)$$

$$NTr = N(1 - T)p + NTr(1 - \lambda)$$

$$T(p + \lambda r) = p$$

$$T = \frac{1}{1 + \lambda r/p}$$

Thus in the equilibrium case, the percentage of tenure is determined by the value of $\lambda r/p$. The table below illustrates this relationship:

$\lambda r/p$	0	0.110	0.250	0.428	0.667	1.000	1.500	2.333	4.000
T	1.0	0.90	0.80	0.70	0.60	0.50	0.40	0.30	0.20

As an example, any combination of values of λ, r, and p that produces a value of 0.250 for $\lambda r/p$ will result in a tenure ratio of 80 percent at equilibrium.

It is instructive to consider not only the limiting value for the percentage of tenure but also the manner in which that limit is approached. Two such cases will be calculated.

Suppose that we begin with the present 433 full-time faculty members of whom 250 are tenured and 183 nontenured, so that the percentage tenured is 57.7 percent. If the limiting value of T is set at 70 percent, then $\lambda r/p$ must be 0.428. If we assume that 95 percent of the tenured vacancies will be filled by nontenured appointments ($\lambda = 0.95$) and that the attrition rate for tenured faculty is 3 percent ($r = 0.03$), then the required value of p is 0.0666 (6.66 percent). Using these values, the year-by-year experience will be as in table 8A-1.

As the second example, consider the same 433 full-time faculty members with an initial tenure percentage of 90 percent (390 tenured, 43 nontenured). The same values for r, p and λ then produce the development in table 8A-2.

Application of the Model to Wichita State University

Historical Data for WSU

It is instructive to review historical data for Wichita State University shown in table 8A-3. Using the average values for r, p, and λ, the limiting percentage of tenure is 75.4 percent. Using the "worst" values of r, p, and λ occurring during the 6-year period, the limiting percentage of tenure is 91.2 percent. Using the "best" values of r, p, and λ from this period, the limiting percentage of tenure is 38.2 percent.

Table 8A-1
Case 1: Tenure Percentage over Ten Years

Year	Tenured Attrition	Tenure Awards	New Tenured Appointments	Number of Tenured Faculty	Number of Nontenured Faculty	T (%)
0				250	183	57.7
1	7.5	12.9	0.4	255.8	177.2	59.1
2	7.7	11.8	0.4	260.3	172.7	60.1
3	7.8	11.5	0.4	264.4	168.6	61.1
4	7.9	11.2	0.4	268.1	164.9	61.9
5	8.0	11.0	0.4	271.5	161.5	62.7
6	8.1	10.8	0.4	274.6	158.4	63.4
7	8.2	10.5	0.4	277.3	155.7	64.0
8	8.3	10.4	0.4	279.8	153.2	64.6
9	8.4	10.2	0.4	282.0	151.0	65.1
10	8.5	10.1	0.4	284.0	149.0	65.6
∞	9.1	8.6	0.5	303.1	129.9	70.0

Table 8A-2
Case 2: Tenure Percentage over Ten Years

Year	Tenured Attrition	Tenure Awards	New Tenured Appointments	No. of Ten. Faculty	No. of Non-tenured Fac.	T (%)
0				390	43	90.0
1	11.7	2.9	0.6	381.8	51.2	88.2
2	11.5	3.4	0.6	374.3	58.7	86.4
3	11.2	3.9	0.6	367.6	65.4	84.9
4	11.0	4.4	0.6	361.6	71.4	83.5
5	10.8	4.8	0.5	356.1	76.9	82.2
6	10.7	5.1	0.5	351.0	82.0	81.1
7	10.5	5.5	0.5	346.5	86.5	80.0
8	10.4	5.8	0.5	342.4	90.6	79.1
9	10.3	6.0	0.5	338.6	94.4	78.2
10	10.2	6.3	0.5	335.2	97.8	77.4
∞	9.1	8.6	0.5	303.1	129.9	70.0

Table 8A-3
Historic Promotion Rates, Wichita State University

Year	r	p	λ	λr/p
1967–1968	.0692	.1617	1.00	.4280
1968–1969	.0629	.2000	1.00	.3145
1969–1970	.0306	.1538	0.80	.1592
1970–1971	.0495	.1538	0.67	.2156
1971–1972	.0289	.0428	0.91	.6144
1972–1973	.0492	.0631	0.86	.6706
Average	.0484	.1292	0.873	.3270

Values Assumed for Key Variables in Using the Model to Suggest Policy

The equilibrium percentage of tenure, (T). This has been set at 70 percent. In most discussions of this problem, the recommended value is 60 to 70 percent. If a faculty were uniformly distributed among the four ranks, 70-percent tenure would allow for all full and associate professors to be tenured, 70 percent of the assistant professors to be tenured, and 10 percent of the instructors to be tenured.

The attrition rate for tenured faculty, (*r*). This has been set at 0.039. This is the average of the values of *r* for the past 2 years. It should be adjusted each year to reflect the average experience over the previous 2 years.

The mix of new faculty appointments (λ). Most new appointments will be made without tenure, but it is necessary occasionally in making a senior appointment to award tenure at the time of the appointment. It is assumed that 95 percent of the new appointments are without tenure. (λ = 0.95)

The Allowable Rate of Tenure Award

Using the values assigned above for *T*, *r* and λ, the value of *p* is determined to be 8.66 percent. With a probation period of 6 years, one sixth of the nontenured faculty would come up for review each year. Tenure awards to 52 percent of this group would represent awards to 8.66 percent of the nontenured faculty. The actual award rate in 1972–1973 was 57.1 percent of the cases reviewed.

Bibliography

Alonzo, Martin V., Chairman, Management Accounting Practices Committee. "Objectives of Financial Reporting by Nonbusiness Organizations." *Management Accounting* (February 1979): 53–56.

Anderson, Richard E. "A Financial and Environmental Analysis of Strategic Policy Changes at Small Private Colleges." *Journal of Higher Education* (January–February 1978): 30–46.

Anthony, Robert. *Financial Accounting in Nonbusiness Organizations.* Stamford, Conn.: Financial Accounting Standards Board, 1978.

Anthony, Robert, and Herzlinger, Regina. *Management Control in Nonprofit Organizations.* Homewood, Ill.: R.D. Irwin, 1975.

Astin, Alexander. "On the Failures of Educational Policy." *Change* (September 1977): 40–43.

———. *Four Critical Years.* San Francisco: Jossey-Bass, 1977.

Balderston, Frederick R. *Managing Today's University.* San Francisco: Jossey-Bass, 1975.

Ben-David, Joseph. *American Higher Education: Directions Old and New.* New York: McGraw-Hill, 1972.

Boulding, Kenneth E. "Quality Versus Equality: The Dilemma of the University." *Daedalus* (Winter 1975): 298–303.

Bowen, Howard R. *Investment in Learning.* San Francisco: Jossey-Bass, 1977.

Bowen, Howard R., and Douglass, Gordon K. *Efficiency in Liberal Education.* New York: McGraw-Hill, 1971.

Bowen, William G., *Economic Aspects of Education.* Princeton, N.J.: Princeton University, 1964.

Breneman, David W. *Graduate School Adjustments to the "New Depression" in Higher Education.* Washington, D.C.: National Academy of Sciences, 1975.

"Can't Somebody Turn the Damn Thing Off?" *Forbes* (August 7, 1978): 47–53.

Carnegie Foundation for the Advancement of Teaching. *More Than Survival.* San Francisco: Jossey-Bass, 1975.

Carter, E. Eugene. *Portfolio Aspects of Corporate Capital Budgeting.* Lexington, Mass.: D.C. Heath, 1974.

Cartter, Allan M., and Solmon, Lewis C. "Implications for Faculty." *Change* (September 1976): 37–38.

Chambers, M.M. *Higher Education—Who Pays? Who Gains?* Danville, Ill.: Interstate Printers and Publishers, 1968, pp. 263–277.

Cheit, Earl F. *The New Depression in Higher Education.* New York: McGraw-Hill, 1971.

179

Cohen, Michael, and March, James. *Leadership and Ambiguity: The American College President.* New York: McGraw-Hill, 1974.

"Colleges and Money: A Faculty Guide to Academic Economics." *Change* (September 1976).

Commission on Academic Tenure in Higher Education. *Faculty Tenure,* William R. Keast, Chairman. San Francisco: Jossey-Bass, 1973.

Committee for Economic Development. *The Management and Financing of Colleges.* New York: CED, 1973.

Common Fund, The, 635 Madison Avenue, New York, N.Y. 10022.

Copeland, Thomas E., and Smith, Keith V. "An Overview of Nonprofit Organizations." *Journal of Economics and Business* (Winter 1978): pp. 147-154.

Dresch, Stephen. *An Economic Perspective on the Evolution of Graduate Education.* Washington, D.C.: National Academy of Sciences, 1974.

Ennis, Richard M., and Williamson, J. Peter. *Spending Policy for Educational Endowments.* New York: Common Fund, 1976.

Ford Foundation, *Managing Educational Endowments: Report to the Ford Foundation.* New York: 1969.

———. *Toward Greatness in Higher Education;* A First Report on the Ford Foundation Special Program in Education. New York, 1964.

Freeman, Richard Barry, and Breneman, David W. *Forecasting the Ph.D. Labor Market.* Washington, D.C.: National Academy of Sciences, 1974.

Freeman, Roger A. *Crisis in College Finance? Time for New Solutions.* Washington, D.C.: The Institute for Social Science Research, 1965.

Gambino, Anthony J. "Planning and Control in College and Universities." *Management Accounting* (January 1979): 53-54.

Gamso, Gary. "An Approach to Cost Studies in Small Colleges." Boulder, Colo.: NCHEMS Publications, 1978.

Geiger, Louis G. "The Impending Crisis of the Liberal Arts Colleges." *AAUP Bulletin* (December 1971): 500-504.

Ghali, Moheb, Miklius, Walter, and Wada, Richard. "The Demand for Higher Education Facing an Individual Institution." *Higher Education* (November 1977): 477-487.

Golloday, Mary A., ed. *The Condition of Education.* Washington, D.C.: National Center for Education Statistics, 1976.

Gordon, Margaret S., ed. *Higher Education and the Labor Market.* New York: McGraw-Hill, 1974.

Grinold, Richard C., Hopkins, David S.P., and Massy, William F. "A Model For Long Range University Budget Planning under Uncertainty." *The Bell Journal of Economics* (Autumn 1978): 396-420.

Grube, R. Cowin, Panton, Don B., and Terrell, J. Michael. "Risk and Rewards in Covered Call Positions." *Journal of Portfolio Management* (Winter 1979): 64–68.

Harris, Seymour E. *Higher Education: Resources and Finance*. New York: McGraw-Hill, 1962.

Higher Education Prices and Price Index. Annual publication of the United States Office of Education.

Hoenack, Stephen A. "Private Demand for Higher Education in California." Unpublished doctoral dissertation. Berkeley: University of California, 1967.

Hoenack, Stephen A., and Weiler, William C. "Cost-related Tuition Policies and University Enrollments." *Journal of Human Resources* (Summer 1975): 332–360.

Hopkins, David S.P., and Massy, William F. "A Model for Planning the Transition to Equilibrium of a University Budget." *Management Science* (July 1977): 1161–1168.

Ibbotson, Roger G., and Sinquefield, Rex A. "Stocks, Bonds, Bills, and Inflation: Updates." *Financial Analysts Journal* (July–August 1979): 40–44.

Ibbotson, Roger G., and Sinquefield, Rex A. "Stocks, Bonds, Bills, and Inflation: Simulations of the Future (1976–2000)." *Journal of Business* (July 1976): 313–338.

Ibbotson, Roger G., and Sinquefield, Rex A. "Stocks, Bonds, Bills, and Inflation: Year-by-year Historical Returns (1926–1974)." *Journal of Business* (January 1976): 11–47.

"Inflation Hit Colleges Harder in Fiscal 1978." *Chronicle of Higher Education* (September 22, 1978): 8.

Jackson, Gregory A., and Weathersby, George B. "Individual Demand for Higher Education." *Journal of Higher Education* (November–December 1975): 623–652.

Jencks, Christopher, and Riesman, David. *The Academic Revolution*. Garden City, N.Y.: Doubleday, 1968.

Johnson, Jane Louise. "Setting Tuition Levels at Public Institutions: The Case of the University of Washington." *Journal of Higher Education*. (March–April 1976): 125–139.

Kaludis, George, ed. *Strategies for Budgeting*. San Francisco: Jossey-Bass, 1973.

Kieft, Raymond N. "Academic Planning: Four Institutional Case Studies." Boulder, Colo.: NCHEMS Publications, 1978.

Kieft, Raymond N., Armijo, Frank, and Bucklew, Neil. "A Handbook for Institutional Academic and Program Planning: From Idea to Implementations." Boulder, Colo.: NCHEMS Publications, 1978.

Kim, Tye. "Investment Performance of College Endowment Funds." *Quarterly Review of Economics and Business* (Autumn 1976): 73–83.

Kolstoe, Oliver P. *College Professoring, or through Academia with Gun and Camera.* Carbondale, and Edwardsville, Ill., Southern Illinois University Press, 1975.

Kreezer, Dexter M., ed. *Financing Higher Education 1960–1970.* New York: McGraw-Hill, 1959.

Ladd, Everett, and Lipset, Seymour. *Professors, Unions and American Higher Education.* Berkeley: Carnegie Commission on Higher Education, 1973.

Lee, Eugene C., and Bowen, Frank, M. *Managing Multi-campus Systems: Effective Administration in an Unsteady State.* San Francisco: Jossey-Bass, 1975.

Livesey, Herbert. *The Professors.* New York: Charterhouse, 1975.

Lorie, James, and Brealy, Richard, eds. *Modern Developments in Investment Management,* 2d ed. Hinsdale, Ill.: Dryden Press, 1978.

Lupton, Andrew H., Augenblick, John, and Heyison, Joseph. "The Financial State of Higher Education." *Change* (September 1976): 21–35.

Maciariello, Joseph A., and Enteman, Willard F. "A System for Management Control in Private Colleges." *Journal of Higher Education* (November 1974): 594–606.

Malkiel, Burton G., and Firstenberg, Paul B. *Managing Risk in an Uncertain Era.* Princeton, N.J.: Princeton University, 1976.

Massey, William F. "A Dynamic Equilibrium Model For University Planning." *Management Science* (November 1976): 248–256.

Monts, J. Kenneth. "The Crisis in Private University Education: A Simulation Experiment." *Behavioral Science* (March 1979): 140–151.

Moyer, R. Charles, and Kretlow, William J. "The Resource Allocation Decision in U.S. Colleges and Universities: Practice, Problems, and Recommendations." *Higher Education* (February 1978): 35–46.

National Center for Higher Education Management Systems (NCHEMS). "Academic Unit Planning and Management—Technical Report 75." Boulder, Colo.: NCHEMS Publications, 1976.

———. "An Introduction to the Identification and Uses of Higher Education Outcome Information—Technical Report 40." Boulder, Colo.: NCHEMS Publications, 1973.

———. "A Reference Guide to Postsecondary Education Data Sources." Boulder, Colo.: NCHEMS Publications, 1975.

———. "An Overview of Two Recent Surveys of Administrative Computer Operations in Higher Education." Boulder, Colo.: NCHEMS Publications 1975.

———. "Exploring Cost Exchange at Colleges and Universities." Boulder, Colo.: NCHEMS Publications, 1974.

————. "Faculty Activity Analysis: Overview and Major Issues—Technical Report 24." Boulder, Colo.: NCHEMS Publications, 1972.

————. "Higher Education Enrollment Forecasting." Boulder, Colo.: NCHEMS Publications, 1975.

————. "Higher Education Facilities Planning and Management Manuals—Technical Report 17." Boulder, Colo.: NCHEMS Publications, 1971.

————. "Higher Education Finance Manual—Technical Report 69" Boulder, Colo.: NCHEMS Publications, 1975.

————. "Higher Education Planning and Management Systems: A Brief Explanation." Boulder, Colo.: NCHEMS Publications, 1972.

————. "Instructional Program Budgeting in Higher Education." Boulder, Colo.: NCHEMS Publications, 1972.

————. "Introduction to the Resource Requirements Prediction Model 1.6—Technical Report 24A." Boulder, Colo.: NCHEMS Publications, 1973.

————. "Introduction to the State Planning System (SPS)—Technical Report 86." Boulder, Colo.: NCHEMS Publications, 1976.

————. "Outcome-Oriented Planning in Higher Education: An Approach or an Impossibility?" Boulder, Colo.: NCHEMS Publications, 1973.

————. "Program Measures—Technical Report 35." Boulder, Colo.: NCHEMS Publications, 1973.

————. "State Postsecondary Education Profiles Handbook." Boulder, Colo.: NCHEMS Publications, 1976.

————. "Statewide Planning for Postsecondary Education: Issues and Design." Boulder, Colo.: NCHEMS Publications, 1971.

————. "Why Planning, Programming, Budgeting Systems for Higher Education?" Boulder, Colo.: NCHEMS Publications, 1970.

Orwig, M.D., ed. *Financing Higher Education: Alternatives for the Federal Government.* Iowa City: The American College Testing Program, 1971.

Radner, Roy, and Miller, L.S. "Demand and Supply in U.S. Higher Education: A Progress Report," *American Economic Review* (May 1970):326–334.

Riesman, David. "The Future of Diversity in a Time of Retrenchment." *Higher Education* (November 1975):461–482.

Rodriguez, Rita M., and Carter, E. Eugene. *International Financial Management,* 2d ed. Englewood Cliffs, N.J.: Prentice-Hall, 1979.

Romney, Leonard. "Measures of Institutional Goal Achievement." Boulder, Colo.: NCHEMS Publications, 1978.

Rubin, Irene. "Universities in Stress: Decision Making under Conditions of Reduced Resources." *Social Science Quarterly* (September 1977): 242–254.

Scheps, Clarence, and Davidson, E.E. *Accounting for Colleges and Universities,* 3d rd. Baton Rouge: Louisiana State University Press, 1978.

Sharpe, William F. *Investments.* Englewood Cliffs, N.J.: Prentice-Hall, 1978.

Silber, John R. "Paying the Bill for College. The 'Private' Sector and the Public Interest." *Atlantic* (May 1975): 33–40.

"University Challenge." *The Economist* (London) (January 27, 1979): 34–35.

"U.S. Colleges: Life and Death Struggle." *U.S. News and World Report* 84 (November 21, 1978): 64–66.

Veysey, Lawrence R. *The Emergence of the American University.* Chicago: University of Chicago Press, 1965.

Vladeck, Bruce. "Why Non-profits Go Broke." *The Public Interest* (Winter 1976): 86–101.

Weathersby, George B., and Jacobs, Frederic. *Institutional Goals and Student Costs.* Washington, D.C.: The American Association of Higher Education, 1977.

West, Richard R. "Tenure Quotas and Financial Flexibility in Colleges and Universities." *Educational Record* (Spring 1974): 96–100.

Wheeler, John W. "Fiduciary Responsibilities of Trustees in Relation to the Financing of Private Institutions of Higher Education." *Journal of College and University Law* (Spring 1975): 210–228.

"A Yellow Light For Options." *Institutional Investor* (February 1979): 83–85.

Zeckhauser, Sally, and Zeckhauser, Richard. "Encouraging Improved Performance in Higher Education." *Daedalus* (Winter 1975): 97–107.

Index

About the Author

E. Eugene Carter is professor and head of the Department of Finance at the University of Illinois at Chicago Circle and is a consultant with various corporate and nonprofit institutions. He is also a director of several corporations, including A.G. Edwards and Sons, Inc. He previously taught at Carnegie-Mellon University, Harvard University, and the Massachusetts Institute of Technology. He has also taught in the Institute for Educational Management of the Harvard School of Education.

Mr. Carter received the B.S. degree from Northwestern University and the M.S. and Ph.D. degrees from the Graduate School of Industrial Administration of Carnegie-Mellon University, where he studied under Woodrow Wilson, National Defense, and Ford Foundation Fellowships.

He has published articles in various academic and management journals. He is author of *Portfolio Aspects of Corporate Capital Budgeting* and coauthor with Rita M. Rodriguez of *International Financial Management.*